The Sermon on the Mount

STUDIES IN THE SYNOPTIC GOSPELS

by Herman Hendrickx, CICM

The Infancy Narratives
The Passion Narratives of the Synoptic Gospels
The Resurrection Narratives of the Synoptic Gospels
The Sermon on the Mount

The Sermon on the Mount

Herman Hendrickx

Geoffrey Chapman
London

A Geoffrey Chapman book published by
Cassell Ltd
1 Vincent Square, London SW1P 2PN

First edition copyright 1979 by East Asian Pastoral Institute, PO Box 1815,
Manila, Philippines
Revised edition © Geoffrey Chapman, a division of Cassell Ltd. 1984

Cum permissu superiorum

This edition first published 1984

ISBN 0 225 66399 6

British Library Cataloguing in Publication Data
Hendrickx, Herman
    The Sermon on the Mount.—Rev. ed.—
    (Studies in the synoptic gospels)
    1. Sermon on the mount
    I. Title   II. Series
    226'.906   BT380.2

Typeset in VIP Times by
D.P. Media Ltd, Hitchin, Hertfordshire

Printed and bound in Great Britain by
Biddles Ltd, Guildford and King's Lynn

Contents

Preface

This book had its beginning in a series of lectures and meditations on the Sermon on the Mount given to several groups of theology students, religious and catechists. The positive response of the public and the kind appreciation expressed in reviews of the previous three books in this series encouraged me to revise my notes thoroughly in the light of recent publications.

In a time of polarization within the Christian community (commitment to the cause of man over against personal surrender to God) it is imperative to ask ourselves what Jesus himself intends for us and wants from us. In this context, the Sermon on the Mount is indispensable. It has inspired – and confused – many throughout the centuries. Some, among them many non-Christians, have found in it a message which they considered extremely timely and relevant to their situation. Mahatma Gandhi, for instance, was delighted by the Sermon on the Mount, which, he said, 'went straight to my heart'. Its words reminded him of the *Bhagvad-Gita* or Celestial Song, the sacred book of the Hindus, a poem of seven hundred stanzas, written between the fifth and second centuries B.C. Others, like Friedrich Nietzsche, experienced it as a strange, unearthly sound in a society in which other things matter and which has no use for anything like the Sermon on the Mount. Innumerable efforts have been made to interpret this intriguing part of the gospel, which has never left people at peace either within or outside the Church.

It is impossible to account in detail for every idea or formulation for which I am indebted to New Testament scholarship, and such an apparatus would be beyond the scope and format of this book. Notes have therefore been kept to a minimum but a full bibliography is included, together with suggestions for further reading. I am deeply indebted to the work of many biblical scholars and I wish to record here my appreciation and thanks. The origin and format of the book make inevitable a certain amount of repetition, e.g., in the considerations on the kingdom of God found in the introductory chapter and in the discussion of various passages. Keeping in mind our broader reading public and the way in which the book will be used, it was thought better to keep it this way rather than to pursue a greater conciseness.

I should like to thank all those who had a share in the publication of this book. I am especially indebted to Rev. John Linskens, CICM, for many valuable suggestions and critical remarks at different stages of its composition; to Rev. John O'Regan, OMI, for reading the manuscript and making a number of stylistic improvements; to the many religious and catechists who by their response and questions challenged me to express my thoughts more accurately, and also very specially to Sister Victorina de la Paz, SCMM, Publications Director in the East Asian Pastoral Institute, whose kind concern was so obvious at all times.

Note on the revised edition

The first edition of this book was published in 1979 and could take into account the literature on the Sermon on the Mount only up to 1978. The author and the publisher, Geoffrey Chapman, therefore decided to complete and update the bibliography and make a few minor revisions of the text. We trust that these changes will make the book more readable and useful for the reading public we have in mind.

I would like to express here my gratitude to Miss Anne Boyd, Chief Editor, without whose interest this second edition would not have been possible, and Miss Fiona McKenzie, Senior House Editor, for her highly expert editing.

1 Introduction

The kingdom of God – beginning of the future

Jesus' promise of salvation is expressed time and again in terms of the nearness of the 'kingdom of God' or the 'kingdom of heaven' (literally, the 'kingdom of the heavens'). The dawning of the kingdom of God is the central theme of Jesus' proclamation. In the centre of the Sermon on the Mount stands the Lord's Prayer in whose centre again we find the petition for the coming of the kingdom (Mt 6:10). The same Sermon is preceded by the message that 'the kingdom is at hand' (Mt 4:17; cf. 4:23), and begins by telling the poor that 'theirs is the kingdom of heaven' (Mt 5:3).

What did Jesus mean by the 'kingdom of heaven'? Although the expression 'the kingdom of heaven/of God' does not occur as an actual phrase in the Old Testament, its roots are solidly embedded there. The idea that 'God rules', that he is 'King' is one of Israel's basic affirmations (Ex 15:18; Deut 33:5; Pss 47[46]:2; 93[92]:1; 96[97]:10; 103[102]:19; 145[144]:13). First-century Judaism states that God's kingly rule is eternal and stretches out over the whole world. Although God's sovereignty is fully acknowledged only in Israel, the day is near when God will break into history to manifest himself as the ruler of all, to free his people from bondage, and to subject all nations to his holy will. Jesus said that the kingdom of God was at hand but, unlike the prophets who *announced* a coming reality, he *brought* the kingdom of God. Where *he* is, *there* the kingdom of God is. In his words and deeds, in his person, he himself is the dawning of the kingdom of God.

Jesus spoke of the kingdom of God in many similitudes and parables, but he never tried to give anything like a definition of it. Even if present-day theology systematized all of Jesus' statements concerning the kingdom, this would not yet be an adequate definition, since the kingdom cannot be contained in the categories of our present world and thoughts. Rather, from the expected future it questions our present world and our present speaking about the kingdom of God.

Jesus spoke of the kingdom of God in contrasted pairs, which complement and correct each other. Firstly he spoke of the kingdom as a present reality (Mt 12:28), but at the same time he said also that it was still to be expected and hoped for (Mt 6:10). Secondly, the kingdom of God means the realization of God's will in this world and the subjection of all opposition to God's claims (Mt 6:10; 7:21); but at the same time the establishment of the kingdom has also tangible dimensions (cf. the proclamation of forgiveness by word *and deed*, and the healing miracles), and it does not limit itself to the life of individual persons, but has also a political dimension. Thirdly, on the one hand, the kingdom of God is a free gift and cannot be earned (Mk 10:15), but on the other hand Jesus demands unlimited openness and undivided commitment (Mt 10:29–36).

Those who receive the kingdom of God have found everything: the treasure hidden in the field (Mt 13:44) and the precious pearl (Mt 13:45). They may address God as Father. Their debts are forgiven. They are invited to the wedding feast and clothed with the wedding garment (Mt 22:1–14). They have received everything.

The kingdom of heaven is often mistakenly identified with 'heaven', but the 'heavens' of which Matthew speaks are simply a reverential circumlocution for God. The kingdom of heaven, therefore, means the same as the kingdom of God, which refers first of all, not to the afterlife, but to the establishment of God's rule, the realization of his saving plan, here on earth. Jesus' promise of the coming of the kingdom is not a bill of exchange for the vague future somewhere in another world, but an event which is to be revealed here and now in our present world. This does not mean, of course, that we have nothing to expect beyond death, but this is to be seen as the definitive fulfilment of what has already begun now, in our time, in human history.

The term 'kingdom' is also often misunderstood. It means first of all God's sovereign rule, his saving activity in the history of man, which he wants to transform into saving history. It is the manifestation of God's unconditional goodness to men, whose integral happiness and salvation he wants, here and now, but also eschatologically. If God's rule is accepted, men can also be their true selves. This applies especially to people who were up to now oppressed in so many ways, for God has a preferential love for them.

And if this is still too vague and too general a description of what will happen when God's rule is fully established, we should look at Jesus himself. His words and deeds express and give stature to what he means by the kingdom of God. The practical content of this concept appears in his behaviour, his message and his whole life. The kingdom of God means, then, to be with and to identify with people, especially the threatened, the oppressed and the downtrodden; to give life to those who have none; to remove all oppressive relationships of one person over another, or one nation over another, to bring them to mutual solidarity; to liberate people from any kind of fear; not to condemn people, not to nail them to their sinful past or negative experiences, but to give them in all circumstances a new future, and hope that brings life; to love people without distinction, without selection, without limits; to oppose what is untrue, what is no longer relevant and has no future, a legalistic mentality which overlooks the actual person and promotes only uninspired conformity, and prayer that is not in spirit and truth but mere routine. In short, Jesus' words and deeds reveal the kingdom of God as God's rule concerned with the radical well-being and humaneness of man.

The kingdom of God is often identified with the Church, but not a single New Testament passage allows for this identification. This does not mean that the kingdom of God is not manifested in the Church, but only as a mustard seed, in poverty and weakness, and also as hope. However, the kingdom of God is not limited to the Church.

The kingdom of God is also often understood as limited to the internal, private human sphere: it concerns our internal attitude, our immediate environment, but does not exceed it. Only recently have theologians emphasized that the kingdom of God has political dimensions (i.e., concerns the *polis*, meaning the city, state or community) and that the great questions which occupy and move the world are within its scope.

Further aspects of the kingdom of God will be developed as we proceed with the explanation of the Sermon on the Mount.

The origin of the Sermon on the Mount

It is generally accepted that with a view to the instruction of its members the apostolic Church collected the sayings of Jesus, and grouped them in collections of varying length. Translated from Aramaic into Greek, these collections, or at least some of them, were incorporated in the gospels, where they now appear as 'discourses' of the Lord, at a point of the narrative appropriate to their contents or to the plan drawn up by the evangelist. One of these 'discourses' is the Sermon on the Mount (Mt 5:1 – 7:29).

The Sermon on the Mount is a composition of traditional passages or pericopes, as can be seen from the following comparison in which the passages in Matthew's Sermon, those found in Luke's Sermon on the Plain (Lk 6:20–49), and those found in other parts of Luke are arranged in parallel columns.

	Matthew	*Luke 6*	*Luke*
introduction	5:1–2	6:20a	

	Matthew	Luke 6	Luke
beatitudes	5:3–12	6:20b–23	
(woes)		(6:24–26)	
salt	5:13		14:34–35
light	5:14–16		8:16; 11:33
Law	5:17–18		16:16–17
and prophets	5:19–20		
killing and anger	5:21–24		
	5:25–26		12:57–59
adultery	5:27–30		
divorce	5:31–32		16:18
oaths	5:33–37		
retaliation	5:38–42	6:29–30	
love of enemies	5:43–45	6:27–28	
	5:46–48	6:32–36	
almsgiving	6:1–4		
prayer	6:5–8		
Lord's Prayer	6:9–15		11:1–4
fasting	6:16–18		
treasures in heaven	6:19–21		12:33–34
single eye	6:22–23		11:34–36
serving two masters	6:24		16:13
on cares	6:25–34		12:22–31
on judging	7:1–5	6:37–38, 41–42	
pearls before swine	7:6		
answer to prayer	7:7–11		11:9–13
Golden Rule	7:12	6:31	
two roads	7:13–14		13:23–24
fruits	7:15–20	6:43–45	
'Lord, Lord . . .'	7:21–23	6:46	13:25–27
hearers and doers	7:24–27	6:47–49	
conclusion	7:28–29	(7:1)	(4:32)

While totally absent from Mark, a good number of the features of the Sermon on the Mount are found in the 'Sermon on the Plain' of Lk 6:20–49. Moreover, except for Lk 6:27–28, 31, these common elements are arranged in the same order: e.g., both begin with a series of beatitudes (Mt 5:3–12; Lk 6:20b–23) and end with the parable of the builders (Mt 7:24–27; Lk 6:47–49). This allows us to infer a common tradition underlying Mt 5 – 7 and Lk 6:20–49. And since the vocabulary of the common passages is often strikingly similar, it seems probable that Matthew and Luke have used the same basic document, referred to as the Q-source (from the German word *Quelle*, 'source').

But, even after doing justice to the redactional changes and insertions which the evangelists have introduced in that basic document, a close study shows that the versions of this document which Matthew and Luke used were probably not identical. A number of variations of style can hardly be attributed to the final editors. And, more specifically, it seems difficult to attribute to them such important differences as are found, e.g., between the 'antitheses' of Mt 5:21–48 and the corresponding material in Luke.

The source reproduced by Matthew seems to have been more developed than that used by Luke (although we must also allow for the possibility that Luke omitted some of the materials found in his source): it was no longer an elementary collection of sayings of Jesus, but rather a more elaborate catechetical work, which, with a number of editorial changes and additions, Matthew inserted in his gospel in order to make it the expression of his theological interests.

The above comparison also shows that most passages of Mt 5 – 7 which have no counterpart in Lk 6 can be found elsewhere in the third gospel, where they are, however, spread over eleven chapters (Lk 6 – 16), often in contexts more probably original. This indicates that Matthew has composed the Sermon on the Mount using a shorter traditional discourse which he has expanded with many passages originally found in other contexts in the tradition.

Matthew derived almost all the materials of the Sermon on the Mount from the Q-source. But this does not mean that he was a mere collector of sayings of Jesus. These were already gathered in the Q-tradition. Rather, Matthew systematically sifted these materials and rearranged them in his own discourse-*composition*. Moreover, he provided this discourse with a meaningful *framework*. Finally, he gave a new accentuation to several of the passages of which the Sermon is composed: in consideration of his readers and their situation, he has provided Jesus' words with new *theological emphases*.

In its present form, then, the Sermon on the Mount is composed by the early Christians and Matthew from isolated sayings of Jesus and occasionally from statements of early Christian prophets. This fact should not disturb us in dealing with the Sermon on the Mount. The people who transmitted and recorded it offer the best guarantee of its authenticity by their life according to Jesus' word. Therefore, the Sermon on the Mount is Jesus' word, the message of Jesus even in sentences which strictly speaking cannot be traced back to the historical Jesus, because they too originated in the continuity of a praxis, a way of life according to Jesus' teaching. The Sermon on the Mount has both healing and liberating power. Its healing power consists in the fact that Jesus creatively resumes the tradition and frees it from its legalistic strait-jacket. Its liberating power lies especially in that Jesus prophetically challenges people to get moving towards the new society of God.

The Sermon on the Mount in the context of Matthew's gospel

In Mt 28:16–20, which is often called the 'key' of the gospel of Matthew, the clause 'teaching them to observe all that I have commanded you' (Mt 28:20a) is generally believed to refer to the Sermon on the Mount which is considered Matthew's summary of what Jesus commanded his disciples to do and, indirectly, to the five great discourses of which the Sermon is the first. The interrelation of these discourses is indicated by a similarly worded conclusion: 'And when Jesus finished . . .'.

Mt 5 – 7	Sermon on the Mount	conclusion:	Mt 7:28
Mt 10	Mission Discourse		Mt 11:1
Mt 13	Parable Discourse		Mt 13:53
Mt 18	Community Discourse		Mt 19:1
Mt 24 – 25	Eschatological Discourse		Mt 26:1

On the other hand, Matthew apparently intends to present Jesus as the Messiah of the Word (Mt 5 – 7) and the Messiah of the Deed (Mt 8 – 9). The Sermon on the Mount is indeed followed by a section in which Jesus' healing activity is demonstrated in a series of ten miracles which, as a comparison with Mark and Luke shows, is also a Matthean composition from traditional miracle stories mostly found in a different context in Mark or the Q-source (Luke).

In Mt 4:17 a new stage of the gospel story is reached ('from that time'). The arrest of John the Baptist (Mt 4:12) has put the proclamation of the kingdom into the hands of Jesus. Mt 4:18–22 illustrates the absolute and urgent character of the demands which the kingdom makes upon men.

Then follows a summary statement, 'And he went about all Galilee, *teaching* in their synagogues and *preaching* the gospel of the kingdom and *healing* every disease and every infirmity among the people' (Mt 4:23). This verse clearly anticipates the juxtaposition of the Messiah's words (Mt 5 – 7) and deeds (Mt 8 – 9), and is repeated at the end of this twofold composition in Mt 9:35, thus constituting a framework for this double intention. Verse 24–25 then relate the resonance (*akoē*) of Jesus' ministry in the surrounding regions, among which 'all Syria' is mentioned in the first place. This is not accidental, since Syria is most probably the country of the evangelist. Mt 4:23–25 should therefore be considered as a summary statement which introduces the Sermon on the Mount (Mt 5 – 7) and the series of ten miracles (Mt 8 – 9).

When Matthew begins chapter 10 by writing that Jesus 'called to him his twelve disciples and gave them authority', he is confident that Mt 5 – 7 and 8 – 9 have established beyond any doubt that Jesus has this authority.

2 The audience of the Sermon on the Mount *(Mt 5:1-2)*

Verses 1–2: Seeing the crowds, he went up on the mountain, and when he sat down his disciples came to him. (2) And he opened his mouth and taught them, saying:

The fact that Mt 5:1 does not mention Jesus by name shows how closely the evangelist relates the Sermon on the Mount to the preceding paragraphs of the gospel. The 'crowds' were already mentioned in Mt 4:25. The reaction to Jesus' initial proclamation was twofold: 'they brought him all the sick' (Mt 4:24), and 'great crowds followed him' (Mt 4:25).

Now, 'seeing the crowds, he went up on the mountain'. When he went up the mountain Jesus bore the crowds in mind. He did not withdraw from them to be alone with his disciples. He addressed his teaching directly to the open group of disciples, but beyond them he addressed it also to the crowds, who were all invited to become disciples. Even though in the Q-source the Sermon may have been understood as instruction for the community, Matthew certainly includes the crowds in Jesus' audience (cf. Mt 7:28). His message is addressed to the whole people, to all peoples (cf. Mt 28:19). It is not a message (and an ethic) for a small circle, an elite, but for all.

As far as our own time is concerned, the Sermon on the Mount is in the first place, but not exclusively, addressed to and intended to be practised by the Christian community. In and to the community it should become clear that and how a different kind of society can come about. Not perfect – that is not given to us; but a continually renewed attempt in the right direction. However, this is not the end of it. Jesus' demands are important for our *whole* society, and also for the society of *nations*. But on this level we cannot expect anything to happen unless some realization can be seen in a *smaller* circle. In this respect we could think in terms of a certain gradation, as with the effect of a stone thrown into a pool: its impact becomes noticeable in ever-widening circles.

The Sermon is addressed to the readers from 'the mountain'. Matthew collects Jesus' sayings not just in any sermon but in a Sermon *on the Mount*. This is emphasized. What does the evangelist mean by this location? The mountain is a place for divine revelation and other important events (Mt 5:1; 14:23; 15:29; 17:1; 28:16). For Matthew, Jesus' words are extremely important; they occupy a very special place. He wants to present Jesus as one who teaches with authority (cf. Mt 7:28–29). If the Sermon on the Mount does not lie heavy as a mountain on us we have not grasped the importance Matthew gives it.

Jesus 'sat down', adopting the customary posture of a rabbi or teacher (cf. Mt 23:2). In other cultures too, e.g., in India, spiritual leaders do not speak without first sitting down, lifting their hand, and opening their mouth. . . . The disciples 'came to him' for instruction. Matthew frequently uses the verb 'to come to' (*proserchomai*) in this sense (cf. Mt 13:10, 36; 15:12; 18:1; 24:3).

Matthew gives full weight to Jesus' words. He could hardly have expressed it in more forcible language: 'And he opened his mouth and taught them, saying . . .'. In the Bible, the words 'he opened his mouth' indicate that someone is taking the initiative to speak after a long silence (cf. Job 3:1) or is going to say important things (Ps 78[77]:2; Dan 10:16; Acts 8:35; 10:34). So this is not just any beginning. Now is the time to listen.

3   The Beatitudes

(Mt 5:3–12)

Introduction

What is a beatitude?

The 'beatitude' is a form of speech which proclaims the happiness or blessedness of one or more persons in certain circumstances or under certain conditions. In the Bible it is found in various contexts: narratives, prophetic oracles, psalms, and wisdom sayings. But a *series* of beatitudes like the one we find in the gospel of Matthew is rare.

As to their meaning, the beatitudes may be divided into two categories. In the first, a person or group is declared happy because of a particular state or an act which exists *de facto*; e.g., Ps 33(32):12, 'Blessed is the nation whose God is the Lord, the people whom he has chosen as his heritage'. In the second category, the proclamation is conditional and amounts to an indirect exhortation to adopt a certain conduct; e.g., Ps 32(31):2, 'Blessed is the man to whom the Lord imputes no iniquity, and in whose spirit there is no deceit'. Matthew's beatitudes belong to the second category, but one may wonder whether this was so in the beatitudes as they were pronounced by Jesus. A closer study of this question will show that Matthew's beatitudes are the result of considerable pre-Matthean literary activity.

Eight beatitudes?

Matthew and Luke present their own version of the beatitudes: Mt 5:3–12 contains eight (nine?) beatitudes, while Lk 6:20–26 offers four beatitudes (Lk 6:20–23), followed by four woes (Lk 6:24–26). Presumably neither of the two has the exact original words spoken by Jesus. Is it possible to determine what was added or omitted by either of them and exactly what belonged to their common source? Let us attentively read the two versions arranged in parallel columns.

TWO VERSIONS

Mt 5:3–12	*Lk 6:20b–23*
3 Blessed are the poor in spirit, for theirs is the kingdom of heaven.	20 Blessed are you poor, for yours is the kingdom of God.
4 Blessed are those who mourn, for they shall be comforted.	
5 Blessed are the meek, for they shall inherit the earth.	
6 Blessed are those who hunger and thirst for righteousness, for they shall be satisfied.	21 Blessed are you that hunger now, for you shall be satisfied. Blessed are you that weep now, for you shall laugh.
7 Blessed are the merciful, for they shall obtain mercy.	
8 Blessed are the pure in heart, for they shall see God.	
9 Blessed are the peacemakers, for they shall be called sons of God.	
10 Blessed are those who are persecuted for righteousness' sake, for theirs is the kingdom of heaven.	
11 Blessed are you when men revile you and persecute you and utter all kinds of evil against you falsely on my account.	22 Blessed are you when men hate you, and when they exclude you and revile you and cast out your name as evil, on account of the Son of man.
12 Rejoice and be glad, for your reward is great in heaven, for so men persecuted the prophets who were before you.	23 Rejoice in that day, and leap for joy, for behold, your reward is great in heaven, for so their fathers did to the prophets.

Lk 6:24–26

24 But woe to you that are rich, for you have received your consolation.

25 Woe to you that are full now, for you shall hunger.

Mt 5:3–12   *Lk 6:20b–23*

Woe to you that laugh now,
for you shall mourn and
weep.

26 Woe to you, when all men
speak well of you, for so their
fathers did to the false
prophets.

THE BASIC TEXT

A critical assessment of the texts of Matthew and Luke leads to the
following reconstruction of the basic text:

(1) Blessed are the poor,
      for theirs is the kingdom of heaven.
(2) Blessed are those who mourn,
      for they shall be comforted.
(3) Blessed are those who hunger and thirst,
      for they shall be satisfied.
(4) Blessed are you when men hate you,
      and when they exclude and revile you
      and cast out your name as evil,
      on account of the Son of man.
      Rejoice and be glad,
      for your reward is great in heaven,
      for so men persecuted the prophets
      who were before you.

This basic text contains four beatitudes. As far as the first three
beatitudes are concerned, the version of Matthew seems to be closer to
the text of the source, after removal of the Matthean additions 'in
spirit' and 'for righteousness'. It is generally accepted that Lk 6:22 has
better conserved the first part of the fourth beatitude ('Blessed are you
. . . on account of the Son of man'); for the second part ('Rejoice . . .
before you'), the text of Matthew again seems closer to the source-text.
      The first three beatitudes of this basic text are very similar in
structure: short, in the third person plural, and twofold. The first part
refers to an existing situation of human misery. The second part
promises a future reversal or compensation. This second part contains
also the motive ('for . . .') why a destitute or mourning person can now
be called blessed. How, or on what ground, the speaker or writer dares
to make such a connection is not immediately clear from the formulation itself. It should be said, however, that the passive mood, found in

the second and third beatitudes ('shall be comforted', 'shall be satisfied') is a reverential circumlocution for divine action. The real meaning is therefore: 'God will comfort them', 'God will satisfy them'.

The fourth beatitude of the basic text is distinguished from the first three by its length (abundance of more or less synonymous words), the address (second person instead of third person in the first three), the exhortation to joy and gladness (imperative!), and the contents (persecution on account of Jesus). These differences require a separate discussion of the two groups of beatitudes. We will consider first the fourth beatitude, and then the first three. Of each group we will ask the questions: who, why, what, when?

The beatitude of the persecuted

It is clear that the disciples are addressed. They will have to suffer hate and scoffing, exile and expulsion. The persecution is Christologically conditioned: 'on account of the Son of man'. This beatitude is not addressed to just anyone who suffers, but to those who suffer on account of Christ.

They are called blessed because their 'reward is great in heaven'. This motivation, which stresses the provisional character of their present situation, can be called eschatological. However, the phrase 'in heaven' should not be understood as referring to a place. It means 'before God'. At the same time there is a salvation-historical retrospect, as it were, an additional consolation: in the past the prophets were no better off! Past and future are within God's saving plan. Jesus reminds his disciples of the persecuted prophets; he thinks of his own destiny and predicts the destiny of his followers who will be persecuted on his account.

In what does the beatitude consist? The metaphor 'reward' certainly has future overtones, but the assumed knowledge of this reason for hope can cause blessedness amidst persecution (now).

It is obvious that Jesus did not pronounce this beatitude at the beginning of his public ministry, but rather in a situation of parting, towards the end of his ministry. He knew what was going to happen to him, and he told his disciples what would be their lot: 'A disciple is not above his teacher' (Mt 10:24). We should refer especially to passages which express the same trend of thought, the same worries which beset the last period of Jesus' life on earth (cf. Mt 23:29–36; Mk 13:9–13).

It seems that not Jesus but the later Christian tradition (the primitive Church, the Q-source) attached the fourth beatitude to the first three. It is a beatitude, but its structure and contents differ greatly from the former. It can be understood in a situation shortly before Jesus' death and, in its present formulation (especially 'on my account', 'on account of the Son of Man'), even better in a situation after Jesus' death. Such a situation is not necessary for the first three beatitudes.

The beatitude of the poor

It is almost generally accepted that the first three beatitudes do not intend to refer to three distinct groups of people: poor, mourners, and those who hunger and thirst. Rather they mention three samples of a large category of destitute and oppressed people found in society. The first beatitude refers to the oracle of Isa 61:1 and what it says of the good news announced to the poor: 'The spirit of the Lord God is upon me, because the Lord has anointed me to bring good tidings to the afflicted (RSV footnote: poor) . . .'. The beatitude of the mourners is inspired by the same oracle: 'to proclaim the year of the Lord's favour . . . to comfort all who mourn' (Isa 61:2). The beatitude of those who hunger and thirst echoes, though in a wider sense, the group of promises of consolation to which Isa 61 belongs; see, e.g., Isa 61:6, 'you shall eat the wealth of the nations', and Isa 49:10, 'they shall not hunger and thirst'.

> To whom, then, does the word 'poor' apply? Is it to those who possess no means and no power? Yes! The text here requires us to change our thinking so as to accustom ourselves to a basic trait of biblical thinking, viz., that God stands on the side of the poor. The salvation that Jesus is proclaiming is a prophetic message from the Holy God, who comforts the poor by lifting them out of the dust and dirt of their existence (Ps 113:7) and cheers them by 'establishing his throne' among them, the downtrodden and the abused (Isa 57:15; cf. 49:13). The concern of God for the poor can be observed throughout the entire Old Testament. One who wishes to enter intimately into the biblical concept of God will have to learn to bear with the severity that lurks in the thought of this partiality of God for one particular class of people. 'Enlightened' religiosity, which looks upon the relationship between God and man as purely a disposition of mind, is frightened by the biblical notion that God takes cognizance of the social position of a person. Anyone who interests himself in the biblical world of ideas must become accustomed to the fact that the relationship of man to God is based entirely on the indivisible being of man.[1]

Why are these poor called blessed? In the fourth beatitude (Q) the persecuted are called blessed: those who suffer *on account of Jesus* will be rewarded. They are called blessed because of a religious, moral quality. However, this does not apply to the first three beatitudes, which call blessed not those who are poor on account of Jesus, but those who are materially poor as such. Therefore, we should not say that the poor are called blessed because of their internal dispositions, as some very renowned scholars have done. The emphasis lies somewhere else.

From the beatitudes appears first of all God's free gift, his grace, which precedes man's response. The reason for the privilege of the poor is to be sought not in their own presumed virtues or internal dispositions, but in God's disposition towards them. It has been shown that throughout the ancient Near East and also in Israel the poor were promised the special protection of the kings. The foundation of what could be called the 'privilege of the poor' is found, not in an idealized conception of their poverty, but in an ideal of the royal function. The same is true in religious texts: the gods are protectors of the disinherited, not because they are more pious than others, but because the gods take a special interest in them. This is especially true in the religion of Israel. Yahweh the Lord God of Israel is the protector and defender of the poor. He assumes this role in virtue of the *justice* which is characteristic of him. This is not a retributive justice which would recompense particular merits of the poor acquired by their presumed piety and trust in God. We have here rather a justice of the 'royal' type: God undertakes to guarantee the rights of persons who cannot protect themselves by their own means and cannot count on anybody else to defend their rights. The blessedness of the poor at the coming of the kingdom is to be found, therefore, not in the justice or piety of these privileged people, but in the justice of God. They are called blessed not because of their poverty, of course, but because of the fact that through God's justice their condition is going to change with the dawning of the kingdom of God. This interpretation is confirmed by a study of other privileged people of the kingdom: the 'little children', and the sinners. Here too, their privileged status is not due to any special dispositions of theirs, but to God's disposition towards them.

Jesus addresses people who are poor, who mourn, and who hunger and thirst. These are in fact variations of one and the same theme. These three beatitudes deal with people who in one way or another live in a miserable situation. They are called blessed, not because of their virtue, their internal disposition, their openness to the kingdom of God, but simply because they are poor and as such benefit from God's disposition towards them.

In a sense, the beatitudes have a function of proof. In Jesus' words and actions is fulfilled what had been predicted by the prophets concerning the poor and the miserable (cf. Isa 61:1–2, etc.). The kingdom is here. The fact that the good news is preached to the poor, that they are called blessed, proves its realization. In words borrowed from Isa 61, the beatitudes say that 'the time is fulfilled and the kingdom of

God is at hand' (Mk 1:15; cf. Mt 4:17). The beatitudes are rightly called 'messianic proclamations'.

In what does this beatitude of the poor consist? The sayings promise inheritance of the kingdom of heaven, consolation and satisfaction. As in the fourth beatitude, this should be understood in an eschatological way. What is the exact meaning of 'theirs *is* the kingdom of heaven'? The close connection between the first three beatitudes has been sufficiently shown. It seems difficult, therefore, to contrast the first beatitude which apparently speaks of a present possession, and the second and third beatitudes whose promises evidently concern the future. The eschatological character of the kingdom argues against opposing the first beatitude to the second and the third. The context therefore seems to impose a future perspective. In fact, it is clear why a future tense is not used in the first beatitude. That would have been to say virtually that God was not yet King! The kingdom of God 'is'; those for whom God destines it do not yet fully experience it, but it 'is' already for them, it is already their heritage. They are called blessed, not simply because the kingdom will come one day, but precisely because its coming is imminent. The beatitudes of the mourning and those who hunger and thirst are given their true meaning in the same perspective. These people must consider themselves blessed, not because they will be comforted and satisfied one day (God knows when!), but because with the appearance of Jesus this day has arrived. The moment for the realization of the promises uttered by Isaiah has come: God is going to establish his kingdom for the benefit of all the miserable.

When did Jesus pronounce these beatitudes? Two possibilities have been considered. Unlike the fourth beatitude, these three may very well have been pronounced either at the very beginning of Jesus' ministry, since he himself proclaims the nearness of the kingdom of God (Mt 4:17), or during the time when he sent the twelve to Galilee. We know from other passages that Jesus taught his disciples short, easily memorized sayings which they had to preach.

MATTHEW'S INTERPRETATION

Discussion of the text
How did Matthew edit the text of his source (Q)? Through comparison with the older Q-text we can get an idea of Matthew's redaction and expansion.

First, in the original beatitudes of Q, Matthew has added the phrases '(poor) in spirit' (Mt 5:3) and '(thirst) for righteousness' (Mt 5:6). Secondly, he (or the pre-Matthean tradition?) has added the five beatitudes of the meek (Mt 5:5), the merciful (Mt 5:7), the pure in heart (Mt 5:8), the peacemakers (Mt 5:9), the persecuted for right-eousness' sake (Mt 5:10).

Matthew has emphasized more strongly the separate character of the fourth Q-beatitude (Mt 5:11-12), but at the same time he connects it again with the other beatitudes. This separation is brought about by the arrangement of the first eight beatitudes (Mt 5:3-10) in two stanzas (Mt 5:3-6 and 5:7-10), the external similarity of which in the Greek text extends itself to the number of words used. The original beatitudes of the poor, the mourning and the hungry are found in the first stanza, while the second mentions another group of addressees (merciful, pure in heart, peacemakers; to this group belong also the meek mentioned in Mt 5:5). The addition of this second group of addressees has not just led to the insertion of Mt 5:5, but has also altered the overall outlook of the first stanza, as the insertion of 'in spirit' (Mt 5:3) and 'for righteousness' (Mt 5:6) indicates. The group of addressees of the first stanza is thus attuned to that of the second stanza.

The two stanzas manifest a remarkable parallelism in overall structure and in detail. The clause 'for theirs is the kingdom of heaven' (Mt 5:10b) corresponds to Mt 5:3b. By means of this repetition, the expression 'for theirs is the kingdom of heaven' becomes, as it were, the theme of the beatitudes, and it may be supposed that the second half of the other beatitudes ('for they shall be comforted', etc.) are mere variations of this theme. The two stanzas are in typically Matthean fashion framed by the key-word 'righteousness' (Mt 5:6a, 10a).

The original beatitudes of the poor, the mourners, and the hungry were remodelled into a series of four beautitudes in which 'the poor' (Hebrew: *ani*) – 'theirs is the kingdom of heaven' (Mt 5:3) correspond to 'the meek' (*anawim*) – 'they shall inherit the earth' (Mt 5:5). The same stylistic device is found in Mt 5:4, 6 (the mourning, the hungry – comforted, satisfied). It is also found in the second stanza in Mt 5:8, 9 (pure in heart, peacemakers – to see God, to be called sons of God). Thus a psalm-like series originated of sayings whose similar sound is further reinforced by the repetition of the emphatic 'for they' at the beginning of the second half of the verse, and by the fact that in the four beatitudes of the first stanza the names of those called blessed all begin in Greek with the letter *p* (*ptōchoi, praeis, penthountes, peinantes*), thus constituting a case of alliteration.

Mt 5:10 does not introduce any new idea; it is an 'excerpt' from Mt 5:11-12 and the previous verses (see the key-word composition by means of the words 'to persecute' and 'for the sake of, on account of' from Mt 5:11, and 'theirs is the kingdom of heaven' from Mt 5:3). Mt 5:10 is apparently a redactional composition of Matthew devised to conclude the two beatitude-stanzas and to connect these stanzas with the following beatitude in prose style, addressed to the persecuted community (Mt 5:11–12), in which the false character of the accusations is stressed.

Change of accent

The Matthean version of the beatitudes is not merely a stylistic and material expansion. The eight (or nine) beatitudes are given a function considerably different from that in the original Q-version.

Although the beatitudes were originally intended as 'messianic proclamations' and did not indicate virtues to be practised, Matthew now stresses the internal disposition. Expressions like 'in spirit', 'pure in heart', 'thirst for righteousness', 'meek', and 'merciful', no longer point first of all to a social group, as was the case with the poor, etc., in the Q-source, but to a certain mentality, a moral disposition.

The first part of the beatitudes ('Blessed are . . .') is no longer a mere establishment of a fact (that they are materially poor, that they mourn, that they thirst): to Matthew it expresses a necessary condition for participation in the promise of salvation. Those referred to are no longer people paradoxically privileged (poor who will inherit, etc.), but virtuous people (poor *in spirit*) who commit themselves morally; in other words, Matthew has transformed a negative life-situation (poverty, hunger) into positive attitudes ('poor in spirit', 'hunger and thirst for righteousness'). In Matthew, the beatitudes have become a description of the virtues which the Christian should practise. The number of beatitudes is certainly related to Matthew's concern for completeness, which is also found elsewhere in the gospel. The beatitudes are an almost complete list of virtues.

It is not only the materially destitute (cf. the first three beatitudes of Q) or the religiously persecuted (cf. the fourth beatitude of Q) who are called blessed. Matthew is so much concerned with the 'spirit' that he almost loses sight of the material level. Meek, merciful, pure in heart, peacemakers can also be found among well-to-do Christians. As a matter of fact, the first three beatitudes were originally addressed to people who were not yet Christians, but Matthew is obviously addressing fellow-Christians in an exhortatory and paraenetic way. The original proclamation that the kingdom of God is at hand and that it is God's undeserved gift to man is no longer timely for the contemporary community. They know this already. Therefore Matthew weakens the messianic character of the beatitudes in order to emphasize the equally necessary human response. However much the kingdom of God may be a free gift of God, it presupposes also a basic attitude in man.

The ethical accentuation of the beatitudes in Matthew is obvious. But two things should be noted. First, it is impossible to ignore the Christological foundation of the beatitudes. The Matthean Jesus is all that the beatitudes describe. He himself realizes this 'Christian' programme. Therefore, the beatitudes should not be defined as a mere catalogue of Christian virtues necessary for salvation. They presuppose faith in the one who by proclaiming them inaugurated the kingdom. Second, the ethical emphasis of the beatitudes is developed in a precise and absolutely fundamental context: the sovereign proclamation of salvation offered for free to all men. The ethical emphasis of the beatitudes is not an arbitrary act of the Matthean community or of the redactor, but has its foundation and meaning in the re-evaluation of eschatology. It is also to be explained by a change of audience, from the materially poor to the Matthean Church, for which the beatitudes are both paraclesis and paraenesis, or consolation and exhortation. The ethical emphasis deriving from Matthew does not weaken the eschatological character of the beatitudes as much as is frequently said.

Exegesis

The first beatitude (Mt 5:3)

Verse 3: Blessed are the poor in spirit, for theirs is the kingdom of heaven.

In view of what we said about the basic text of the beatitudes and their Old Testament background, we should do justice to the fact that the God of the Bible is on the side of the poor, or even biased in favour of the materially poor, before we start speaking of the 'poor *in spirit*'. Lk 6:20 calls the poor blessed as such, and almost all biblical scholars agree that Jesus too was addressing the materially poor, and that the phrase 'in spirit' was added by Matthew.

In secular Greek, the term 'poor' (*ptōchos*) means materially destitute. However, in the Bible and other Jewish literature *ptōchos* and its Hebrew equivalents *ebion* and *ani* can have several meanings. Firstly, they can mean 'poor' in the sense of destitute, as in Deut 15:4, 11, 'But there will be no poor among you. . . . For the poor will never cease out of the land.' Secondly, it may mean people who are downtrodden and oppressed because of their poverty, as in Amos 8:4, 'hear this, you who trample upon the needy, and bring the poor of the land to an end'. Thirdly, the poor and oppressed have no influence, no power, no prestige. Their rights are not vindicated by men. There remains only God, and because of their situation God shows special attention to the poor, and decides 'to bring good tidings to the poor' (Isa 61:1). Subordinately, therefore, *ptōchos* and its Hebrew equivalents come to describe people who, because they have nobody on earth to defend their rights, have put their confidence in God. In Ps 69(68), the 'oppressed' and 'needy' (Ps 69[68]:32–33) are also those 'who seek' the Lord (Ps 69[68]:6). Closer to the Christian era, the apocryphal *Psalms of Solomon* express the same ideas.

In this line of thought the Septuagint repeatedly translates the words *ani* and *anaw(im)* by *praüs*, 'meek', or 'modest', although in themselves these Hebrew words have no moral or religious meaning. Hence the need for specification in order to make their moral connotations explicit. Moreover, the Hebrew language not infrequently spiritualizes a physical or material quality by means of the addition of the words 'spirit' or 'heart' to an adjective. Thus in Isa 29:24, 'those who err in spirit' are those who leave the ways of truth. Similarly, Matthew (or the pre-Matthean tradition) specified the 'poor' by the addition of the phrase 'in spirit'.

The only parallel known to Matthew's 'poor in spirit' is found in the *Rule of War* of Qumran: 'By the poor in spirit . . . the hard of heart, and by the perfect of way all the nations of wickedness have come to an end; not one of their mighty men stands' (1 QM 14, 7). In this text the phrase 'poor in spirit' has a moral and spiritual meaning which may be rendered as 'humble'. The same is true for Matthew, who is presenting here an essential aspect of the programme of discipleship which he offers to his Church: humility, an attitude of which Christ, 'gentle and lowly (humble) in heart' (Mt 11:29), is the example.

In adding the phrase 'in spirit', Matthew is not adding something totally new. He wants to explicitate what seems to him the real meaning of Jesus' word, taking into account the religious implications of the word 'poor' in Jewish piety. This explicitation tallies perfectly with the didactic preoccupation characteristic of the Matthean redaction. By the addition of the phrase 'in spirit', Mt 5:3 becomes the self-designation of the pious. The beatitudes refer to them as they live up to the norm of piety. In line with this, and by means of Mt 5:5, 7–10, the beatitudes have been developed into a catechism of discipleship. Saint Jerome paraphrased: 'Blessed are the poor in spirit, those who by the Holy Spirit are voluntarily poor'. More recently suggested translations are: 'those who know their need for God (and for their neighbours)', and 'blessed are those who choose to be poor' (in Spanish, *dichosos los que eligen ser pobres*).

The promise 'for theirs is the kingdom of heaven' is equivalent to the expression 'for to such belongs the kingdom of heaven' (Mt 19:14). The meaning of the 'kingdom of heaven' has been explained above. This kingdom is now promised to the 'poor in spirit'. Matthew is no longer talking about people who live in material destitution, as the original beatitude did, but about people who live in the right disposition. The beatitude is no longer intended as a messianic proclamation, but as catechesis and paraenesis, i.e. exhortation to a virtuous Christian life. Matthew no longer emphasizes first of all the imminence of the kingdom of God, but rather the conditions for participation in it. In doing so he stresses the 'spirit' so much that he almost forgets the material level. 'Poverty' is interiorized; it becomes renunciation. Matthew invites his readers to a change of mentality. They should distance themselves from their possessions in order to be open to the values of the kingdom. Poverty in spirit is not necessarily opposed to possessions, but it is always opposed to attachment. However, this does not mean that Matthew is exclusively concerned with a mentality. The latter is the more important, but Matthew knew that internal detachment is impossible in practice without freeing oneself from possessions (Mt 19:16–30).

The second beatitude (Mt 5:4)

> **Verse 4:** Blessed are those who mourn, for they shall be comforted.

The terminology of this beatitude is borrowed from Isa 61:2, '. . . to comfort all who mourn', where those who mourn are the same people as the 'poor' of Isa 61:1. We should also refer to texts like Isa 60:20, '. . . your days of mourning shall be ended'; Isa 66:10, 'Rejoice with Jerusalem . . . rejoice with her, all you who mourn over her'; and especially Sir 48:24, 'By the spirit of might he saw the last things, and comforted those who mourned in Zion'.

In the Bible, the Greek word *penthein* is used for mourning for the dead (Gen 23:2), national catastrophe (Isa 3:26), and fear of divine punishment (Amos 5:16). But mourning may also be the result of oppression (I Macc 1:25–27; 2:24, 39). The term is often associated with weeping (*klaiein*, the verb used in Lk 6:21), e.g., in Mk 16:10, '. . . as they mourned and wept'; Rev 18:11, 'And the merchants of the earth weep and mourn for her'. See also Rev 18:15, 19 and Jas 4:8f.

It follows from the Old Testament texts cited that Jesus did not intend to call a simple spiritual disposition blessed. Like Isa 61:2, he announced the eschatological counterpart of a real human suffering, whatever its origin might be: unconditional messianic comfort. As the Messiah, sent and inspired by God, he chooses the side of the poor, the mourning, the hungry, the little ones. Where he passes, mourning changes into joy, the sick are cured, lepers are cleansed and restored to the community. Jesus shows an uncompromising solidarity with outcasts and all those who in one way or another are victims of discrimination.

But what did Matthew have in mind, and what, according to him, was the object of the affliction? Lk 6:21b reads: 'Blessed are you that weep now', and the presumption is that (under the influence of

Isa 61:2?) Matthew changed 'weep' into 'mourn'. And in Mt 9:15 the evangelist writes: 'Can the wedding guests *mourn* as long as the bridegroom is with them?', while Mk 2:19 has: 'Can the wedding guests *fast* . . . ?' In both cases Matthew softens the physical aspect and uses a more general expression. According to Mt 9:15, the suffering is caused by the bodily absence of Jesus. Similarly, one may envisage in Mt 5:4 the Church during its earthly existence: subject to the vicissitudes of the world, it mourns while waiting for its accomplishment. However, this mourning also expresses faith and hope. If those who mourn should not be distinguished from the poor (in spirit), they are also people who expect their consolation entirely from God. Matthew calls the disciples to such an attitude.

Blessed are the disciples who mourn because God gets so little chance in their lives, because they are so far removed from the ideal of the gospel. Blessed are the disciples of Jesus who mourn because the world, beginning with their everyday environment, shows so little of the realization of God's kingdom, because God's will is not yet done on earth. Blessed are the Christians who do not resign themselves to the situation of injustice and oppression which prevails in so many parts of the world, who are still shocked by the many spiritual, social and material obstacles which prevent the realization of the kingdom.

Those who mourn are called blessed, not because of their mourning, of course, but because 'they shall be comforted', because with the coming of the kingdom their situation will change, and because their tears will be wiped away (cf. Rev 21:4). How they will be comforted is not immediately clear, but the passive form in which the promise is cast is a 'theological passive', a reverential circumlocution for divine action: 'for God will comfort them'. This must be understood eschatologically: echoing the prophetic oracles, the verb *parakalein* contains the fullness of the divine intervention in the eschatological times. However, this consolation has already become a reality in God's action in the person of Jesus, who *is* 'the consolation of Israel' (Lk 2:25). In Jesus, who untiringly responded to all human misery, God's consolation received a human face to such an extent that he could be truly called 'God with us' (Mt 1:23).

The third beatitude (Mt 5:5)

Verse 5: Blessed are the meek, for they shall inherit the earth.

In many manuscripts this beatitude is found in the second place, immediately after the beatitude of the poor. The Hebrew word *anawim* may be translated in Greek as 'poor' as well as 'meek, gentle'. In favour of the second place is the parallelism: to the poor belongs the *kingdom of heaven* – the meek will inherit the *earth* (i.e., the land, in Greek: *gē*).

The vocabulary and idea of this beatitude is borrowed from Ps 37(36):11, 'But the meek shall possess the land, and delight themselves in abundant prosperity'. In the New Testament the word 'meek' (*praüs*) is found three more times: Mt 11:29, 'Take my yoke upon you, and learn from me; for I am gentle (meek) and lowly in heart . . .'; Mt 21:5, '. . . Behold, your king is coming to you, humble (meek), and mounted on an ass . . .'; and finally I Pet 3:4, 'but let it be the hidden person of the heart with the imperishable jewel of a gentle (meek) and quiet spirit, which in God's sight is very precious'. The Matthean texts have no parallels in either Mark or Luke.

The word *praüs* is devoid of all sociological and economic nuances. It expresses an ideal of which Jesus is the unmistakable model (cf. Mt 11:29; 21:5). If Matthew did not compose this beatitude – many biblical scholars say he did – it should be admitted that it fits perfectly into the spiritualized character of his redaction, and allows him to reinforce the moral import of the beatitude of the poor, 'meek' being almost synonymous with 'poor' (in Hebrew, *anawim* and *ani*). Some scholars (e.g. J. Dupont) hold that the first and the third beatitude have basically the same meaning.

Like the 'poor in spirit', the 'meek' are people who have surrendered themselves completely to God. They have broken through the narrow circle of their own wishes and dreams and have opened their hearts to the dream of the kingdom of God to come. Instead of enlisting God into the service of their own short-sighted desires, they have entered into God's service. This attitude of mind is not the same as passive resignation or servile conformism. The beatitude demands a great readiness and creative commitment to a future which God wants to realize through men. The meekness which is called blessed has nothing to do with any opium of the people devised to keep them subservient. The meek are all intent on service to their fellow-men. But unlike the 'hard men', the 'hawks', they do not fight to obtain a better situation. Not that they do not want a better situation, or are not committed to the realization of a more humane world, but they have decided not to use violence to obtain it. At the risk of seeming naive, they are confident that in order to inherit the land they should be meek, and are convinced that violence is a way that does not lead to the land which God promises. Mahatma Gandhi, Martin Luther King, Helder Câmara are indisputable examples of this meekness.[2]

To possess the land was the original hope of the nomadic ancestors of Israel, and possession of land was God's first promise to his people. Indeed, land is a central theme of biblical faith, and Israel's history can be described as a dialectic of landlessness and landedness.

As a landless people, Israel is presented as sojourners (Abraham, Jacob), wanderers (the Exodus), and Israel in exile. All these images present the land as *promise* to the landless. Over against them stands the landedness of the settlement in Egypt under Joseph, the monarchy, and the restoration under Ezra after the exile. It has been correctly said that the Bible is the story of God's people with God's land.

The core of the gospel proclamation is the end of one age and the beginning of a new one. The theme of 'kingdom' is decisive for the understanding of the New Testament. Among many other things it includes the idea of historical, political, physical realm, that is, land, and it is never spiritualized to the extent of totally denying this aspect. However rich and complex the concept of the kingdom may be, the coming of Jesus implies a reference to the theme of radical inversion of landed and landless (cf. Lk 1:51–55; 6:20–26; 19:1–10).

> The action, the preaching, and the person of Jesus, all attest to new land now being given. But the land being newly given is land presented in an acutely dialectical way. The way to land is by loss. The way to lose land is to grasp it. The way to life in the land is by death. Thus at the heart of the reversal of land/landless is a scandal. It is not a new scandal, for it is precisely what the whole history of Israel evidences in terms of gift and grasp. But now that whole dialectic is encompassed in one person. On the one hand it will not do to treat the New Testament as though it is uninterested in the land. On the other hand it will not do to treat the New Testament as though it contains a simple promise of the land. . . . Rather the New Testament has discerned how problematic land is; when the people are landless, the promise comes; but when the land is secured, it seduces and the people are turned toward loss. Thus the proclamation of Jesus is about graspers losing and those open to gifts as receiving.[3]

> We have yet to face how odd and discomforting is the biblical affirmation that God wills land for his people and he will take it from others for the sake of the poor. We have failed to maintain the land/landless dialectic, so that we are immobilized on the issue without power to invite the landed to landlessness or to include the landless in the land. The good news is not that the poor are blessed for being poor, but that to them belongs the kingdom, that is, the new land. Similarly the meek are not simply blessed but are identified as heirs of the land.[4]

For Matthew the original meaning of 'land' has grown pale. 'To inherit the land' has become a formula expressing the gift of eschatological salvation. It describes the true identity and security which man finds in God. The promise of this beatitude is an answer to a fundamental longing for 'land', a 'space' in which men can be themselves and totally free.

The fourth beatitude (Mt 5:6)

Verse 6: Blessed are those who hunger and thirst for righteousness, for they shall be satisfied.

We indicated that the beatitudes of the 'poor' and 'those who mourn' were inspired by Isa 61:1–2. Without referring to any such precise text, the beatitude of 'those who hunger (and thirst)' seems to come from the same context of the Book of Consolation (Isa 40 – 66). It is therefore permissible to think that the 'poor', 'those who mourn', and 'those who hunger (and thirst)' originally referred to one and the same group of destitute people. Isa 61:6 reads: '. . . you shall eat the wealth of the nations, and in their riches you shall glory'. But reference should especially be made to Isa 49:8–13, taken from an oracle closely related to that found in Isa 61. 'Thus says the Lord, "In a time of favour I have answered you. . . . They shall feed along the ways, on all bare heights shall be their pasture; *they shall not hunger or thirst*. . . ." For the Lord has comforted his people, and will have compassion on his afflicted' (Isa 49:8–13 *passim*). From these and other texts it is clear that the weak and the suffering will profit from the great divine intervention. There is no insistence on the virtues and merits of the 'poor', 'mourners', and 'hungry', on their trust in God and their patience in the midst of suffering. They are not considered under this aspect, no more than the prisoners and oppressed, the blind and the deaf, who are often mentioned in the same context. We are faced here with oppressed people to whom God wants to show his mercy, because he decides to be on their side.

A comparison with Lk 6:21 reveals two differences. First, while Luke writes, 'you that hunger now', Matthew has: 'those who hunger and thirst'. It is not certain whether Matthew added 'and thirst', although it may be said that Luke's text seems to fit better in the original context: the poor are hungry, while thirst is not especially reserved for them. Moreover, in the second part of the beatitude we find only one verb, 'be satisfied' (*chortazesthai*), which refers only to hunger. While not excluding the possibility that Luke abbreviated the original text, it seems preferable to hold that Matthew amplified the text under the influence of the traditional pair: hunger–thirst, as found, e.g., in Isa 49:10 cited above, and Isa 32:6, '. . . to leave the craving of the hungry unsatisfied, and to deprive the thirsty of drink'. 'Behold, the days are coming, . . . when I will send a famine on the land; not a famine of bread, nor a thirst for water, but of hearing the words of the Lord' (Amos 8:11). Besides, in the Bible thirst is often the symbol of an ardent desire for God. 'As a hart longs for flowing streams, so longs my soul for you, O God. My soul thirsts for God, for the living God' (Ps 42[41]:1–2); 'O God, you are my God, I seek you, my soul thirsts for you' (Ps 63[62]:1).

Secondly, Matthew adds the object of their hunger and thirst: righteousness. 'Righteousness' is a very important key word in Matthean theology. It is found seven times in the gospel (Mt 3:15; 5:6, 10, 20; 6:1, 33; 21:32; never in Mark, once in Luke), all of which should most probably be attributed to the evangelist. The term occurs for the first time in the conversation of Jesus and John the Baptist on the question of who should baptize whom. Jesus settles the argument saying: 'Let it be so now; for thus it is fitting for us to fulfil all righteousness' (Mt 3:15). 'Righteousness' refers here to God's saving will, God's saving will as expression of his faithfulness to the covenant people. Just as God defends the rights of the poor, and consoles those who mourn, so he also allays the hunger of those who place their hope in the justice of the covenant. In Isaiah and the Psalms, 'righteousness' is often a synonym for 'salvation'. For example, Ps 17(16):15, 'As for me, I shall behold your face in righteousness, when I awake I shall be satisfied (*chortazesthai*) with beholding your form' (note the use of 'righteousness' and 'to be satisfied' in the same verse); Isa 11:4f., 'but with righteousness he shall judge the poor and decide with equity for the meek of the earth. . . . Righteousness shall be the girdle of his waist, and faithfulness the girdle of his loins' (note the parallelism of 'poor' and 'meek', and of 'righteousness' and 'faithfulness'). The prophet Isaiah speaks here of salvation and justice for the poor and the wretched.

In the present beatitude too, 'righteousness' seems to be something to be received from God ('they shall be satisfied' = God will satisfy them), rather than something to be achieved by men. But it refers also to the ethical response of the disciple who should 'seek first his (= God's) kingdom and his (= God's) righteousness' (Mt 6:33). He should seek the realization of God's saving plan without ceasing, in order to achieve an ever-growing righteousness which 'exceeds that of the scribes and the Pharisees' (Mt 5:20). Righteousness is therefore both a demand and eschatological salvation; it is a God-given attitude which corresponds to the kingdom and admits to it.

The addition of 'for righteousness' must be attributed to Matthew's catechetical concern which makes him emphasize the moral import of the beatitudes. By speaking of 'righteousness' in the beatitudes, he announces the theme which he will develop in the continuation of the Sermon on the Mount and thus creates a closer link between the beatitudes and the rest of the discourse. Originally, and together with the beatitudes of the poor and those who mourn, the beatitude of those who hunger was essentially a messianic proclamation; it was just another way of saying that 'the kingdom of God is at hand' (Mk 1:15; Mt 4:17). In this context the notion of 'practising your righteousness' (Mt 6:1; RSV translates 'piety') seems somewhat dissonant. This emphasis can be understood only on the level of Matthew's composition and his concern for ethical response to the initial messianic proclamation.

Those who ardently desire the vindication of what is right or the triumph of God's cause are called blessed, 'for they shall be satisfied'. The passive is again a reverential circumlocution for divine action: God will satisfy them. The idea is found in Ps 17(16):15 cited above; in Ps 107(106):9, 'for he satisfies him who is thirsty, and the hungry he fills with good things'; and Ps 132(131):15, 'I will abundantly bless her provisions: I will satisfy her poor with bread'. 'Satisfaction' is often used to express the joy which results from the divine gift, an idea expressed in particular in Ps 17(16):15. In the New Testament Jesus can say: 'He who comes to me shall not hunger, and he who believes in me shall never thirst' (Jn 6:35), because he has 'the words of eternal life' (Jn 6:68). With his whole person he refers to God who does not leave any of his promises unfulfilled. He can and will satisfy man's hunger for justice or righteousness. By the addition of 'righteousness' or 'justice', hunger and thirst receive a meaning which goes beyond a material need, but also includes that need. Those who hunger and thirst are the victims of the injustice of men, and their suffering thus becomes the hunger and thirst of the justice of God.

The fifth beatitude (Mt 5:7)

Verse 7: Blessed are the merciful, for they shall obtain mercy.

With this beatitude we enter into the second stanza of Matthew's beatitudes, which has no counterpart in Luke. Moreover, while in the previous beatitudes we could discover a physical or sociological condition underlying Matthew's spiritual interpretation, this is no longer the case here: we are dealing now with Christian attitudes, with Christian ethics which are, however, based on the most fundamental demands of the gospel. This is especially true of the beatitude of the 'merciful' which is found in another form in Lk 6:36, 'Be merciful, even as your Father is merciful'. In the Greek, Matthew and Luke use a different adjective (*eleēmōn* and *oiktirmōn*), but their meaning is practically identical.

Except for Heb 2:17 where it is said of Christ, the word 'merciful' is found only in the present beatitude in the New Testament. In the Septuagint, it is used quite often for God as well as for men. Mercy is very often mentioned in Jewish literature, sometimes in formulations which are quite similar to our beatitude, e.g., *Sifre Deut* 13:18, 'As long as you are merciful to men, heaven will show mercy to you'.

The Hebrew word *chesed* which underlies the Greek *eleēmōn* is practically intranslatable. It is first of all an attitude of the God of the covenant himself, but he expects the same attitude also from men. It does not mean to pity or to feel sorry for someone in trouble. It means rather the ability to get into another person's skin until one can see and feel things as the other sees and feels them, in other words, the ability to identify with the other person. The unmerciful, on the other hand, insist on their own rights.

Divine mercy extended to those who are merciful is one of Matthew's favourite themes. The parable of the unforgiving servant (Mt 18:23–35), which is found in Matthew alone, states that God's mercy, which we have experienced, expects that we too show mercy to our fellow-man: 'and should not you have had mercy on your fellow servant, as I had mercy on you?' (Mt 18:33). And from Hosea 6:6 Matthew borrows the idea that God wants mercy: 'I desire mercy, and not sacrifice' (Mt 9:13; 12:7; both texts are found in Matthew alone). In fact, we may say that the one great command running through Matthew's gospel is that of mercy (cf. Mt 5:7; 9:13; 12:7; 18:33; 25:31–46). in the Letter of James this idea is found in a catechetical context: 'So speak and so act as those who are to be judged under the law of liberty. For judgment is without mercy to one who has shown no mercy; yet mercy triumphs over judgment' (Jas 2:12–13).

Undoubtedly this demand for mercy can be traced beyond Matthew to Jesus himself (cf. Lk 6:36). The overall context of Jesus' message clearly excludes any kind of calculating mercy. Men cannot earn God's mercy by their own practice of mercy. God's mercy always remains a gift, and men's mercy should be a spontaneous response to the divine mercy which is freely and undeservedly extended to them.

The merciful 'shall obtain mercy', literally 'shall be shown (or given) mercy'. The passive form of the verb is again a reverential circumlocution for divine action: God will show mercy to them. The allusion to the final judgment is clear. Matthew does not intend to say that the merciful will enter into eternal life purely out of compassion: Mt 25:31–46 shows clearly that there is a relationship between people's acts and their reward. But the second half of this beatitude of the merciful means that before God the disciples who have practised mercy will in a very special way benefit from the divine mercy which they too, like any person, will need.

The sixth beatitude (Mt 5:8)

Verse 8: Blessed are the pure in heart, for they shall see God.

The popular and moralistic interpretation of this beatitude may be paraphrased as 'Blessed are those who keep the sixth commandment, for they will enjoy the beatific vision'. But what did Matthew really mean by the 'pure in heart' and by 'seeing God'?

Purity and impurity were important realities for Israel, also for Judaism in Jesus' time. For twentieth-century people who clearly distinguish hygiene and morals it is hard to understand and to appreciate a way of thinking in which these two were closely related. Hygienic prescriptions received a cultural, religious and moral meaning, and religious and moral demands were incarnated in hygienic practices. In the course of the centuries the list of commandments and prohibitions was constantly expanded and this led to a very elaborate casuistry and endless discussions about what was permitted and forbidden, obligatory or not obligatory.

However strange these prescriptions and casuistry may look to us, they had their use in Israel. They promoted a moral atmosphere and contributed to the maintenance of monotheism and the sense of God's infinite holiness among the Israelites. But for all their positive aspects they were not without dangers, the most serious of which was formalism. People often simply performed the external ritual without any conversion of heart.

The prophets reacted vehemently against this. We read in Hos 6:6: 'For I desire steadfast love and not sacrifice, the knowledge of God rather than burnt offerings'. Amos 5:21–26 states: 'I hate, I despise your feasts, and I take no delight in your solemn assemblies. . . . But let justice roll down like waters, and righteousness like an ever-flowing stream.' And Jer 7:3–7 insists: '. . . Amend your ways and your doings, and I will let you dwell in this place. Do not trust in these deceptive words: "This is the temple of the Lord, the temple of the Lord, the temple of the Lord." For if you truly amend your ways and your doings, if you truly execute justice one with another, if you do not oppress the alien, the fatherless or the widow, or shed innocent blood in this place, and if you do not go after other gods to your own hurt, then I will let you dwell in this place, in the land that I gave of old to your fathers for ever.'

The Psalms too, protest against this situation by passing over the prescriptions of purity almost in silence while emphasizing God's moral demands. Thus we read in Ps 24(23):3f.: 'Who shall ascend the hill of the Lord? And who shall stand in his holy place? He who has clean hands and a *pure heart*, who does not lift up his soul to what is false, and does not swear deceitfully.' Ps 51(50):10 says: 'Create in me a *clean heart*, O God, and put a new and right spirit within me'. And Ps 73(72):1 states: 'Truly God is good to the upright, to those who are *pure in heart*'. In this last verse we find the phrase 'pure in heart' used as a parallel for 'upright'. In the New Testament, Jas 4:8 exhorts: '. . . Cleanse your hands, you sinners, and purify your hearts, you men of double mind'.

Jesus radically pursued this line of interiorization (see Mt 15:1–19; 23:23–28). He made short work of the mere ritual and cultural purity which was so much emphasized by the scribes and Pharisees, but which had no value in the kingdom of God.

'Pure in heart', then, are those who are upright, whose motives are unmixed, whose minds are utterly sincere, who are completely and totally single-minded, whose interests are undivided. To be 'pure in heart' does not mean to be sinless, and should certainly not be interpreted in terms primarily of chastity.

To the pure in heart, the beatitude promises that 'they shall see God'. In the Old Testament the expression 'to see God' refers first of all to the Temple cult: to appear before God, to experience God's presence in the Temple worship, especially during the great festivals (cf. Ps 24:3f.). It expresses the sum total of what the faithful experience in terms of peace and joy, of help and strength, of protection and intimacy. See Ps 17(16):15, 'As for me, I shall behold your face in righteousness; when I awake, I shall be satisfied with beholding your form', and Ps 42(41):2b, 'When shall I come and behold the face of God?' If we take away the Temple context, 'to see God' means: an internal and intimate experience of God's presence, as the result of a life which is totally open to God's will. The rabbis spoke about 'seeing God' especially in an eschatological sense: the pious will see God in the coming age.

In the New Testament too 'to see God' often has an eschatological meaning, as, e.g., in I Jn 3:2, '. . . we shall see him as he is'; Rev 22:4, 'they shall see his face . . .', and Heb 12:14, 'Strive for peace with all men, and for the holiness without which no one will see the Lord'. But Jesus, through whom the coming age enters our world, calls the pure in heart blessed here and now, because they already experience God's presence. However, this experience is not yet final, 'for now we see in a mirror dimly, but then face to face' (I Cor 13:12). In this sense the beatitude contains a promise for the future.

The seventh beatitude (Mt 5:9)

Verse 9: Blessed are the peacemakers, for they shall be called sons of God.

The Greek word *eirēnopoios*, 'one who makes peace', is found only here in the whole Greek Bible, and the verb *eirēnopoiein*, 'to make peace', appears only once in the New Testament (Col 1:20). We find it also in Prov 10:10 LXX which differs from the Hebrew text and states: 'he who boldly reproves makes peace', a text which will prove very important for determining the true meaning of 'peacemakers'. The word *eirēnē*, 'peace', occurs many times and is a biblical key concept.

The Hebrew word *shalōm* is very rich in content and is hard to translate, as can be seen from the Septuagint, where more than twenty-five different words are used to render it. *Shalōm* is derived from a root which means: 'complete', 'intact', 'to be or to be in the process of being fulfilled'. To biblical man, 'peace' is the sum total of all that makes people contented (in German: *zufrieden*, literally, 'to peace', or 'at peace'). It is the condition of those who live in complete harmony with themselves, with their fellow-men, with nature, and with God. 'Peace', therefore, is not the opposite of war (cf. II Sam 7:11, where a liberation war is called *eirēnē*, 'peace'!), but of everything which disturbs the well-being and prosperity of individuals and the community. This 'peace' cannot be achieved without justice, and so we read in Jer 6:13–14, 'For from the least to the greatest of them, every one is greedy for unjust gain; and from prophet to priest, every one deals falsely. They have healed the wound of my people lightly, saying, "Peace, peace," when there is no peace.' But in messianic times peace and justice will be the people's 'overseers' (Isa 60:17), and God 'will extend prosperity (in the Greek *eirēnē*, 'peace') to her like a river, and the wealth of the nations like an overflowing stream' (Isa 66:12). Indeed, 'righteousness (justice) and peace will kiss each other' (Ps 85[84]:10b). And one should certainly not fail to read Ps 72(71):

> Give the King your justice, O God,
> and your righteousness to the royal son! . . .
> In his days may *righteousness* flourish,
> and *peace* abound, till the moon be no more! . . .
> For he delivers the needy when he calls,
> the poor and him who has no helper.
> He has pity on the weak and the needy,
> and saves the life of the needy.
> From oppression and violence he redeems their life;
> and precious is their blood in his sight.

In the New Testament too, 'peace' is one of the most important characteristics of the messianic kingdom which has come among us in the person of Jesus, and keeps coming towards its fulfilment at the end of time. This is especially emphasized by Luke (cf. 2:14; 19:38). The seventy-two disciples are sent to announce peace to whatever house they enter. If the owner is open to peace, then he will experience the gift; but if he rejects it, the peace will return to the heart of the announcers, who should in no case become exasperated (Lk 10:5-6). Not all people will accept the message of peace, and so Jesus can say that, however much he intended to bring peace, he has in fact brought the sword of division, because many, then and now, reject peace, thus causing division, sometimes even between close relatives (Lk 12:51-53; Mt 10:34-36).

Who, then, are the 'peacemakers'? From the previous considerations it should be clear that 'peacemakers' is not a synonym for the 'peaceful', the 'peaceable'. We are dealing with peace-*makers*, not with peace-*keepers*! Many peace-keepers ultimately succeed only in causing trouble, not peace, by allowing a threatening and dangerous situation to develop, their defence being that for the sake of peace they do not want to take action. The peace of the Bible is not achieved by evading issues, but by facing them and effectively dealing with them. The beatitude is addressed to people who actively commit themselves to bring about peace in its full biblical sense explained above, people who are prepared to face the issues, to tackle the obstacles which prevent such peace, if necessary by direct action.

Concern for peace is one of the basic characteristics of the Christian existence. The present beatitude has too often been interpreted as peace of man with his God, or as a private peace which does not exceed the boundaries of family or neighbourhood. The biblical concept of peace does not allow such limitations. God's peace concerns the total person and the whole world. As an aspect of the kingdom of God it cannot be confined to the private sphere. Like the kingdom it is both a gift and an urgent task for the Christian. And today this task means especially concern for social justice, progress and peace for all peoples.

The peacemakers 'shall be called sons of God'. In a biblical-Semitic way of speaking, 'to be called' is a synonym for 'to be'. The passive refers to God's action and should be understood as meaning: God will call them. When God calls people by a new name, it is more than just a name-giving. It means that they will *be* sons of God. For the same meaning of 'to be called' see Mt 5:19, '... shall be called least ... great in the kingdom of heaven'; Mt 21:13, '... My house shall be called a house of prayer'. To be 'a son of God' means: to be accepted in the peace and friendship of God, to be close to God. It is practically a synonym for 'elect', applying to eternal life the idea of the covenant according to which the members of Israel were designated as 'sons of God' (Ex 4:22; Deut 14:1; 32:19f.; Hos 11:1, compare Mt 2:15). In the New Testament the phrase 'sons of God' becomes a typical description of the eschatological gift, e.g., 'so that you may be sons of your

Father who is in heaven' (Mt 5:45; parallel in Lk 6:35; see also Lk 20:36; Rom 8:14; 9:26; II Cor 6:18; Gal 3:26). See especially the interesting parallel I Jn 3:1, 'See what love the Father has given us, that we should be called children of God; and so we are'. Again, something of what is promised is already realized, but the full realization is expected in the future.

The eighth beatitude (Mt 5:10, 11–12)

Verse 10: Blessed are those who are persecuted for righteousness' sake, for theirs is the kingdom of heaven.

Verses 11–12: Blessed are you when men revile you and persecute you and utter all kinds of evil against you falsely on my account. (12) Rejoice and be glad, for your reward is great in heaven, for so men persecuted the prophets who were before you.

The eighth beatitude constitutes a transition (Mt 5:10) which concludes the series of the preceding beatitudes (Mt 5:3–9) and at the same time introduces the following one (Mt 5:11–12). On the one hand, it is closely related to the previous beatitudes by means of the apparently intentional repetition of Mt 5:3b, 'for theirs is the kingdom of heaven', thus constituting an inclusion, i.e., a marking off of a section by repeating the words from the beginning of it at the end. On the other hand, the mention of the 'persecuted' is borrowed from the following verses, as also the phrase 'for righteousness' sake', which is inspired by 'on my account' (or, 'for my sake'), while at the same time underlining the end of the second stanza of the Matthean beatitudes by means of an obvious parallelism with Mt 5:6, 'for righteousness', which concludes the first stanza.

The final beatitude (Mt 5:11–12) is more developed than the preceding ones. The first verse, Mt 5:11, describes the treatment which awaits the disciples. In Matthew we find three kinds of bad treatment: revilement, persecution, and calumny, while in Luke we have four: hatred, exclusion, revilement, casting out of the name. Matthew seems to have introduced the following changes in his source:

(1) The idea of 'persecution' seems to have been substituted for the more descriptive expressions found in Luke, 'when men hate you, and when they exclude you'.
(2) Matthew also avoids the technical expression 'cast out your name as evil' and renders it in a more general way: 'utter all kinds of evil'.

(3) By adding that all this is done 'falsely'. Matthew apparently wants to emphasize that the accusations levelled against the disciples are false, or that the disciples must live in such a way that the accusations are false.

(4) It is also probable that Matthew has abridged the formula indicating the motive of the bad treatment inflicted on the disciples: 'on my account' is substituted for the expression 'on account of the Son of man'. As far as this verse is concerned, the formulation of Luke is to be preferred as closer to the source.

The second verse, Mt 5:12, says almost the same as Lk 6:23, but there are constant divergences of detail, of which some may be attributed to Luke's intention to write well. Luke's expression 'in that day' should be related to the adverb 'now' found in the second and the third beatitude (Lk 6:21) as well as in the second and third woe-saying (Lk 6:25), and is to be considered as a Lucan addition. The expression 'leap for joy' must also be attributed to Luke. The final phrases, 'for so men persecuted the prophets who were before you' (Matthew) and 'for so their fathers did to the prophets' (Luke), though not very different in expression, have a rather different meaning. Luke's Greek readers would have had a hard time understanding 'the prophets that were before you'. For the last verse, therefore, the preference must go to Matthew as closer to the source.

Suffering for justice is frequently found in the Psalms, e.g., Ps 22(21) and Ps 34(33):19–20. But it is especially clear in Wisdom 2:10–20: 'Let us oppress the righteous poor man. . . . Let us lie in wait for the righteous man. . . . Let us test him with insult and torture, that we may find out how gentle he is, and make trial of his forbearance. Let us condemn him to a shameful death, for, according to what he says, he will be protected.' The same idea is emphasized in the New Testament. In I Pet 3:13–14 we read: 'Now who is there to harm you if you are zealous for what is right? But even if you do suffer *for righteousness' sake*, you will be *blessed*. Have no fear of them, nor be troubled.' And in I Pet 4:13–14: 'But rejoice in so far as you share Christ's sufferings, that you may also *rejoice and be glad* when his glory is revealed. If you are reproached *for the name of Christ*, you are *blessed*, because the spirit of glory and of God rests upon you.' These and similar texts show that a statement like that in Mt 5:10, 11–12 was familiar in the early Church. The parallel use of 'for righteousness' sake' (Mt 5:10) and 'on my account' (Mt 5:11), and of 'for righteousness' sake' (I Pet 3:14) and 'for the name of Christ' (I Pet 4:14) implies that for Christians to dedicate their lives to justice should be the same as to give their lives to Jesus and to accept persecution for his sake. God's righteousness takes shape in the person of Jesus, and ultimately a Christian suffers not for *something* but for *somebody*.

'Blessed' means both an extension of congratulations and a call: Congratulations and keep it up! Of the different forms of bad treatment mentioned only 'to revile' (*oneidizein*) is found both in Matthew and Luke, and can therefore be traced to their source. The term is repeatedly found in the Old (I Sam 17:10, 25, 26, etc.) and the New Testament (Mt 27:44, etc.). United with his Lord, 'bearing abuse (*oneidismos*) for him' (Heb 13:13), the Christian relives the experience of the just one who in Ps 69(68):7, 9 addresses himself to God saying: 'For it is *for your sake* that I have borne reproach (*oneidismos*), that shame has covered my face. . . . for zeal for your house has consumed me, and the insults of those who insult (*oneidismoi tōn oneidizontōn*) you have fallen on me.'

The disciples will also be 'persecuted' (*diōkein*), a verb often used in the New Testament to describe all kinds of maltreatment suffered by Christians because of their faith (Mt 10:23; 23:34, etc.; compare Mt 13:21). But it would certainly be too one-sided to attribute the roles of persecutor and persecuted once and for all to the 'world' and the Church as such. The Church too is not completely secure against the possibility of making use of power politics and various forms of terror.

Instead of Luke's 'cast out your name as evil', i.e., denunciation, which reminds us of Deut 22:14, 'and brings an evil name upon her', Matthew writes: 'utter all kinds of evil against you *falsely*'. This emphasis seems to be related to Matthew's redaction of the trial before the Sanhedrin where Mark's reference to false witnesses (Mk 14:56–57) is carried further by attributing to the judges the intention to find 'false testimony' (Mt 26:59). The disciple, who is not better than the Master (Mt 10:17–25), will suffer the same treatment. It is also possible that Matthew added the word 'falsely' because in the Church not all accusations were uttered falsely (see Mt 24:12, 'and because wickedness is multiplied, most men's love will grow cold').

The clause 'rejoice and be glad' describes more explicitly what is implied in the 'blessing' formula. Then follow two reasons for this joy. First, 'your reward is great in heaven', i.e., with God. The New Testament, including Paul, does not hesitate to speak about reward. But this is not a claim and should not lead us to calculate our reward because, when we have done everything possible, we should still say: 'We are unworthy servants; we have only done what was our duty' (Lk 17:10). Moreover, this reward is not in proportion to what we have done, but rather a 'hundredfold' (Mt 19:29). All reward is a reward of grace, or, as it has been expressed very adequately: 'a surprise thankfully accepted'. The reward is ultimately God himself, as expressed in the eightfold promise of the beatitudes, from the 'kingdom of heaven' (Mt 5:3) to divine sonship (Mt 5:9).

The second reason for joy is that 'so men persecuted the prophets who were before you'. Apparently Matthew took 'who were before you' as referring to the prophets, while Luke thought it referred to the persecutors and therefore has 'for so their fathers (= those who were before you) did to the prophets'. The disciples should rejoice in their sufferings because they are on the right track, they are in good company: as persecuted they are the successors and imitators of the prophets, men of God *par excellence*. Originally, this passage was most probably related to the theme of the tragic fate of the prophets (cf. Mt 23:29–37; Acts 7:52, etc.), but this seems no longer the case on the level of the Matthean redaction, where 'prophet' has become a title and a word of encouragement.

By their direct address 'blessed are you', Mt 5:11–12 constitute a transition to the next pericope, Mt 5:13–16, 'You are the salt of the earth. . . . You are the light of the world.'

4 Salt of the Earth and Light of the World *(Mt 5:13–16)*

Mt 5:13–16 can fairly easily be recognized as a redactional or editorial composition. Similitudes of different origin have been brought together to form a short address to the disciples, as the twofold 'you are' in Mt 5:13a, 14a, and the concluding *houtōs*-clause ('so'; Mt 5:16) especially show. Two sayings from the Q-source (Mt 5:13bc paralleled by Lk 14:34–35; cf. Mk 9:50 and Mt 5:15 paralleled by Lk 11:33) are each time introduced by an affirmation of the redactor (Mt 5:13a, 14a). Moreover, Mt 5:14a is commented upon by a saying which is found in Matthew only (Mt 5:14b; but see the apocryphal *Gospel of Thomas* 32). The paraenetic application of the whole (Mt 5:16) is also to be attributed to the redactor. The whole paragraph, therefore, is highly redactional.

The formal structure of the pericope is similar to that of Mt 16:17–19: to present the mission of the disciples and that of Peter, Matthew uses the same model, which presupposes similar conditions.

Mt 5:(11–12)13–16	*Mt 16:17–19*
macarism	*macarism*
11–12 Blessed are you when men revile you. . . .	17 Blessed are you, Simon Bar-Jona. . . .
new function	*new function*
13–15 You are the salt of the earth. . . . You are the light of the world. . . .	18 You are Peter, and on this rock. . . .
command of mission	*command of mission*
16 Let your light so shine before men. . . .	19 I will give you the keys of the kingdom . . . and whatever you bind on earth. . . .

The position of these sayings following the beatitudes is due to Matthew, who thus continues the personalizing of the beatitudes which started with the shift from the third person to the second person plural in Mt 5:11, 'Blessed are you . . .', identifying the recipients of the beatitudes with the circle of disciples who are now directly addressed. The introductory phrases 'you are the salt of the earth – you are the light of the world', which emphasize discipleship as a whole (probably with emphasis on witnessing) rather than any single quality, should also be attributed to Matthew. The close relationship of these sayings with the beatitudes is important for the interpretation of the former. The disciples who are called the salt of the earth and the light of the world are none other than the poor and the powerless to whom the beatitudes are addressed. And as the beatitudes constitute a perfect correspondence between grace and demand, so the unmotivated and gracious declaration of Christ installing his disciples as witnesses (Mt 5:13–15) precedes the exhortation and mission of verse 16.

You are the salt of the earth (Mt 5:13)

> **Verse 13:** You are the salt of the earth; but if the salt has lost its taste, how shall its saltness be restored? It is no longer good for anything except to be thrown out and trodden under foot by men.

This saying has its Q-parallel in Lk 14:34f., but it is also found in another form in Mk 9:50. On the basis of a detailed comparison of these three versions, it has been suggested that the original form of the salt-saying was as follows: 'Salt is good; but if the salt becomes tasteless, with what do you salt it? It is good for nothing any more. They throw it away. Whoever has ears to hear, hear!' Originally a threat directed against Israel as a whole or its religious leaders, it was later used in a wide variety of contexts by the evangelists.

By means of the clause 'You are [not: you ought to be!] the salt of the earth', Matthew inserted the saying into the context of the Sermon on the Mount. The address 'you' should most probably be understood in a communitarian sense: all of you together, as a community, and not: each of you separately. Next he writes literally: 'but if the salt becomes foolish' (*mōranthēi*; same in Luke). He, and apparently Q before him, seems to anticipate the interpretation of the saying as referring to the (foolish) disciples: not the salt, but the disciples intended by the salt, can become foolish. Mark writes more appropriately: 'If the salt loses its salinity'. Both versions can be traced back to the same Hebrew or Aramaic substratum. The next clause, 'how shall its saltness be restored', is more or less the same in the three versions.

But then, unlike Mark, Matthew and Luke add a description of the fate of the salt which has lost its taste.

The general meaning of the saying is that the function of the disciples is similar to the function(s) of the salt. But what specifically does Matthew mean?

A survey of the Old Testament shows that in Jewish life salt was used in many ways. It was used to season tasteless food (Job 6:6); it was sprinkled on various Temple offerings (Lev 2:13; Ez 16:4; 43:24). Elisha used it to purify the spring of Jericho (II Kings 2:19–22). Abimelech sowed Shechem with salt (Judg 9:45; cf. Deut 29:22; Jer 17:6; Zeph 2:9; Job 39:6), to bring a curse of barrenness or an anathema on the city. Salt was also used as a figure of permanent friendship: 'a covenant of salt' (Num 18:19; II Chron 13:5). We know that it was also used to preserve food and as fertilizer.

Referring to Pliny, who cites the maxim 'Nothing is of greater benefit to the whole body than salt and sun', and who asserts that 'without salt a really civilized life is impossible', and to a similar statement in Sir 39:26, 'Basic to all the needs of man's life are water and fire and iron and salt', it has been pointed out that salt is essential to human existence. In its Matthean version, then, the salt-saying would intend to portray discipleship as involving a very important, almost essential role in daily life, which, if not fulfilled, would cause the disciples to be rejected.

To clarify further the image of salt becoming tasteless or losing its function and being thrown into the street, it has been pointed out that the ancient Semites – as Arab bakers sometimes still do – covered the floor of their ovens with slabs of salt to promote the combustion of poorly burning fuel like dried camel dung. After about fifteen years the catalytic effect of the salt wore out and it was thrown into the street. In this connection it has been noted that one of the Semitic words for 'oven' (*arca*) is similar to the Semitic word for 'earth', and that 'earth' might have been read where the original meant 'oven': 'you are the salt of the oven'. However, this explanation is not so helpful for the text of Matthew since it overlooks the parallelism 'salt of the *earth* – light of the *world*', which would be broken if the suggestion were to be followed. Moreover, the ancient Semites used salt as fertilizer. Therefore, the expression 'salt of the *earth*' is quite natural, especially if we pay attention to what is apparently the older version, 'it is fit neither for the land nor for the dunghill' (Lk 14:35). The disappearance of the 'dunghill' from Mt 5:13 softens the agricultural connection; the metaphor refers more directly to the reality of the disciples, and the 'land', now parallel with 'world' (Mt 5:14), no longer means 'cultivable soil' but 'universal mankind'.

But how do the disciples act as fertilizer? The Jewish treatise

Sopherim states: 'The Torah is like salt, the Mishnah like pepper, the Gemara like spices. The world cannot exist without salt, or without pepper, or without spices. So also the world cannot exist without Scriptures, and the Mishnah, and the Gemara' (15:8). Without attributing too much importance to this late Jewish treatise which compares the Law to salt that allows the world to subsist, one may think in analogous terms when interpreting Mt 5:13, especially because of the continuation of the text, 'but if salt has lost its taste, how shall its saltness be restored?' Matthew and Luke write literally, 'but if the salt becomes foolish', and their translation of the original is most probably intentional: it provides the basis for an allegory. The disciples are the salt of the earth by their knowledge of the time of fulfilment. The parallelism between salt and the light of revelation (Mt 5:14) confirms this interpretation, and Col 4:6, 'let your speech always be gracious, seasoned with salt', points in the same direction. The disciples, who have the knowledge of God's saving will, should remain what they are by a life in harmony with what they have received. Otherwise, 'how shall their saltness be restored?' Christians who 'become foolish', who become adulterated by compromise with the world, who lose their distinctiveness in the world, are no longer capable of fulfilling their function towards the world, i.e., they can no longer transform it.

Therefore, they will be 'thrown out and trodden under foot by men'. These features are part of the parabolic element of the text and should not be literally applied to the final fate of the unfaithful disciples. But the expression 'thrown out' has a double meaning. It appears as such in Mt 13:48, where the bad fish are thrown out, and, in equivalent terms, in other Matthean passages which deal with eternal damnation. With the exception of Mt 8:12, they all speak of sinful mankind in general (Mt 13:42), or more often of unfaithful Christians (Mt 7:19; 13:48, 50; 18:8, 9; 22:13). Christ warns his disciples, and invites them not to betray their vocation as a conserving and stimulating entity, as people who give orientation to the world.

They are really the salt of the earth and the light of the world. They should not doubt, even if others try to make them believe that they are an insignificant little group who are socially as well as religiously unrepresentative. They are truly the preservers of society and an orientation for the human community, no matter what others may say. They are the bearers of a new society, to them belongs the kingdom of heaven.

To fulfil this role, 'salt' should not organize itself in separate movements and institutions, but mix with what it is supposed to serve. However, to be salt means also to live critically: 'critical' in the sense of distinct, i.e., to have priorities, to emphasize certain values, often in a way diametrically opposed to what 'everybody' says, thinks, and does.

You are the light of the world (Mt 5:14–16)

Verses 14–15: You are the light of the world. A city set on a hill cannot be hid. (15) Nor do men light a lamp and put it under a bushel, but on a stand, and it gives light to all in the house.

The saying of a city on a hill (Mt 5:14b) has no synoptic parallel, but in Oxyrhynchus Papyrus 1:7 = *Gospel of Thomas* 32 we find: 'Jesus said: a city which is set on the summit of a high hill, and on a firm foundation, cannot be brought low, nor can it be hidden'. The parable of the lamp on the stand is also found in Lk 11:33; Mk 4:21 and Lk 8:16. On the basis of a detailed comparison of these four texts, it has been suggested that the original wording of the lamp-saying was as follows: 'What does it seem to you: the lamp comes in, and they place it under a bushel and they do not place it on the lampstand? (Whoever has ears to hear, hear!)' The original context of this saying was most probably the attempt of Jesus' opponents to prevent him, the light, from preaching the good news. But the lamp has been lit, the light is shining; not in order to be put out again, but in order to give light to all. This saying was then used in a variety of contexts by the evangelists.

In Mark, the saying is found in the 'parable discourse' (Mk 4:1–34) and illustrates the theme of messianic revelation, first hidden, then brought into the open. Luke has the saying in the same context (Lk 8:16), using it as a prelude to an exhortation to be attentive to the message. But he uses it a second time in Lk 11:33, where the lamp could refer to Jesus, who is implicitly mentioned in Lk 11:32, 'and behold, something greater than Jonah is here', while the light would symbolize the truth of the gospel.

Matthew, or the pre-Matthean tradition, has combined the saying of the lamp (Mt 5:15) with that of the city on the hill (Mt 5:14b). Light cannot become 'lightless', but its illuminating power can be taken away by putting it under a bushel, so that it no longer lights the house. If, however, the bushel is inverted and made to serve as a lampstand, then the light can fulfil its role, and it can give light to all in the simple Palestinian house which has only one room. This light cannot be overlooked, just as a city set on a hill (Mt 5:14b) cannot be overlooked.

The lamp which must provide light is first of all a reference to doing good works (Mt 5:16). Anybody who refuses or fails to do good works is like a man who lights a lamp and then hides it under a bushel. But those who do good works will be a light only when they do them in such a way that anybody who sees them is led to glorify God. This runs counter to the attitude of those who have no intention of being a light to the world but only of maintaining their own purity. Discipleship is always founded on its function: service to others, service to the world of men. Without such service there is no true discipleship.

> This brief parable in its Matthean form, then, charts a clear course between sectarian withdrawal from the world, on the one hand, and simple conformity to it, on the other hand. Without service in the world the Church becomes a self-serving institution, Christians an irrelevant group of high-minded people – Christians without Christianity, salt without salinity, light that illumines nothing. The world, correspondingly, does without one thing above all else that the Church could bring to it – the life-preserving, light-giving presence of God among his own.[5]

The conclusion to be drawn from verses 13–15 is evident: it is proper to salt to season/preserve/stimulate, and proper to light to illuminate. What then is proper to disciples who are real disciples – since they are called both salt and light? The condition of the disciple is envisaged with regard to the world (*gē, kosmos*). In the light of the secular and biblical symbolism attributed to salt and light, it seems that both of these belong to the category of witness. Verse 16, which says that the 'good works' of the disciple allow the world to recognize and praise God, confirms this interpretation.

Two further considerations should be added. Firstly, as is illustrated by the violent contrast in verses 13b, 14b, 15, this witness is not a function reserved to a particular group within the community. It belongs constitutively to the condition of discipleship and, therefore, to the whole community. Secondly, this condition of witness is presented as both indicative ('you are . . .') and imperative ('let your light so shine . . .'). The disciples are not admonished to accomplish a task which will bring them to the desired state, but rather to be or become what they already are.

The disciples are the salt of the earth and the light of the world if they constantly live according to the Sermon on the Mount, the life style of Jesus himself. But we should add another consideration. The Church is the salt of the earth and the light of the world; this sounds familiar, doesn't it? But should we not rather invert the picture? Should we not say that the Church is there where people live according to the Sermon on the Mount, being salt and light for each other? This may also be found among people who are not church-goers or who do not belong to the so-called official Church, but who nevertheless live in a way which resembles the ideal of the Sermon on the Mount, while within the official Church we may observe a number of 'saltless' and 'dark' spots. Matthew's words, then, may also be intended to purify our concept of the Church.

No! This does not allow for the sinfulness which is truly part of us!

Verse 16: Let your light so shine before men, that they may see your good works and give glory to your Father who is in heaven.

The disciples let their light shine by doing good works. The phrase 'good works' is derived from the religious vocabulary of Judaism. Distinct from the 613 precepts of the Law, they included almsgiving and various charitable works: hospitality, assistance to prisoners, etc. But Matthew enlarges the notion of 'good works', by which he means the totality of Christian conduct, an authentic way of life, as the continuation of the Sermon on the Mount shows, although in view of the immediate context, he may be thinking especially of witness. Moreover, he does not mention reward here, but refers only to the glory of God. This glory is attained indirectly, through the agency of 'men', before whom the good works are done. The same idea is found in the Old as well as the New Testament (Isa 45:14–15; I Thess 4:12). But the only close parallel is I Pet 2:12, 'Maintain good conduct among the Gentiles, so that in case they speak against you as wrong-doers, they may see your good deeds and glorify God on the day of visitation'.

However, one should not do good works 'in order to be seen by men' (Mt 6:1, 16, 18; 23:5, 28). The disciples should beware of all ostentation. They should be faithful, and God will take care of his own glory! Thus understood, Mt 5:16 does not contradict the instructions of Mt 6:1–18. The two passages are addressing themselves to two different problems. In Mt 5:16 the evangelist warns against the danger of keeping one's light hidden, while in Mt 6:1–18, he deals with self-seeking ostentation. It is the motive that makes all the difference: if the light shines for human glory, it is ostentation; if it shines for the glory of the Father, it is true piety.

To give glory to the Father is to reveal his true being as it has been manifested in Jesus. If we had not seen Jesus' 'good works', we would not have known that we can approach God as a 'dear Father' (*Abba*). Similarly, our 'good works', our commitment to men, especially to the poor, should lead people to Jesus and the Father. In the course of time the image of God has often been obscured by 'isms', and our time has its share of them. The only hope the world has to see God as he really is lies in the life witness of fully committed Christians. In conclusion, it should be said again that it is the poor of the beatitudes who are called salt of the earth and light of the world.

5 Jesus and the fulfilment of the Law *(Mt 5:17–20)*

After Mt 5:13–16, verses 17–20 appear as a new beginning. They provide the introduction to the series of six antitheses (Mt 5:21–48), or rather, they announce the *general principle* of which the antitheses are the illustrations. As such, they occupy an important place within the Sermon on the Mount. A careful study of the passage shows that it is composed of four distinct sentences each representing a different viewpoint on the question of the value of the Law in its relation to the gospel. Verse 17 deals with the relation of the Law to Jesus. Verse 18 speaks of the persistence of the Law in its smallest details, while verse 19 concerns fidelity to teaching the Law in its smallest parts. Verse 20, finally, serves as a bridge between the general principle (Mt 5:17–19) and the illustrations which follow (Mt 5:21–48), and thus seems to sum up what precedes and to initiate what follows.

> **Verse 17:** Think not that I have come to abolish the law and the prophets; I have come not to abolish them but to fulfil them.

The verb 'think not' is an aorist subjunctive and therefore does not imply that Jesus supposed the following thoughts to be present in the minds of his listeners, but rather that they should not begin to think, or should not let it enter their minds that. . . . The warning is addressed to the disciples first of all, but other listeners are not excluded (cf. Mt 5:1).

We have a very interesting parallel to our present verse in Mt 10:34 (both Mt 5:17 and 10:34 belong to Matthew's special material):

Mt 5:17	*Mt 10:34*
Think not that I have come	Do not think that I have come

| to abolish the law and the prophets;
I have come not
to abolish them
but to fulfil them. | to bring peace on earth;
I have not come
to bring peace
but a sword. |

The sequence 'think not that I have come' appears only in Matthew, and may be attributed to his redaction. The pre-Matthean form of the saying would have begun simply with 'I did not come' (cf. Mk 2:17 = Mt 9:13).

The gospels contain a whole series of statements in which the phrase 'I have come' or 'the Son of man has come' is found. This phrase always describes the mission of the eschatological figure who will bring about the denouement of salvation history and whose action will constitute a reversal of the expectations of men concerning his mission. In this particular instance it is said that Jesus' eschatological mission does not consist in doing away with 'the law and the prophets', but in giving them their eschatological fullness.

'To abolish', applied to the Law, is rare in the New Testament, but it is found in II Macc 2:22, 'the laws that were about to be abolished'; 4:11, 'and he destroyed (abolished) the lawful ways of living'. Similar expressions are found in IV Macc 5:33; 17:9. These texts refer not simply to an abolition of a particular law, but to a total rescinding of law which leads to the destruction of the people of God as a separate people. Therefore, the phrase 'to abolish' should be understood in the sense of the total destruction of the whole Law.

The expression 'the law and the prophets' refers to the whole of the Scriptures and occurs ten times in the New Testament, though not always with exactly the same meaning. Sometimes the aspect of ethical norm is emphasized (e.g., Mt 7:12; 22:40); at other times, their prophetic value as witnesses to Christ (e.g., Mt 11:13). It has been shown that Matthew understands the Law in the light of the prophets, meaning that the prophetic message of mercy and love must serve as a critical principle for interpreting the Law. But, as we will see below, more may be involved.

While most exegetes agree on the general meaning of *plēroō* as 'to fill completely', 'to fulfil', they are greatly divided over the more specific meaning of the verb. Out of the sixteen occurrences of the verb in Matthew, twelve are found in fulfilment quotations (e.g., Mt 1:22, 'to fulfil what the Lord had spoken by the prophet'), one in the context of the martyrdom of the prophets (Mt 23:32), one speaking of Jesus and John playing their appointed roles at the moment of (prophetic) fulfilment (Mt 3:15). In one instance, it has the non-theological meaning of 'filling up' a net (Mt 13:48). It is thus very difficult to avoid the conclusion that the prophetic note in 'fulfil' in Mt 5:17 is unmistakable. In view of Matthew's general interest in prophecy, his redaction of Mt 5:18 (see below), and the awkwardness of 'to abolish . . . the prophets', a phrase nowhere else found in the Septuagint or the New Testament, we may attribute the phrase 'and the prophets' to Matthew's redaction. And since 'to fulfil the law' is found only a few times in Paul, while anywhere else in the New Testament we have 'to do the law', 'to practise the law' (in Greek, *poiein*, a verb found in Matt 5:19), the original form of the saying may very well have been: 'I came not to abolish the law but to do it', which, as far as form is concerned, is very similar to 'I came not to call the righteous, but sinners' (Mk 2:17b).

But why should Matthew have added the phrase 'and the prophets' and changed the verb 'to do' into 'to fulfil' to fit this addition? His redactional activity in verse 17 (and, as we shall see, in verse 18 as well) seems to have aimed at modifying a traditional statement about the Law so that the emphasis of the saying would be shifted from keeping the Law to prophetic fulfilment. This implies attributing to Matthew a concept of the Law as prophetic. We find this concept expressed in Mt 11:13. It appears clearly if we compare the verse with the parallel text of Lk 16:16a:

Mt 11:13	*Lk 16:16a*
For all the prophets and the law prophesied until John.	The law and the prophets were until John.

Matthew apparently changed the usual order of 'law and prophets' to 'all the prophets and the law', an order unknown to the rest of the New Testament or the whole of the Septuagint, thus emphasizing the importance of the prophets. This is confirmed by the use of the verb 'prophesied', nowhere else found with 'the law' as subject. Matthew could not subsume the Law under the prophets more clearly than this. With the coming of Jesus, both the prophets and the Law lost their function of pointing ahead to him. They now rather witness to and confirm what has already been fulfilled. Jesus has become the norm of interpretation. This is the point of the antithesis (Mt 5:21–48) and of the concluding parable of the Sermon on the Mount which emphasizes not the keeping of the Law, but the words of Jesus as the focus of Christian living. 'Every one then who hears these words of *mine* and does them . . .' (Mt 7:24). For the disciple, the person of Jesus, who is God-with-us, takes the place of the Law as the centre of the Christian's life (cf. Mt 1:23; 18:20; 28:20).

But this Jesus has also come to fulfil the Law and the prophets. This

> means that he 'establishes' or 'upholds' the Torah by interpreting it definitively on the basis of God's primordial will, which is epitomized in the dual command to love. He thus both confirms its abiding validity and modifies its actual form. And his definitive [prophetic] interpretation becomes the basis for a new obedience, the higher righteousness, which leads to salvation. Jesus thus 'actualizes' God's plan of salvation-history, promised in the scriptures as a whole, precisely by facilitating that genuine righteousness which defines the life of the kingdom.[6]

In his eschatological message of the kingdom Jesus announces that God has turned himself to man in unlimited mercy and loving forgiveness.

Verse 18: (a) For truly, I say to you,
            (b) till heaven and earth pass away,
            (c) not an iota, not a dot, will pass from the law
            (d) until all is accomplished.

In the New Testament *Amēn* (here translated 'truly') is used as a liturgical acclamation and can be found at the beginning or the end of a prayer. Jesus' usage of *Amēn* stands out as unique because he alone has the phrase before his own sayings. Only Matthew has the formula 'for truly, I say to you' (Mt 5:18; 10:23; 13:17; 17:20). The fact that the conjunction *gar* ('for') is used to express a variety of meanings should make us hesitate to take a causal link between verses 17 and 18 for granted.

Some scholars have understood 'pass' in the sense of perishing in an eschatological context. As for the passing of heaven and earth, both rabbinic and apocryphal literature reflect two different views. It is understood either as a purification and transformation of the earth or as a complete annihilation to be followed by a 'new creation' in the strict sense.

The combination of 'heaven and earth' refers to the whole of creation seen as a unity. In the light of a number of Old and New Testament passages where 'the heavens' and/or 'the earth' occurs with reference to their passing away or re-creation[7] and the Jewish interpretation of 'passing away' mentioned in the previous paragraph, it is not so clear that 'till heaven and earth pass away' should be understood as 'never', as a number of scholars believe. Others understand Mt 5:18 as linking the existence of the Law with the existence of the first heaven and earth. Both 'heaven and earth' and the Law are signs of stability in the present time, but they will ultimately pass away.

The Greek word *iōta* is used to translate *yod*, the smallest letter of the so-called square Hebrew alphabet. The Lucan parallel, Lk 16:17, which precedes Lk 16:18 (the prohibition of divorce), reads: 'But it is easier for heaven and earth to pass away, than for one dot of the law to become void'. Mt 5:18, however, has '*not an iota*, not a dot . . .'. This 'one iota' could be understood only by those who knew that the *yod* was the smallest letter in the Hebrew or Aramaic alphabet. No wonder then that Luke, writing for Greek readers, dropped it. But it is exactly that iota that explains why Lk 16:17 and 18 were connected in the preceding Aramaic tradition. A rabbinical text runs as follows: 'Who accused Solomon? Rabbi Jehoshua ben Levi said: the Yod in "yarbeh". Rabbi Simeon ben Jokai taught: The Book of Deuteronomy ascended into heaven, prostrated before God and said: Lord of the world, You have written in your Law: each testament of which one prescription is violated is totally violated. Behold Solomon seeks to destroy a yod of mine. And God answered: *Solomon and a thousand like him will pass away but no single word/stroke/yod of yours shall pass*.'[8] There can be no doubt that this text refers to Deut 17:17 which read: *lo' yarbeh-lo nashim*, 'he (the king) shall not multiply wives for himself'. What does to 'destroy the yod of this law' mean? Omitting the yod of this law one gets: *lo' arbeh-lo nashim*, 'to multiply his wives', i.e., according to this rabbinical interpretation, exactly the opposite. This seems to indicate that this text about the iota and the dot was used in discussion about polygamy and Solomon, the typical polygamist of the Old Testament, who was accused of having overturned the meaning of Deut 17:17. Instead of a law against polygamy (according to a certain rabbinical interpretation) it became a law in favour of polygamy. This could be achieved by blurring out in the text of Deut 17:17 the yod or iota, the smallest letter of the Aramaic alphabet. So, to say that not a single iota of the Law will be dropped means the rejection of the polygamic interpretation of Deut 17:17. Thus it becomes clear why in the Aramaic tradition the sayings of Lk 16:17 and 18 belonged together. It also shows what was the original context of the reference to the iota.

The rabbinic story can be understood as asserting the eternal validity of the Law by comparison with Solomon who passes away. Other similar stories compare the Law with one or another thing. In this light it is remarkable that Mt 5:18 juxtaposes a phrase usually denoting the eternal validity of the Law with the limitation of an eschatological *terminus ad quem*.

The word *keraia* (here translated 'dot') literally means a horn, a projection, and then, figuratively, a hook as a part of a letter. The word was used in Greek to refer to accents, and, figuratively, to something quite insignificant. It is a matter of discussion what *keraia* would denote in the Hebrew alphabet and whether 'iota' and 'dot' are referring to two different things or should be understood as an example of Hebraic parallelism.

Faced with the question whether *nomos* should be translated as Law, Pentateuch (Torah), or Scripture, we prefer here the meaning of Torah (Pentateuch). Reasons for this choice are: (1) the use of *nomos* as opposed to 'the prophets' in verse 17; (2) the reference to teaching or relaxing commandments in verse 19; (3) the rabbinic parallels about Deuteronomy mentioned in connection with the meaning of *iōta*. It has been shown that for Matthew *nomos* means 'the Torah of the Old Testament seen as a whole, both as the revelatory Word of God and as a normative Law'.[9] 'Not an iota, not a dot will pass from the law' means then that even the smallest element of the Law is an integral and inalienable part of the whole Law.

'Until all is accomplished' is strongly reminiscent of some of the introductions to the fulfilment quotations in Matthew, e.g., 'All this took place to fulfil ...' (*plērōthēi*, Mt 1:22; cf. *plērōsai* in Mt 5:17). Should it be understood as 'until all has taken place, i.e., is past' (W. Bauer) or 'until all has been done or obeyed' (W. Trilling)?

Verse 18 is the only verse in Mt 5:17–20 which has a clear parallel, namely Lk 16:17. Most commentators agree that Matthew and Luke are using the same source (Q) here. 'For truly, I say to you' seems to be an introduction formula added by Matthew. It can be attributed to Matthean redaction. The same should be said of 'until all is accomplished' which Matthew added for his own theological purpose. We are left with Mt 5:18bc and Lk 16:17 as two different adaptations of an earlier Q-logion (or dependent on two different versions of Q?):

Mt 5:18bc	*Lk 16:17*
	a But it is easier
b till heaven and earth	for heaven and earth
pass away,	to pass away,
c not an iota, not a dot,	b than for one dot
will pass from the law.	of the law to become void.

We have here an affirmation of the lasting validity of the Law in all its parts and in its smallest details, either for ever or till the end of this age. In Luke all temporal connection has disappeared and we get a comparison between two events which could happen only with the greatest difficulty. But since Luke says elsewhere that 'heaven and earth will pass away' (Lk 21:33), the same is true of the Law: it will pass away, though not without difficulty. All this fits very well into Luke's redaction (cf. Lk 16:14–18). Mt 5:18bc seems to represent a more primitive form of the saying. On the level of the Jewish-Christian community this saying could mean either that the Law will never pass or that the Law will pass only at the end of this age. What it means for Matthew becomes clear when we compare the present saying with Mt 24:35:

Mt 5:18acd	*Mt 24:35*
b till heaven and earth pass away,	a Heaven and earth will pass away,
c not an iota, not a dot, will pass from the law.	b but my words will not pass away.

Mt 24:35a shows that, for Matthew, heaven and earth will certainly pass away, as predicted by Jesus. But while in Mt 24:35 this passing away is opposed to the permanence of Jesus' words, in Mt 5:18 the passing away of heaven and earth becomes the time limit up to which the Law in all its details will maintain its force. Matthew, therefore, interprets the primitive form of Mt 5:18bc as an affirmation of the Law's validity within a limited time period. But what time period?

The answer is to be found in Mt 5:18d, 'until all is accomplished'. The basic meaning of *ginomai* (RSV, 'to accomplish') is the occurrence of an event, and Matthew uses it frequently to refer to the fulfilment of events predicted by the prophets. 'But how then should the scriptures be fulfilled that it must be so (literally, 'that so it must *happen*' = *genesthai*). . . . But all this has taken place (*gegonen*), that the scriptures of the prophets might be fulfilled' (Mt 26:54, 56; note the expression 'the scriptures *of the prophets*'). That this is characteristic of Matthean redaction and theology is confirmed by the apocalyptic discourse, more precisely in Mt 24:34, the verse which immediately precedes Mt 24:35 quoted above. In fact, it seems justifiable to say that in Mt 5:18 Matthew has re-edited a Q-saying by introducing into it material from Mk 13:30–31 = Mt 24:34–35. Mt 5:18 and 24:34 are very similar in both structure and vocabulary:

Mt 5:18acd	*Mt 24:34*
a For truly, I say to you, . . .	a Truly, I say to you,
c not an iota, not a dot, will pass from the law (*ou mē parelthēi* . . .)	b this generation will not pass away (*ou mē parelthēi*)
d until all is accomplished (*heōs an panta genētai*).	c till all these things take place (*heōs an panta tauta genētai*).

It appears clearly that 'will not pass away . . . till all these things take place' certainly does not mean 'this will never happen'. The passing away is taken for granted and the emphasis is on what constitutes the time limit which in Mt 24:34 seems to be the fulfilment of prophesied events in an apocalyptic context. It seems, then, that Mt 5:18d, 'until all is accomplished', contains the idea of the fulfilment of prophecy as the time limit of the Law. Nothing in the Law will lose its binding force until all that is prophesied has come to pass in the eschatological event. But while in Mt 24:34 the reference is to a series of Old and New Testament prophecies dealing with the destruction of Jerusalem, the coming of the Son of man in glory, etc., Mt 5:18 is preceded by Old Testament prophecies which, in keeping with Matthew's historicizing interests, are presented as mapping out the 'life of Jesus'. Thus Mt 5:18d seems to refer to the prophecies which are fulfilled in Jesus' life, culminating in his death-resurrection, which is the turning point between the old and the new age. And the binding force of the Torah as an inviolable whole has passed with the passing of the old creation.

In its present form, then, Mt 5:18 is not a strict affirmation of the lasting validity of the Mosaic Law for all time. Rather, Matthew has re-edited an originally strict saying on the Law so as to adapt it to his own understanding of salvation history. The Mosaic Law as a whole and in so far as it is Mosaic lasts up until the apocalyptic event of the death-resurrection of Jesus. After this decisive turning point, the norm for the disciples is 'all that I have commanded you' (Mt 28:20). Jesus adopts an attitude of sovereign distance toward the Law. For him the distinctive principle of action is not the Law but the reign of God already proclaimed. Only the fulfilment of the Christologically interpreted Law leads to the greater righteousness which obtains entrance into the kingdom of heaven. Within this perspective, however, Matthew seems to respect the Law as much as possible.

Verse 19: (a) Whoever then relaxes one of the least of these commandments and teaches men so,

(b) shall be called least in the kingdom of heaven;

(c) but he who does them and teaches them

(d) shall be called great in the kingdom of heaven.

The verb *luō* (here translated 'to relax') has various meanings: loose, untie bonds, set free, break up, destroy, tear down, bring to an end, abolish. Applied to commandments and laws it means: repeal or annul. It is not immediately clear whether the verse speaks of relaxing or annulling by teaching or by doing, but the idea of breaking by action seems to be better suited to the context.

All six of Matthew's usages of the word *entolē* suggest a reference to an individual commandment rather than the Law as a whole. The predicate 'least' is probably to be understood in the sense of the rabbinic 'light' commandments, as contrasted with the 'heavy' ones. But the 'light'–'heavy' distinction could mean a number of things. As far as Matthew's tradition is concerned, it most probably reflects the distinction between unimportant and important commandments. Practically speaking, then, the 'least of these commandments' most probably refers back to the iota and dot of verse 18. We have to admit that they are not 'commandments' in the strict sense of the word, but they can be used metaphorically for the whole. At any rate, the adjective 'these' refers to something relatively near.

The clause 'shall be called least in the kingdom of heaven' has been interpreted in terms of exclusion from the kingdom. But a survey of the usage of *elachistos* in the New Testament does not reveal a single usage which would imply a negative judgment on the part of God, exclusion from the kingdom, or damnation. This conclusion is confirmed by a survey of the related words *mikros* ('small') and *mikroteros* ('smaller'). The closest parallel to our present verse is Mt 11:11, '. . . he who is least in the kingdom of heaven', which certainly implies inclusion in the kingdom. The true superlative sense of *elachistos* is rather rare, the more usual sense being elative: very small, quite unimportant. The latter sense is certainly possible in Mt 5:19, where applied to the person mentioned it probably means 'very insignificant', 'very unimportant'. The idea of exclusion from the kingdom is certainly not found in Mt 5:19.

Nine of the fourteen Matthean usages of *didaskō* ('to teach') refer to the teaching activity of Jesus, and the disciples are never said to teach; only at the very end of the gospel (Mt 28:20) are the disciples charged to teach all the nations whatever Jesus has commanded. Before the resurrection, Jesus alone teaches. Is Mt 5:19 then referring to the teaching activity of Christians after the resurrection? This is possible. But it should be noted that doing and teaching are combined in verse 19, and that by placing doing before teaching Matthew may be emphasizing the former. *Didaskō* means for Matthew that function initiated by Jesus (Mt 22:16; 4:23; 9:35; 11:1) and carried on by the Church (Mt 28:20), whereby the 'law and the prophets' are interpreted in terms of their fulfilment by Jesus (Mt 5:17; cf. 5:1f.; 7:28f.). *Didaskō* emphasizes that the gospel of the kingdom is also conditioned by the (Christologically interpreted) Law and the greater righteousness it demands.

In the New Testament, 'to call' very often has a theological meaning, especially in cases like Mt 5:19 where the future tense suggests an eschatological context and the passive is a circumlocution for divine activity. When God calls a person something, he makes that person what he calls him; 'to be called' approaches 'to be'. Matthew may be referring here to the eschatological declaration at the last judgment which assigns a definitive state to those judged.

Scholars are divided over whether 'he who does them' refers to the official teachers of the community or to every disciple. The fact that 'teaching' appears in both the positive and the negative part of the statement makes it likely that the official teachers of the community are meant.

Matthew uses the adjective 'great' about twenty times in a wide variety of contexts, the closest to Mt 5:19 being 'whoever would be great among you must be your servant' (Mt 20:26), but even this passage is not close enough to allow any firm conclusion as to the precise sense of 'great' in Mt 5:19. Since Hebrew and Aramaic lack proper superlatives, *megas* ('great') might be taken as superlative, as is *elachistos* ('least'). But since the latter probably has an elative meaning *megas* could have a meaning such as 'very great', 'very important'.

Among all New Testament writers Matthew alone uses the phrase 'the kingdom of heaven', or literally, 'the kingdom of the heavens', 'the heavens' being a circumlocution for the divine name. It is interchangeable with 'the kingdom of God'. Matthew's concept of the kingdom of heaven is rather complex, referring to a reality which in one sense is already present and in another sense is a future reality. In Mt 5:19 the emphasis is on the future aspect: the final kingdom at the end of this age. Fidelity in doing and teaching the commandments will be rewarded in the future kingdom of heaven.

The style of Mt 5:19 is that of a legal statement: not only does the *content* concern law, but also the *form* of the statement is legal. It has been form-critically classified as a 'sentence of holy law' (in German: *Satz heiligen Rechtes*), another example being Mt 16:19, 'I will give you the keys of the kingdom of heaven, and whatever you bind on earth shall be bound in heaven, and whatever you loose on earth shall be loosed in heaven'. See also Jn 20:23, 'If you forgive the sins of any, they are forgiven; if you retain the sins of any, they are retained'.

Practically all scholars agree that Mt 5:19 comes from pre-Matthean tradition. But was this verse already joined to Mt 5:18, to which it seems to stand in a certain tension? One should not exaggerate the unevenness between the two verses and one should certainly not speak of a contradiction which would make the union of the two verses in the tradition impossible. A number of scholars have presented positive arguments for the union of Mt 5:18 and 19 in Q. In fact, Mt 5:19 looks like a conclusion to a thesis expressed in Mt 5:18, at least in its primitive form Mt 5:18bc:

Mt 5:18b Till heaven and earth pass away,
  c not an iota, not a dot, will pass from the law. . . .
 5:19a Whoever then relaxes one of the least of these commandments and teaches men so,
  b shall be called least in the kingdom of heaven.

But what is the origin and situation in life (*Sitz im Leben*) of Mt 5:19? Several scholars have traced the verse and its union with Mt 5:18 back to debates among various tendencies within the primitive Jewish-Christian community. In Mt 5:18bc we have an expression of strict Jewish-Christian tendencies, while Mt 5:19 is the corrective of a more moderate Jewish-Christian group. In an attempt to determine the situation in life more exactly, it has been suggested that the concern with teaching and doing, the distinction between great and small commandments, and the idea of different degrees of rewards in the kingdom point to a catechetical or paraenetic setting. Beside its corrective purpose, the verse perhaps also served as an exhortation and admonition to the official teachers of the community to be faithful in teaching and action.

For Matthew himself, the verse may have meant first of all that during his public ministry Jesus not only observed the Law himself, but also exhorted others to faithfulness (cf. Mt 23:2–3). Secondly, Matthew may have addressed this verse as an exhortation to the teachers of his Christian community: although they no longer proclaim a number of Old Testament prescriptions as binding, they should be faithful in action and in teaching to all that Jesus commanded (cf. Mt 28:20), as this includes important parts of the Mosaic Law.

Except for the phrase 'of heaven', it is very difficult to identify with certainty traces of Matthean redaction. It is just possible that Matthew formulated Mt 5:19cd, 'but he who does them . . . kingdom of heaven', to complement verse 19ab with a more positive expression of the same sentence of holy law. It is also possible that by means of the whole verse Matthew intended to soften the radical character of verse 20 ('you will never enter').

> **Verse 20:** For I tell you, unless your righteousness exceeds that of the scribes and Pharisees, you will never enter the kingdom of heaven.

The phrase 'for I tell you' may be intended to make the following saying an emphatic summary of all that has been said in the previous verses (Mt 5:17–19). It is both a summary and a new beginning.

The verb *perisseuō* used intransitively means: to be present in abundance, to be more than enough, to abound, to grow, to exceed. In the New Testament it is used most of the time of spiritual abundance in the sense of a fullness present and proclaimed in the age of salvation, or a new standard which is required in the new age. The latter sense fits in well with the eschatological flavour of Mt 5:17–19 and the ethic of the Sermon on the Mount as a whole. The righteousness which is required for entering the kingdom of heaven must exceed the best performances of the past as exemplified by the scribes and the Pharisees. As can be seen from the following antitheses (Mt 5:21–48), the new righteousness should exceed the old both quantitatively and qualitatively.

In Matthew, 'righteousness' may have either of the two Old Testament meanings of the term: the saving will and activity of God, or the moral activity of men who do the will of God. In Mt 5:20 we find the second meaning. Christian righteousness differed from the popular rabbinic approach which emphasized the meticulous fulfilment of legal prescriptions with a view to gaining enough merit to outweigh one's guilt at the final judgment. Whoever succeeded in this was considered righteous in God's eyes. Though interior dispositions were not entirely disregarded, they were accidental. Jesus is presented as opposing to this, not a better Pharisaism, a more meticulous observance of even the smallest points of the Law, but an attitude illustrated in the following antitheses. The exceeding righteousness consists in a radical and total obedience to God in complete self-giving to one's fellow-man, which carries the ethical intent of the Law to its God-willed conclusion, even when this means in some instances abrogating the letter of the Law. All this is possible because of the eschatological character of Jesus' presence; in other words, what is new about Christian righteousness is Christ himself and his radical demand, 'Follow me' (Mt 19:21). That this righteousness is not simply a matter of human achievement is suggested by the petition of Mt 6:10, 'your will be done'.

Matthew's use of 'the scribes and the Pharisees' is clearly redactional. It is a fixed theological formula in which the scribes and the Pharisees are understood to be the official representatives of Jewish theology and piety. Matthew, whose view is certainly influenced by the debate between Jewish Christianity and Judaism after A.D. 70, does not give us a fair picture of the scribes and the Pharisees as they were during the life of Jesus.

The expression 'to enter the kingdom of God/heaven' is based on two Old Testament images. The first image is the entrance of Israel into the promised land understood as either the historical (Deut 4:1) or the eschatological entrance (*Psalms of Solomon* 11:2–6). The second image is connected with demands of ritual purity and ethical righteousness for entrance through the Temple gate or the city gates of Jerusalem, used as an apocalyptic image in Isa 26:2f. The latter seems to be more important in Mt 5:20.

'The kingdom of heaven' is here most probably to be understood in the final, eschatological sense. But, as said before, it has also a past and present stage, and Matthew understands the Church as in some way having the kingdom, without, of course, being totally identified with it.

Mt 5:20 has been form-critically classified both as a 'sentence of holy law' (*Satz heiligen Rechtes*) and as an 'entrance-condition' (in German: *Eingangsbedingung*). The verse has a double function: it sums up everything that precedes it and is also an immediate introduction to the antitheses, while Mt 5:17–20 as a unit constitutes the larger introduction to the antitheses.

Scholars are divided over the question whether Mt 5:20 is redactional or traditional. A good number of them, among them Bultmann, Descamps and Dupont, argue quite convincingly that the verse is a Matthean creation composed to form both a summary and an immediate introduction to the antitheses. The opposite opinion has more recently been defended by Wrege and Banks. We incline to the opinion which considers Mt 5:20 redactional.

For Matthew, then, Mt 5:20 has a twofold sense. On the level of his paraenesis addressed to Christians the verse expresses his deep concern for a sincere commitment to the spirit of the Law. Insofar as Matthew attributes these words to Jesus, he understands them as an expression of Jesus' fidelity to the Mosaic Law during his earthly life, a fidelity which, according to Matthew, he also impressed on his disciples.

The basic line of thought of the pericope Mt 5:17–20 in its final form has been summed up as follows:

> After the beatitudes (5:3–12) and the metaphors of salt and light (5:13–16), there is a clear break. *Mt 5:17* begins a new theme: the Law and the prophets, the centre of OT faith, in their relation to Jesus, the centre of Christian faith. Jesus immediately warns against thinking that his activity concerning Law and prophets is purely negative or destructive (as a facile reading of the antitheses might indicate). No, he comes as the eschatological fulfiller. He gives this eschatological, prophetic fulfillment (which preserves yet transcends, even revokes) to both Law and prophets. *Mt 5:18* explains this relationship or analogy. With the solemnity of an apocalyptic prophet, Jesus assures his audience that, until the eschatological passing away of heaven and earth which signals the new age, not the slightest part of the Law will pass, until all prophesied events have come to pass. As Mt shows by his whole ordering of salvation-history, his arrangement of the public ministry of Jesus, and his depiction of the apocalyptic events at the

death-resurrection, this passing away of heaven and earth which marks the fulfillment of all prophecy occurs at the death-resurrection, *die Wende der Zeit*. The death-resurrection of Jesus is the apocalyptic terminus prophesied in 5:18. *Mt 5:19* draws the conclusions from this thesis. On the level of the sacred past of Jesus' public ministry, 5:19 inculcates faithfulness to the Torah while the old aeon lasts. On the level of Mt's parenesis to the community, it inculcates the importance of fidelity on the part of the Christian teacher to all Jesus commanded (cf. Mt 28:20). *Mt 5:20* then sums up 5:17–19 and forms the immediate introduction to the antitheses. The theme of Law is subtly shifted and reinterpreted in terms of Christian justice. The eschatological mission of Jesus, the economy of salvation-history (and the Law's place within it), the fidelity of the teacher, all aim at one practical goal: *dikaiosynē*, the moral life of the Christian. This *dikaiosynē* means perfect conformity to God's will, a moral life that far transcends the legalism, minimalism, lovelessness, and hypocrisy of the scribes and Pharisees. It is that abundant Christian justice, opposed to the justice of the scribes and Pharisees . . . which is now unfolded in 5:21–48.[10]

What is meant by the 'righteousness of the scribes and Pharisees' may receive further specification in Mk 7, where Jesus said to them, 'Well did Isaiah prophesy of you hypocrites, as it is written, "This people honours me with their lips, but their heart is far from me; in vain do they worship me, teaching as doctrines the precepts of men." You leave the commandment of God, and hold fast the tradition of men.' And he said to them, 'You have a fine way of rejecting the commandment of God, in order to keep your tradition!' (Mk 7:6–9). Jesus then used the example of how they misused the *corban* (Temple offering) to violate God's concern about sharing resources with the needy, in this case one's parents. The scribes and Pharisees had created a religion based on the practice of their own norms (who would venture to say that today's 'religion' is free from similar distortions?). As a result of what Jesus refers to as their transgressions of God's basic commands, injustice was sanctioned as a religious act. Referring to such perversion of justice – all in the name of a 'religion' defined by its institutional leaders – Jesus is clearly calling for a conversion to greater justice not merely of individual persons, but of the system with all its underpinnings and supports. Jesus' words should make us aware that leadership in ecclesial and religious institutions continues at times to reinforce the injustice of the system in our time.

Summing up, we may say that in their present Matthean form, and setting, Mt 5:17–20 form a unit which serves as a 'vestibule' to the antitheses. It is often stressed that Matthew is in fact fighting on two fronts here. While Mt 5:20 clearly opposes the attitude of the scribes and the Pharisees and their understanding of the Law (still present in the early Church?), verses 17–19 formulate Matthew's attitude towards disciples who tend to reject the Law.

6 The Antitheses

(Mt 5:21–48)

Introduction

The six antitheses are the first section of the Sermon on the Mount to
be developed at length. As they stand now in the gospel of Matthew
they are the product of Matthean composition. In their present context
they constitute the unfolding of what the evangelist understands by the
'exceeding righteousness' of which Mt 5:20 speaks. This context is the
work both of the pre-Matthean tradition and especially of Matthean
theological activity.

The introductory formula

Although the antitheses are heterogeneous not only in origin, but also
in content, structure and form, Matthew has welded them together into
a unit, first of all by means of the introductory formula. Indeed they are
marked by the repetition of the same formula: 'You have heard that it
was said. . . . But I say to you. . . .' This, at least, is the formula of
verses 27–28, 38–39 and 43–44, namely the second, fifth and sixth
antitheses. The first adds '(You have heard that it was said) *to the men
of old*', a normal explicitation at the beginning of a series. Although,
except for the fourth, the other antitheses do not repeat it, they always
suppose it.

There is an 'anomaly' only in the third and fourth antitheses. The
introductory formula of the third is considerably shorter, 'It was also
said' (Mt 5:31), and the fourth adds the adverb '*again* you have heard
that it was said to the men of old' (Mt 5:33). The third antithesis is
different from the others in its contents, too. It consists mainly of
the saying about divorce which is also handed down by the tradition
in other contexts (see Mt 19:9; Mk 10:11–12; Lk 16:18;
I Cor 7:10–11). This saying is introduced by a quotation from
Deut 24:1. 'Whoever divorces his wife, let him give her a certificate of
divorce' (Mt 5:31), from which Matthew has also borrowed the restric-

tive incision 'except on the ground of unchastity' which characterizes his redaction of Mt 5:32. Moreover, the third antithesis appears as a complementary explanation of the second antithesis about adultery. All these remarks make us think that the third antithesis was inserted by the pre-Matthean tradition or by Matthew himself into an original series of five antitheses. If so, we can understand why the third antithesis does not have a more developed introductory formula – being only an 'appendix' to the second antithesis – and that the return to the source in the fourth antithesis is indicated by the adverb 'again' in an attempt to connect the interpolation more strongly with the context.

For the rest, Matthew's intention in distributing the differently worded introductory formulas may have been more artistic than theological. The full formula is found in the first and the fourth (with resumptive 'again') antitheses. It is followed by the medium formula in the second and the fifth antitheses, and by the short formula in the third antithesis. It is not clear why the pattern is broken in the sixth and final antithesis. It is possible that Matthew felt that the sixth, being both the final and the second longest antithesis, deserved a longer introduction than the terse 'it was also said', which suited the third and shortest antithesis. At any rate, the variation in the introductory formula does not seem to have any theological importance and, whatever its length may be in a given antithesis, it must always be understood in the light of the full formula.

The meaning of the antithetical formula

The introductory formula of the antithesis is twofold. In its full expression the first part of the formula, 'You have heard that it was said to the men of old', is found only in Mt 5:21 and 5:33. What is its precise meaning?

The second person plural 'you' refers primarily to the disciples but indirectly also to the crowds (cf. Mt 5:1). 'You have heard' could refer to hearing the scriptures as read in the synagogue, and also to the comments on these scriptures given by the Jewish teachers. A look at the antitheses, where the first thing cited is always one or more passages from the Torah, reveals that the first meaning is certainly included. The passive 'that it was said' is a respectful circumlocution for the divine name, so that we should understand: 'that God said'. The expression can certainly not be made to refer only to the teaching of the scribes.

'The men of old' are first of all the generation that stood at Mount Sinai, but can also include the following generations and especially the chain of teachers of tradition which the scribes traced to their own time. What was said 'to the men of old' is the Torah. But the Torah is quoted in the context of the tradition of the fathers.

The first part of the antithetical formula means therefore: 'You have heard (in the synagogue) that God said to the men of old at Sinai (and to the teachers who passed down the tradition) that. . . .'.

The second part of the introductory formula with which the antithesis proper begins, 'but I say to you that', has a number of parallels in rabbinic discussions. The words 'but I say' introduce a statement which contradicts or departs from the opinion of a recognized authority. The speaker's opinion about the meaning of a particular scripture passage is opposed to another person's opinion about the same passage, and by quoting other scripture passages the speaker tries to decide the discussion in his own favour. But neither in Judaism nor in Qumran is the opinion of a teacher ever placed in contrast to the Torah, not even in statements which constitute a stiffening of the Law. This, however, happens in the 'but I say' of the antitheses. Here the speaker is opposing the commandment itself, not just the interpreter of the Law. He places his 'I' beside the name of God contained in the formula 'It was said'. He claims that his proclamation brings a new interpretation of the will of God. What was said before is no longer simply valid; it should be said and understood in a new way. The word of Jesus stands at times in contrast to the word of God as expressed in the Torah; and whenever this happens the word of Jesus is to be the decisive norm for the disciples' life. It is usually said that it remains to be verified in each individual case whether Jesus' new interpretation should be understood in terms of mere radicalization or actual abrogation. The first, second and sixth antitheses would simply radicalize the Torah, while the third, fourth and fifth would revoke the letter of the Torah.

However, a closer study of the antithetical formula shows that Jesus' words are not presented as (radical) interpretations of the Torah, but, rather, are opposed to well-known Torah commandments. *N B* His words have an independent authority which is not derived from the Torah, but is guaranteed by the speaker himself. Therefore, the antitheses are not presented as radicalizations of the Torah but confront it. They should be understood as demands of Jesus which by their radical character surpass the Torah, but not as radicalizations of the Torah. This character is shared by *all* the antitheses.

The authority of Jesus' words is ultimately founded on his proclamation of God's eschatological 'action'. The reign of God ('the kingdom of God is at hand') means God's limitless grace and forgiveness for man which calls for man's 'reaction', a limitless service and dedication to man, which can no longer be founded on the Torah but is made possible by God's eschatological intervention.

Concluding, we may say that whatever many parallels the single elements of the introductory formula may have in contemporary Judaism, the statement 'but I say to you' expresses an unparalleled claim, and therefore that the formula as a whole has no parallel in Jewish literature. On this ground it may be concluded that Jesus himself used it. With this formula Jesus affirmed that he did not speak as a self-willed rabbi, but as one who knows the will of God as nobody else knows it, and who proclaims it as nobody else does.

Exegesis

The first antithesis (Mt 5:21–26)

The antithesis proper is usually limited to Mt 5:21–22. But most probably Mt 5:22bc should also be considered secondary. Firstly, because of the presence of *sunedrion* (22b) and *gehenna* (22c), *krisis* would otherwise have to be given the unusual meaning of 'local court'. Secondly, Mt 5:22bc considerably weakens the (original) antithetical character of the statement. Therefore, Mt 5:21–22a seems to be the original antithesis, which has been secondarily expanded by Mt 5:22bc. It is followed by two sayings: the first recommends reconciliation with one's brother before presenting one's offering (Mt 5:23–24); the second is the short parable of the two litigants (Mt 5:25–26). Although the contents of these sayings may go back to Jesus, he certainly did not pronounce them together with the antithesis about killing. It is difficult to determine whether or not these sayings belonged already to Matthew's source.

The antithesis proper (Mt 5:21–22a)

Verses 21–22a: You have heard that it was said to the men of old, 'You shall not kill, and whoever kills shall be liable to judgment.' (22a) But I say to you that every one who is angry with his brother shall be liable to judgment;

The first antithesis quotes the fifth commandment, 'You shall not kill' (Ex 20:13). Although the next clause still depends on 'you have heard that . . .', it does not contain an Old Testament quotation. It must undoubtedly be understood as a summary of the punishment for killing stated in the Old Testament: 'Whoever strikes a man so that he dies shall be put to death' (Ex 21:12). If this is so, then the meaning of Mt 5:21b, 'and whoever kills shall be liable to judgment', and especially of the Greek word *krisis*, is established. It must mean 'death penalty' or 'capital punishment', and not 'judgment' (RSV) or '(local) court' (JB), so that we should translate: 'and whoever kills shall be meted out the death penalty'. The same must then be true of the antithesis: 'But I say to you that every one who is angry with his brother shall be meted out the death penalty'. Only thus is the sharpness of the antithesis clearly expressed: not only killing and murder, but also anger and hatred deserve capital punishment! Murder, anger, and hatred are placed on the same level. Not only actually killing, but even in anger denying somebody the right to live, is acting as one who takes a life.

The phrase 'brother', inherited from Israel, designates here a member of the Christian community, the new people of God united by the bonds of love. In Matthew, this concept seems to be enriched by a reference to God's fatherhood, a theme which is very dear to the evangelist. In fact, he brings the two together in Mt 23:8-9, 'But you are not to be called rabbi, for you have one teacher, and you are all *brothers*. And call no man your father on earth, for you have one *Father*, who is in heaven'. The theme of God's fatherhood is ultimately founded on that of the (eschatological) reign of God.

Liability to council and hell (Mt 5:22bc)

Verse 22bc: whoever insults his brother shall be liable to the council, and whoever says, 'You fool!' shall be liable to the hell of fire.

With the words about 'judgment' (RSV), or more correctly about 'death penalty', the antithesis seems to be complete, but Matthew 'opposes' two more sentences to the commandment of Ex 20:13. It may seem that these two clauses bring the first part of the antithesis to a climax: from anger to insult and then to calumny, and correspondingly, from 'local court' to the council and then to divine judgment. But since it was established that *krisis* means 'death penalty' and not 'local court', there is no question of a climax, especially since *sunedrion* does not refer here to the Sanhedrin or the Jewish Supreme Council, nor to the council of the Christian community charged with the administration of justice. Neither is there a climax from anger to 'calling one's brother *raka*' and calling him 'fool'. The apparent climax and distinctions are of purely rhetorical value. The mistake has often been made of interpreting this passage from the point of view of ecclesiastical law, while it is concerned with the moral and eschatological order.

The precise meaning of *raka* (RSV translates 'insults his brother' instead of 'says *raka* to his brother') is doubtful. It is most probably a transcription of the Aramaic word *reiqa*. The vocalization of the first syllable (*raka* instead of *reika*) is possibly due to the influence of the Syriac *raqa* ('mean', 'contemptible'). *Raka* is undoubtedly a vocative form and has a connotation of emptiness, which Jerome translated appropriately as 'brainless'. It seems probable, therefore, that Matthew is talking about calling somebody stupid.

The term 'fool' in the Bible has a religious sense: one who deliberately refuses to honour God (cf. Ps 14[13]:1, 'The fool says in his heart, "There is no God"'). There is no essential difference between anger and its expression in an insult, neither is there any important distinction between the two words 'raka' and 'fool'.

Gehenna (translated by RSV as 'hell') is the Greek transcription of the Aramaic *gehinnam* derived from the Hebrew *gei hinnom*, the name of the valley west and south-west of the western hill of Jerusalem. In the history of Israel this place acquired an evil reputation as the scene of idolatrous sacrifices offered during the time of Ahaz and Manasseh (II Kgs 16:3; 21:6; Jer 7:31–32; 19:6). This explains why the authors of apocalypses like I Henoch situated the fire of hell in this place, and why others like the writer of IV Esdras identified it with hell. It was at this stage that the New Testament took over the use of the term (cf. Mt 5:22, 29–30; 10:28; 18:9; 23:15, 33, etc.) to designate the eternal punishment of the damned.

We must conclude that the three clauses of Mt 5:22 are parallel statements. But if the second and the third clauses do not add anything to our understanding of the antithesis, questions may be raised as to their origin. Indications point to the post-Easter Christian community which wanted to accept and practise Jesus' statements of Mt 5:22, and as a competent body pronounced judgment on evildoers. However, as we can see from a number of New Testament passages, the community did not execute this judgment, since they believed that it would have its fulfilment in God's judgment (cf. I Cor 5:4f.). So we can say that the Church's acceptance of Jesus' saying is expressed in Mt 5:22a, 'but I say to you that every one who is angry with his brother shall be liable to judgment (better: shall be meted out the death penalty)', while its practice and belief are expressed in Mt 5:22bc, 'whoever insults his brother shall be liable to the council, and whoever says, "You fool!" shall be liable to the hell of fire'. Similar statements are found in rabbinic Judaism and at Qumran.

In this and similar statements Jesus is not just concerned with a new disposition or with the fundamental *right* (which implies 'my right' and the possibility of insisting on it), but with the other *person* as such, whose well-being should be pursued without limitations, regardless whether these are justified or not. Therefore, Jesus does not consider whether the anger is justified or not. Whenever our anger threatens our limitless concern for men, we are liable to judgment. The Torah commandment and its scribal interpretation are hereby declared insufficient, and the possibility of basing relationships with our fellow-men on a legal position is taken away. At the same time it becomes impossible to interpret Jesus' demand in a legalistic sense, i.e., as a radicalization of a law extending it to the realm of inner disposition. Jesus' word is founded on the demand for a radical and limitless concern for men, which is made possible by God's eschatological action as it is proclaimed in Jesus' message. The greater righteousness is not to keep our hands off, it is to hold our hands out to our fellow-men.

Jesus does not mean to say that those who bear anger or hatred in their heart should receive the death penalty. He does not take a stand on the question of capital punishment, nor does he say that capital punishment is a 'divine right'. But he means that manslaughter and murder have their origin in anger and hatred and that where in their minds men sever all loving relationships with their neighbours, a process begins which may end in murder. Such feelings cannot be regulated by law, but definitely fall under the eschatological demand of Jesus.

The two additional sayings (Mt 5:23–26)
> **Verses 23–24:** So if you are offering your gift at the altar, and there remember that your brother has something against you, (24) leave your gift there before the altar and go; first be reconciled to your brother, and then come and offer your gift.

At first these verses do not seem to have much connection with the preceding. Most scholars believe that they were inserted here by the evangelist or by an earlier redactor whose heritage Matthew has taken over. It is true that the style of these verses differs considerably from that of verse 22, but nevertheless it still belongs to the style of Jewish legislation (*mishpatim*), and the images referring to the Temple worship are no stranger than those of the fourth antithesis (Mt 5:35). In fact, a good look at the following antitheses, especially the fourth and fifth, is very helpful. The prohibition is superseded first in three formulas which remain in the same line; then follows a positive directive (Mt 5:37; cf. 5:42). If this is taken into consideration, it seems unsurprising that in the first antithesis Jesus not only sets the prohibition of anger against the prohibition of murder, but also adds a positive statement on the duty of reconciliation.

At any rate, Matthew saw in these verses an application of the preceding statement. His characteristic emphasis on mercy instead of sacrifice (Mt 9:13; 12:7) leads him to the imagery of sacrifice. There should be nothing to divide brothers, i.e., Christians, lest they be incapable of worship. If there is dissension between Christians, then the relationship between God and them is also affected. The example does not deal with a case in which you have something against another, but with an instance in which 'you remember that your brother has something against you'. Then it is you who must make the first move toward reconciliation: you must 'go' and restore peace, and this must be done 'first'. The kingdom of God demands that you always take the first step, because you have been forgiven for free. Only when this has been done can you go and offer your gift properly. The 'vertical' relation with God is destroyed when the 'horizontal' relation with fellow-men is broken.

Similarly, the Mishnah stated that the rites of the Day of Atonement could not atone for sins against a neighbour unless one first made peace with that neighbour. According to Jewish teaching sacrifices could be interrupted for ritual reasons, but not on account of a neighbour, since the emphasis was entirely on the ritual. When Jesus asked that an act of worship be stopped for the sake of one's neighbour, he fundamentally set aside all cultic ideology. But, as verse 24 shows, worship *cannot be reduced to* love for one's fellow-men. Worship rather *presupposes* love for one's neighbour.

Jesus requires here an act which, if it is literally interpreted, is at the limit of the practicable. It is indeed hard to imagine Galileans leaving their offerings before the altar and going all the way back to Galilee to reconcile themselves with an offended brother, and then coming back a week later to offer their sacrifice. This is not something that I can demand from others, but an invitation and challenge to do it myself. In fact, Jesus does not mean to legislate in ritual matters, concerning the conditions for the validity of a sacrifice, but is telling a parable in which the scene is imagined purely in function of his teaching. Without opposing the official worship, this teaching nevertheless insists on an aspect of religious life which, because it is more important, conditions the legitimate exercise of this worship. Understood in this way, Jesus' words are not so different from those of the prophets (cf. Isa 1:13–17; Jer 6:20; 7:21–23).

Although a contemporary Christian might easily apply this saying to the Eucharist, it is quite improbable that Matthew thought in these terms, for 'the altar' he spoke of was certainly the altar of the Temple of Jerusalem. The Eucharist was celebrated at that time around a 'table' (I Cor 10:21), and the 'altar' mentioned in Heb 13:10 symbolizes the sacrifice of the New Covenant and does not refer to an 'altar' in the real sense of the word. The 'altar' is mentioned for the first time among the objects of Christian worship in Ignatius of Antioch's letter to the Philadelphians, very early in the second century.

Verses 25–26: Make friends quickly with your accuser, while you are going with him to court, lest your accuser hand you over to the judge, and the judge to the guard, and you be put in prison; (26) truly, I say to you, you will never get out till you have paid the last penny.

These verses constitute a parable-like story which is also found in Lk 12:57–59. But while in Luke the parable has a clearly eschatological character (cf. Lk 12:58f.), in Matthew it seems to have a predominantly paraenetic character. The original purpose of the parable was probably to indicate the imminence of the final crisis and the corresponding critical situation of the hearer. But Matthew uses it mainly as an illustration of the need for reconciliation. The exhortation 'be reconciled to your brother' applies also when he has become an opponent in a legal dispute. One should try to be on good terms with one's opponent, while one is 'on the way' ('to court' is not in the Greek text), i.e., during one's lifetime. The mention of 'paying' should not be taken literally: there is no allusion here either to the possibility of making compensation, or to purgatory. The emphasis is on reconciling oneself with one's brother while there is still time. It is a matter of making the first move as soon as possible. The phrase 'truly, I say to you' in verse 26 emphasizes the consequence for those who did not make the first move in good time, i.e., while there were still 'on the way'. The parable exhorts the readers to seize the opportunity for a fruitful encounter with their neighbour granted by God during their lifetime.

It is clear that the story is not ultimately about a court case over debts: according to Mt 5:21–22, the object of the threat is God's eschatological punishment. However, we should not allegorize the details of the text: the 'guard' is not to be identified with the devil, and the 'prison' does not symbolize hell, since the debtor can hope to leave the place after paying the debt, while hell is 'eternal' (cf. Mt 18:8; 25:41). The evangelist is saying more or less the following: whenever, by your own fault, you are involved in a court case with one of your brothers, try to get his pardon as soon as possible, otherwise God will condemn you at the last judgment. Thus understood, the 'parable' constitutes a practical application of the preceding teaching.

The second antithesis (Mt 5:27–30)

The antithesis proper is contained in Mt 5:27–28. It is followed by a saying which is found again in Matthew's Community Discourse (Mt 5:29–30 = Mt 18:8–9) and in Mk 9:43–47, where it is transmitted in the form of *three* parallel recommendations concerning one's foot, hand and eye. The latter is apparently the primitive form of the saying. In Matthew it has probably been introduced in its present context on the level of the redaction of the Sermon on the Mount. The source probably contained only verses 27–28, which are probably very close to the original form of Jesus' saying. The phrase 'in his heart' may be a Matthean addition.

The antithesis proper (Mt 5:27–28)

Verses 27–28: You have heard that it was said, 'You shall not commit adultery.' (28) But I say to you that every one who looks at a woman lustfully has already committed adultery with her in his heart.

The quotation in verse 27 is literally taken from Ex 20:14, 'You shall not commit adultery'. Unlike the first antithesis, the punishment for adultery is not mentioned, although it is clearly stated in Lev 20:10 (cf. Deut 22:20): 'If a man commits adultery with the wife of his neighbour, both the adulterer and the adulteress shall be put to death'.

Verse 28 is closely related to the kind of explanations which the sixth commandment received in the haggadic (rather than the halachic) sections of the Jewish tradition.[11] For example, 'Resh Laqish has said: You shall not say that only he who with his body breaks the marriage bond, is called an adulterer; also he who breaks the marriage bond with his eyes is called an adulterer'. However, the contemporary practice was based almost exclusively on externally established criteria.

The verb *moicheuein* in these texts is used only in connection with a married woman. Both she and the other man commit a sin against the rights of the husband. The sin of adultery, therefore, consists not so much in unchastity as in an offence against the husband's rights of possession.

In line with this contemporary approach, Jesus is concerned in the first place with the well-being of the husband: one should be radically concerned with the well-being of the other husband. Indirectly, Mt 5:27–28 also expresses a certain consideration for women in that, unlike Judaism and Qumran, Jesus' words are not based on any kind of depreciation of women as a 'danger' or on an appeal for ascetism. His approach to women is totally unprejudiced.

By opposing his statement to the Torah Jesus declares that the Torah, and at the same time any other juridically fixed regulation of relations to another person, here another husband, is insufficient. The starting-point for this authoritative statement of Jesus is to be found in the authoritative proclamation of the reign of God which demands radical concern for fellow-men. Where one meets a fellow-man in his capacity of a husband, his well-being in his marriage is the first and sole criterion of one's relationship to him. Whenever this absolute concern for his well-being is legally or otherwise restricted, this criterion is disregarded. Concern for fellow-men is already in jeopardy when, long before reaching the legal limits, one looks lustfully at the wife of one's fellow-man.

The phrase translated by RSV 'lustfully' is *pros to epithumēsai autēn*, literally, 'with a view to desire her'. Recently it has been pointed out that when *autēn* is taken as the logical object of *epithumēsai* ('to desire'), the saying would read: 'every one who so looks at a (married) woman that she becomes (or: should become) desirable, has already misled her to adultery in his heart'. Thus the uniqueness of Jesus' statement would be that instead of warning men about the danger of women (which anyway Jesus does not intend!), it would warn men against aggressive behaviour towards married women. But in the context of verse 27b (= Ex 20:13LXX; Deut 5:17LXX) *epithumein* is almost certainly an allusion to Ex 20:17; Deut 5:21 where the Septuagint likewise expresses the object of the desire in the accusative. Therefore, the suggestion that Jesus is warning men specifically against aggressive behaviour towards women seems to lack solid ground. Notwithstanding the seemingly legalistic language, Jesus' words mean that one falls short of the goal of being concerned for the well-being of another as a married person long before reaching the stage of actions against which laws can be formulated.

As in the first antithesis, Jesus' statement should not be understood as a radicalization of the Torah. Rather, it declares the Torah insufficient in view of the proclamation of God's eschatological intervention on behalf of men which calls for and makes possible a radical concern of man for man.

The additional saying (Mt 5:29–30)

Verses 29–30: If your right eye causes you to sin, pluck it out and throw it away; it is better that you lose one of your members than that your whole body be thrown into hell. (30) And if your right hand causes you to sin, cut it off and throw it away; it is better that you lose one of your members than that your whole body go into hell.

As already mentioned, Matthew also introduces this saying in a variant form in another context (Mt 18:8–9), where it is part of a Marcan sequence which is not at all related to the prohibition of adultery (cf. Mk 9:43–48). Matthew has tried to make this saying refer to adultery by placing the mention of the eye first and thus relating it to the verb 'look' in verse 28. This may also explain the omission of the reference to the 'foot' (cf. Mk 9:45).

Verses 29–30 are intended to make clear how serious Matthew (and Jesus) is about the prohibition of adultery. Jesus and his disciples certainly spoke about hell: men have the dangerous power to ruin their existence totally. But no New Testament book, not even the Book of Revelation, ever developed the facile symbolism of the sufferings of hell (cf. Rev 20:15). Their reserved character contrasts favourably with the products of a morbid imagination found so often in later literature.

The precision with which Matthew speaks of the *right* eye and the *right* hand is intended to emphasize the importance of the sacrifice one should be willing to bring. In fact, this insistence seems to reflect the general assumption that the right is the more important side of the body, and so damage to it is more serious. The eye also stands here for what is most precious.

The eye is the 'seeing' part, while the hand is the 'doing' part of man as a whole ('the whole body'). Therefore, it makes no sense to remark that the left eye and the left hand still remain, or that Jesus' word does not concern the left eye and the left hand! The saying refers to a part that stands for the whole: eye and hand, i.e., seeing and doing. Via the eye and the hand the whole man can be induced to sin, i.e., can stumble and fall in his own marriage as well as damaging another's. This is the force of the verb *skandalizein*, which does not just mean 'scandalize', but rather 'to entice to sin', 'to cause to sin'. No price should be too high to avoid this.

The third antithesis (Mt 5:31–32)

Verses 31–32: It was also said, 'Whoever divorces his wife, let him give her a certificate of divorce.' (32) But I say to you that every one who divorces his wife, except on the ground of unchastity, makes her an adulteress; and whoever marries a divorced woman commits adultery.

THE ORIGINAL FORM OF THE SAYING ON DIVORCE

Mt 5:31 is generally considered Matthean. This may also be the case for 'but I say to you' (Mt 5:32) which is absent from the parallel text, Lk 16:18. The phrase 'except on the ground of unchastity' did not belong to the Q-text either, so that the latter would have read as follows: 'Every one who divorces his wife, makes her an adulteress; and whoever marries a divorced woman, commits adultery'.

How does this Q-text compare with Mk 10:11–12, which is at present the conclusion of Mk 10:1–9? Mk 10:12, which presupposes Hellenistic-Roman marriage law, is certainly secondary, so that only Mk 10:11 remains for comparison:

Q-text	*Mark*
Every one who divorces his wife,	Whoever divorces his wife, and marries another,
makes her an adulteress; and whoever marries a divorced woman, commits adultery.	commits adultery against her.

According to Mk 10:11 a man commits adultery only when he 'marries another', while the Q-logion forbids sending away one's wife, since this will practically force her to remarry and thus to commit adultery, for which Mt 5:32a holds the husband responsible.

Compared with the Q-logion, Mk 10:11 is to be considered secondary; so is its connection with Mk 10:10. The controversy in Mk 10:2–9 has often been ascribed to the Greek-speaking Jewish-Christian community. Its starting-point is certainly Mk 10:9, which many hold for an original Jesus-saying: 'What therefore God has joined together, let no man put asunder'. While Mk 10:9 is speaking of the inseparable union willed by the Creator which man cannot break up, Mk 10:11(–12) refers to divorce and remarriage. However, the two do not contradict each other if one considers their actual form: the former is an apodictic or incontrovertible prohibition, whereas the latter is a (conditional) statement: '. . . he commits adultery'. Mk 10:9 was understood as a theologoumenon or theological statement, but also as a regulation (not a law!) for practical application so that it led to the rule expressed in verse 11: in the case of a separation, remarriage is forbidden. As can be seen from I Cor 7:10–11, this combination was already known before Mark. In light of the same text (especially I Cor 7:11a), it is also clear that Mark's addition, 'and marries another' (Mk 10:11), should be understood as a 'concession' in practice with regard to the basic statement in Mk 10:9. It should be noted that both in Mk 10 and I Cor 7 the apodictic prohibition of divorce is an absolute principle and norm of Christian marriage. But it is not understood as a law which has to be enforced in all circumstances.

Unlike Mk 10:11 (Lk 16:18; I Cor 7:11a), where divorce and remarriage are rejected, Mt 5:32 and parallel (Q) and Mk 10:9 forbid only divorce. While Mt 5:32 par. (Q) cannot have originated outside a Jewish milieu, Mk 10:9 is thinkable in both a Jewish and a Hellenistic one. The latter statement is an attempt to apply the former to both Jewish and Hellenistic milieus. In the following paragraph, then, we can concentrate on Mt 5:32 par. (Q) as reconstructed above.

THE MEANING OF JESUS' SAYING ON DIVORCE

Jewish divorce laws knew only of dismissal by the husband through a certificate of divorce on the ground of Deut 24:1. This text was interpreted in a stricter sense by the school of Shammai as referring to 'unchastity', and in a looser sense by Hillel as 'everything displeasing the husband'. Refusing to enter into this discussion, Jesus says that what is subject to debate is not the *interpretation* of Deut 24:1, but rather the *very claim* of Deut 24:1 as a legal ground for divorce. Therefore, Jesus' word is in the first place an attack on the legally protected privileged position of the husband: every man who claims this right commits injustice (Mt 5:32a)! At the same time Jesus speaks up for women. He is not so much defending their *rights* against the rights of men – notwithstanding the apparently legalistic formulation, which is used in a provocative way – as speaking up for the *person* of the woman herself. His word disqualifies justice as the appropriate way of regulating marriage relationships. In a paradoxical and provocative way Jesus refers the husband to his irrevocable responsibility for his wife which does not end with legal claims.

Thus Jesus' prohibition of divorce is in line with the other antitheses. It deals with the radical concern for the other person which cannot be fixed within legal restrictions. Jesus' words, therefore, do not constitute a new 'law'. They are based on his proclamation that in his eschatological concern for men God claims no rights but turns toward men with unlimited love. Therefore, men too can be concerned only with the well-being of their fellow-men. Even an appeal to the Law is no longer adequate in this context. Jesus' stand against divorce ultimately reveals a sovereign stand towards the Torah.

JESUS' SAYING AND EARLY CHRISTIAN PRACTICE

Jesus' statement about divorce is much more than a law. It is not just a rule of thumb with which to 'solve' all kinds of moral-theological cases. In fact, Jesus' statement does not give an answer to a number of practical questions, since Jesus ultimately wants to appeal to love and faithfulness. Christian marriage is essentially a radical responsibility for one's partner which can be traced to the Creator himself (cf. Mk 10:9). The tradition-historical study of Mt 5:32 and Mk 10:9 shows that the early Christian communities did not understand these words as inflexible 'laws'. They should not be applied as 'laws' to cases where through human weakness further marital union has become impossible, because this would mean to use against people a directive which is entirely intent on their well-being.

In the practice of the early Church, as it is reflected in Mk 10:11–12 and I Cor 7:10–11, the prohibition of remarriage is understood as a drastic reference to the responsibility for one's partner which still exists after separation, and a warning to the one who has taken the initiative for the separation to remain open for the possibility of actively resuming this responsibility through reconciliation. But even the prohibition of remarriage was not understood by Paul as a 'law' applicable to all cases, as is clear from I Cor 7:12–15.

THE PRACTICE OF THE MATTHEAN COMMUNITY

Matthew too shows that Jesus' directive was not understood as an inflexible 'law'. He considerably reformulates the wording of the Marcan as well as the Q-version of the divorce-saying. Again we have here an application in practice which, because of the difference of community and situation, is different from that found in Mk 10:11–12 and I Cor 7:10–11.

Nowhere, except in Mt 5:32, is the statement about divorce expressed in antithetical form. This form seems to be the work of the pre-Matthean tradition, and it seems also that in the course of the tradition the whole of Mt 5:31 was placed before the divorce logion, which certainly comes from Jesus himself. Apparently this divorce logion did not have a fixed place in the early Christian tradition and could therefore be quoted in different contexts. In the pre-Matthean tradition it was attached to the antithesis about adultery, so that it now appears as a complementary statement, which in the course of the process was given the same antithetical form as the one found in Mt 5:27–28. Mt 5:31–32 is now a continuation of the antithesis about adultery: divorce is in a sense a case of adultery.

While in all other antitheses we find references to Exodus and Leviticus, Mt 5:31 quotes Deut 24:1, 'When a man takes a wife and marries her, if then she finds no favour in his eyes because he has found some indecency in her, and he writes her a bill of divorce and puts it in her hand and sends her out of his house . . .'. As already said, according to the school of Hillel almost anything was sufficient reason to send one's wife away, while the stricter school of Shammai insisted on some weightier matter. The text of Deuteronomy also plays a role in the discussion about divorce in Mt 19:1–9, where it is used by the Pharisees as an objection against Jesus' authoritative explanation of Gen 1:27 and 2:24. This seems to be the more original setting for the saying concerning divorce.

The Law said: 'Whoever divorces his wife, let him give her a certificate of divorce' (Mt 5:31). This is certainly meant to be a quotation of Deut 24:1. Properly speaking, the point of the Hebrew text of Deut 24:1–3 was neither to permit divorce nor to establish its grounds or to determine its procedure. The text intended only to decide on a particular case in which divorce with its conditions and formalities was supposed. Here in Matthew, it becomes a prescription about the procedure! The legality of divorce is unquestioned on condition that this procedure is followed. The 'certificate of divorce' gave the wife the right to remarry and protected her against possible injustice. The husband who sent her away could not claim her any longer as his, and the second husband could not be considered as encroaching upon the rights of the man who had sent her away. Throughout these considerations the possibility of divorce was taken for granted.

Jesus now says: 'Every one who divorces his wife, except on the ground of unchastity, makes her an adulteress; and whoever marries a divorced woman commits adultery' (Mt 5:32). The first part of this saying is somewhat different from Mt 19:9, 'whoever divorces his wife, except for unchastity, *and marries another*, commits adultery (and he who marries a divorced woman commits adultery)'. In Mt 19:9 the second marriage is called adultery. In Mt 5:32, however, the second marriage is not mentioned, but it is said that by sending away his wife a husband leads her into a situation where she may very well commit adultery, for which he is then considered co-responsible. Throughout this reasoning it is presupposed that the husband observed the old prescriptions concerning the grounds and the procedure of divorce. If, in spite of that, the wife by marrying another commits adultery, as is implied in the first part of the saying, this can only be because the first marriage bond was not dissolved. The second part of the saying, speaking of the adultery committed by the second man who marries her, expresses what is already implied in the first part.

The indissoluble character of the marriage bond constitutes the newness of this statement. Otherwise there would be nothing really new, and this saying would be just another reproduction of the old Law. Any interpretation that would deny this would strip the emphatically antithetical structure of the passage of all meaning. But this antithetical structure was elaborated by the pre-Matthean tradition or by Matthew himself. And so it would be quite illogical to ascribe to either of them the addition of an exception ('except on the ground of unchastity').

Therefore, we find it hard to understand the phrase 'except on the ground of unchastity' as a real exception, either accepted by Jesus himself (which scarcely anybody defends), or introduced by the early Christian tradition or by Matthew (which is accepted by a number of Protestant scholars and, in mitigated form, by some Catholics). The reasons for our hesitation to accept this interpretation are the following:

(1) The early post-apostolic tradition apparently did not know of any such exception until the middle of the third century. There is no evidence whatsoever that up to that time anybody accepted adultery as grounds for a divorce in the real sense of the word.

(2)   When Paul states the doctrine of absolute indissolubility of marriage (I Cor 7:10–11), he explicitly appeals to a word of the Lord handed down to him.

(3)   There is no trace of such an 'exception' in Lk 16:18 and Mk 10:11–12, the parallel texts of Mt 5:32 and 19:9.

(4)   The two Matthean texts themselves, if considered in their context and in their own particular perspective, do not admit of such an interpretation, which would amount to accepting a clear-cut contradiction in the texts themselves.

The different interpretations given to 'except on the ground of unchastity' can be summed up as follows:

(1)   The *inclusive interpretation* is held by scholars who try to prove that, grammatically, the clause does not have an exceptive but an inclusive meaning: 'besides – including – the case of unchastity'. If this interpretation were correct, all the problems would be solved. Unfortunately, the grammatical arguments adduced for this explanation are untenable and have rightly been called linguistic gymnastics.

(2)   The *preteritive interpretation* maintains the exclusive character of the clause, but says that it is an exception to the proposition as a whole, not simply to the verb 'to divorce' or 'to send away'. Such a clause is really parenthetical and is called a preterition. Scholars who defend this interpretation do not translate 'every one who divorces his wife – except on the ground of unchastity – makes her an adulteress', but 'every one who divorces his wife – setting aside the case of unchastity – makes her an adulteress'. There is indeed a difference between making an exception to something and setting aside the consideration of it. In the latter case one neither includes or excludes the matter, but simply leaves it out of consideration. Grammatically, there is no objection against this interpretation. But why by-pass precisely the case that was under discussion, namely the validity of 'adultery' as a ground for divorce? Even the modified form in which this interpretation has recently been proposed cannot be accepted.

(3)   The *interpretative or biographical interpretation* also maintains the exclusive character of the clause. According to this interpretation the absolute indissolubility of marriage is strictly upheld in this saying, but in the phrase 'except on the ground of unchastity' Jesus nevertheless proceeds to take sides in the Jewish dispute about the grounds for divorce, and to interpret Deut 24:1–3 in favour of the stricter school of Shammai. For the time being, the concession mentioned is operative for the chosen people until the definitive promulgation of the gospel.

There are no grammatical objections to this interpretation, but it seems to go against the emphatic character of the Matthean text. Jesus would still be taking sides in a dispute which he has declared to belong to the past. To decide between two rival interpretations of a superseded legislation within the framework of a statement whose formulation is strongly antithetical would be entirely beside the point.

Some present-day scholars have attributed this 'interpretation' to Matthew, whose redaction would have to be understood in the light of the Jewish-Christian context in which his gospel originated. Used to their Jewish ideas, the Jewish Christians took some time to realize the full implications of the words of Christ. They did not realize that they violated Jesus' prohibition of divorce by not applying it to the case of adultery. They did not regard this non-application as a real exception to Christ's word. Again we cannot accept this *interim interpretation* because of our understanding of Matthew's overall redaction.

(4) The *traditional interpretation* is still held by an impressive number of Catholic scholars. It understands the Matthean clause as a permission, explicitly given by Jesus himself, for the separation from bed and board on the ground of adultery, without the right to remarry. The main objection to this interpretation is that in the Bible 'to put away one's wife' or 'to divorce one's wife' has no other meaning than the Jewish practice of divorce with a certificate of divorce and the right to remarry.

Some present-day scholars have tried to modernize this traditional interpretation by attributing the clause to Matthew. We agree that the clause should be attributed to the Matthean redaction (or the pre-Matthean tradition), but not that the verb *apoluein* ('to put away') is used in other than the current sense of divorce. These scholars give the term a new Christian meaning: a repudiation which does not break the marriage bond and consequently does not imply the right to remarry. According to this interpretation, the very point of the text would not only be to announce a new doctrine, but also to establish an entirely new meaning for the verb *apoluein*. The evidence given for this thesis is unconvincing. Moreover, this interpretation, as all previous ones, is left with the problem of explaining the use of the word *porneia* (RSV, 'unchastity') within a context which repeatedly uses *moicheuein* ('to commit adultery').

Summing up, we may say that all previous views come up against the difficulty of correctly explaining the meaning of *porneia* and convincingly defining the clause's situation in life within the synoptic tradition.

(5) But there is a fifth interpretation which can be traced back to the

nineteenth century. In the past thirty years it has been supported by J. Bonsirven (who understands *porneia* as including all invalid or illegitimate marriages) and further developed by H. Baltensweiler. Their interpretation is followed by a considerable number of scholars.

The four interpretations previously mentioned all understand the word *porneia* as unchastity or adultery. But if Matthew wanted to exclude the precise case of adultery, the use of the word *porneia* was certainly not the best possible choice. He could have used the term *moicheia*, especially since he used the verb *moicheuein* in the immediate context, while citing the Decalogue in Mt 5:27, to broaden the concept of adultery in Mt 5:28, and again within the present antithesis itself to declare remarriage after divorce adultery. In fact, we find one of the two (three if we include Jn 8:3) New Testament usages of *moicheia* in Matthew: 'For out of the heart come evil thoughts, murder, adultery (*moicheiai*), fornication (*porneiai*), theft, false witness, slander' (Mt 15:19, paralleling Mk 7:21). So Matthew knew both terms and he distinguished between them. In the light of these considerations it seems inadmissible to make *porneia* in Mt 5:32 mean 'adultery', when the proper term for this appears in the same context. Moreover, it has recently been shown that there is no evidence in traditional or contemporary usage of the word *porneia* that takes it to mean what we call 'fornication' today. But if *porneia* in Mt 5:32 does not mean 'adultery' or 'fornication', what does it mean?

The interpretation under consideration offers an answer to the philological question as well as to the question of the situation in life of the use of *porneia* in the proposed sense. It is suggested that *porneia* in Mt 5:32 and 19:9 refers to an incestuous marriage within the degrees of consanguinity or affinity prohibited by Lev 18:6–18.

The situation in life for this particular usage of *porneia* would be the following. Outside Jewish and Roman circles marriages which were incestuous according to the rules of Lev 18 were not uncommon. At times, this created a problem for a Gentile convert to Judaism, and the same problem apparently also occurred in Matthew's Church, which was at first mainly composed of Jewish Christians, but gradually accepted more and more Gentiles into its ranks. To the question whether Jesus' prohibition of divorce helped justify the continuance of an incestuous marriage, the answer was a radical no, and this judgment was inserted into Jesus' prohibition.

The same problem and a similar solution (with the word *porneia* meaning 'incestuous marriage') are found in the New Testament, especially at the end of the so-called Apostolic Decree (Acts 15:29; cf. 15:20; 21:25) promulgated by the 'Council of Jerusalem'. Addressing the Gentile Christians of Antioch, Syria and Cilicia, it prohibits four practices, all forbidden by Lev 17 – 18: eating food sacrificed to idols, drinking blood, eating strangled meat (i.e., without drawing the blood from it), and *porneia* (RSV, 'unchastity'). In this context, *porneia* probably means an incestuous marriage. The same may be said of the use of *porneia* (in connection with food offered to idols!) in the so-called letters to the seven churches, from which appears that there were Christians in the churches of Pergamum and Thyatira who rejected the legislation of the 'Council of Jerusalem' (Rev 2:14, 20–21).

But there is also firm proof that *porneia* was used to describe an incestuous marriage during the New Testament period. In I Cor 5:1, Paul writes: 'It is actually reported that there is immorality (*porneia*) among you, and of a kind that is not found even among pagans; for a man is living with his father's wife'. Here *porneia* clearly means an incestuous union of the type forbidden in Lev 18:8.

A paraphrastic translation of Mt 5:32 in accordance with this interpretation would read: 'But I say to you that every one who divorces (sends away) his wife, *except for the case that it is a marriage contracted in contravention of the laws of Lev 18:6–18*, makes her an adulteress; and whoever marries a divorced woman commits adultery'.

Summing up again, we may say that only two interpretations remain in contest: the one that interprets the phrase 'except on the ground of unchasity' as a real exception, and the one which understands *porneia* as a marriage within the forbidden degrees of kinship. Although the latter is supported by very convincing arguments, it has recently been questioned on two grounds. First, it is said that this interpretation does not explain why the Jewish-Christian community would have insisted on a strict observation of Lev 18, while this was not the case in contemporary Judaism. Secondly, it has been pointed out that in Mt 19:9 *porneia* almost certainly refers to an exception, in view of the significant reformulation of the question. 'Is it lawful for a man to divorce his wife?' (Mk 10:2) into 'Is it lawful to divorce one's wife *for any cause?*' (Mt 19:3). The change in the question corresponds to a change in the answer, i.e., the addition of 'except for unchastity' (Mt 19:9; cf. Mk 10:11).

The translation of these data into contemporary canon law goes beyond the competence of the exegete. Nevertheless it may be said here that canon law too should avoid interpreting Jesus' statements as a strict 'law'. It should not be reduced to a merely negative prohibition of divorce which has to be implemented at all costs. Certainly, the Church has to formulate certain practical rules concerning marriage, but it should see that its regulations and their presentation in pastoral practice clearly show that they are at the service of a radical concern for people which by his provocative word Jesus also applied to marriage.

The credibility of the Church's marriage laws will depend on whether it itself practises a radical concern for people even where – with or without guilt – they are no longer capable of living up to what is undoubtedly the fundamental understanding of Christian marriage (cf. Mk 10:9).

It is written: 'What therefore God has joined together, let no man put asunder' (Mt 19:6; cf. Mk 10:9). We have read: 'Whom the Church has joined together'. This is not exactly the same. 'What therefore God has joined together', said by Jesus in the context of the creation narrative, refers to the mystery of the man–woman relationship. 'Whom the Church has joined together' refers rather to a juridical arrangement by the Church concerning people who have entered into a contract. By his statement, 'What therefore God has joined together, let no man put asunder', Jesus does not formulate an additional commandment, but asks people to respect the original mystery in the man–woman relationship. For righteousness which exceeds that of the scribes and Pharisees (cf. Mt 5:20), this is the ideal and the norm. But what is presented to me as an ideal of righteousness to be pursued I cannot just impose on others as a juridical demand when their man–woman relationship is in crisis. A purely juridical approach to the man–woman relationship whereby a marriage once concluded is made indissoluble can be as hard and legalistic for the man and woman concerned as the scribes and Pharisees were in Jesus' time.

The fourth antithesis (Mt 5:33–37)

In this antithesis, the absolute prohibition of swearing (Mt 5:34a) is followed by a list of forbidden formulas (Mt 5:34b–36) which recalls the anti-Pharisaic polemics of Mt 23:16–22 and derives from rabbinical discussion. Verses 34b–35 contain a series of allusions to the Old Testament, while Mt 5:36 is comparable to other Jesus-sayings (Mt 6:27, 10:30). Mt 5:34b–36, therefore, are considered as a secondary illustration of Mt 5:34a. Mt 5:37 constitutes a special problem. Verse 37a does not altogether exclude swearing, but opposes a simpler formula to verses 34b–36, while verse 37b with its 'anything more' implies a limitation, but not an abrogation of swearing. This suggests a secondary change which tried to cut Jesus' absolute prohibition of swearing down to the size of a practicable rule by interpreting it as a prohibition of the oaths mentioned in Mt 5:34b–36. In light of what is said above it appears that Jas 5:12b, '. . . let your yes be yes and your no be no', is closer to Jesus' original words than Mt 5:37b. The original antithesis may then have consisted of Mt 5:33–34a and the saying found in Jas 5:12b.

The antithesis proper (Mt 5:33–34a and Jas 5:12b)

Verses 33–34a: Again you have heard that it was said to the men of old, 'You shall not swear falsely, but shall perform to the Lord what you have sworn.' (34a) But I say to you, Do not swear at all. . . .

Jas 5:12b: Let your yes be yes and your no be no.

The quotation in verse 33 is made up of a number of citations or allusions from the Torah: 'You shall not take the name of the Lord your God in vain' (Ex 20:7); 'And you shall not swear by my name falsely, and so profane the name of your God' (Lev 19:12); 'Or when a woman vows a vow to the Lord, and binds herself by a pledge . . .' (Num 30:3); 'But if you refrain from vowing, it shall be no sin in you' (Deut 23:22); 'pay your vows to the Most High' (Ps 50[49]:14). As can be seen from these texts, the word 'oath' covers what we would call an oath as well as what we would call a vow.

In verse 34a, Jesus authoritatively places his word over against the Torah: 'Do not swear at all'. This is the basic command of the fourth antithesis, and everything which follows must be understood in its light. Therefore, verses 34b–36 cannot be understood as forbidding only those oaths which Jesus explicitly lists. The absolute directive which precedes them shows that the four oaths mentioned are an illustrative and not a comprehensive enumeration. This is confirmed by the placement of the fourth oath, after the three that contain indirect references to God: not even such an apparently harmless oath is to be allowed.

This prohibition of swearing has its predecessors in Judaism. Wisdom literature as well as rabbinical literature warns against frivolous oaths. Oaths are forbidden by the Essenes and Philo, but the latter's motive is clearly an attempt to avoid the name of God. Jesus, however, is concerned with trustworthiness in relationships with fellow-men, here especially the relationship with other people in oral communication. This relationship must be radically truthful, and any legal restriction of truthfulness is rejected.

The secondary illustrations (Mt 5:34b–37)

Verses 34b–37: (Do not swear at all), either by heaven, for it is the throne of God, (35) or by the earth, for it is his footstool, or by Jerusalem, for it is the city of the great King. (36) And do not swear by your head, for you cannot make one hair white or black. (37) Let what you say be simply 'Yes' or 'No'; anything more than this comes from evil.

In verse 34b we have a more or less literal quotation of Isa 66:1, 'Thus says the Lord, "Heaven is my throne and the earth is my footstool"', and verse 35 is a citation from Ps 48(47):2b, 'Mount Zion, in the far north, the city of the great King'. The three oath formulas mentioned in these verses are rejected with the help of Old Testament citations. Nowhere else in Mt 5:21–48 is an Old Testament text set against another Old Testament text. It has been suggested that these verses contain the arguments which the Christian community used in discussion with the scribes concerning Jesus' fundamental directive: 'Do not swear at all'. The three oaths in Mt 5:34b–35 have in common their indirect reference to God. They avoid a direct naming of God, while still trying to involve him as a witness to the truthfulness of a statement.

Verse 36 goes further: the oath by one's own head, i.e., by one's life, is also forbidden. Those who pledge their own existence for the truthfulness of a statement pretend that they are masters of their own life, although in reality they cannot even change the colour of one hair on their heads. The art of hairdyeing was well known in Jesus' time, but what is intended here is not a matter of artifice. In fact, the verse recalls Mt 6:27, 'And which of you by being anxious can add one cubit to his span of life?' An oath by one's head is forbidden out of deference to God who alone controls our life, growth, and final fate. In Matthew's mind, then, oaths are wrong in the first place because they affect God's sovereign right to be God. Men should not attempt to control God by forcing the all-truthful One to bear witness to their sometimes (and to some extent) truthful statements. Therefore, all oaths, no matter how indirect their reference to God, are to be rejected.

It should not be objected to this interpretation that in Mt 23:16–22, a passage in several respects similar to Mt 5:34b–35, Jesus apparently presupposes the legitimacy of oaths. First, it has been shown that Mt 23 is made up of very heterogeneous material, coming from different levels of the tradition. And secondly, Mt 23:16–22 does not belong to an address to the disciples, but is part of a sharp polemic against the scribes and the Pharisees (cf. Mt 23:13), in which Jesus, presupposing the practice of oaths, almost mockingly shows its inconsistency. Thirdly, Mt 23:22 cannot possibly be understood as affirming the legitimacy of swearing by heaven, after Matthew has explicitly rejected that type of oath in Mt 5:34b.

All these considerations should be taken into account in the discussion of verse 37a, 'Let what you say be simply "Yes" or "No"'. Tradition-critical studies generally lead to the conclusion that a more primitive stage of the tradition is represented by Jas 5:12, 'But above all, my brethren, do not swear, either by heaven or by earth or with any other oath, but let your yes be yes and your no be no, that you may not fall under condemnation'. Unlike the latter text which means 'let your yes be a genuine yes and your no a genuine no', Mt 5:37 has both *nai*s ('yes') and both *ou*s ('no') as predicate nominatives: 'let your speech be yes, yes, no, no'. On the basis of some Jewish texts it is sometimes claimed that the double yes and the double no are to be considered as equivalent to an oath. Reference is made to *Slavonic Enoch* 49:1, 'I swear to you, my children, but I swear not by an oath, neither by heaven nor by earth, nor by any other creature which God created. The Lord said, "There is no oath in me, nor injustice, but truth". If there is no truth in men, let then swear by the words "yea, yea", or else "nay, nay".' But *Slavonic Enoch* could be as late as the seventh century A.D. and it shows Christian influence. Moreover, the swearing by 'yes-yes', 'no-no' is explicitly said not to be a real oath. Therefore, the text should not be used to establish the meaning of Mt 5:37a.

Jesus demands truthfulness, not for the benefit of self-consciousness and individual conscience, but for the benefit of the human community. For only where there is no need to live in distrust and fear of falsehood can the community develop fully. With his demand for truthfulness Jesus looks toward a world in which a truly human community can live, since it has basically left behind the threat of falsehood. Ultimately this demand is nothing but a practical expression of the radical concern demanded by and expressed in God's eschatological action. It constitutes the objective foundation for the radical contents of the antithesis and gives men the possibility to commit themselves to the realization of the demand.

Again, Jesus' demand should not be understood as a 'law'. The answer to the question whether Jesus' word forbids oaths altogether is that Jesus is not giving such prohibitions or commands. He is not a lawgiver but a liberator. In the present case he refers to the ultimate in truthfulness: we should not just say or do the truth in particular instances; we should *be* true and truthful. Therefore, this saying cannot be used to demand the abolition of oaths which the State requires in its effort to establish the truth. However, it is worth recalling that in the Church oaths are used to an extent which sometimes exceeds the practice of the State. One may indeed doubt whether the repeated oaths and swearing in the present life of the Church correspond to the normative directive of the Sermon on the Mount. Beside many other oaths in their priestly life some priests have been obliged to take the oath against modernism more than fifty times. Such practices certainly do not create an atmosphere in which a simple yes is actually understood as such.

On the other hand, it should also be noted that the truth is not a possession conquered once and for all, but a living reality. It is not a ready-made recipe, but an attitude of the whole person which must time and again be rediscovered by word and deed – especially by deed.

One should always avoid looking at the truth and the witness to the truth as a mere matter of words; it is essentially action too. One's whole existence can be a lie or witness to the truth. Moreover, if the truth is infinite as God himself, it follows that we cannot *have* it but that we must always seek it, just as we do not simply have God, but must always seek him. Here too the 'law' of poverty prevails. One should not think that one *has* the whole truth, but should always be open to, hunger and thirst for, God's greater truth. This attitude surpasses all mere 'isms': the citizen of the kingdom lives by God's freedom, not by human theories which are always man-made, and thus ultimately idols. It also prevents all fanaticism. God is not only greater than our intellect, but also greater than our heart.

The fifth antithesis (Mt 5:38–42)

A comparison of Mt 5:38–42 and Lk 6:29–30 leads to the following conclusions. The antithetical form (Mt 5:38–39a) is to be attributed to Matthew. For the rest, Matthew has in general conserved the original version, except for verse 41 and the construction with *hostis* ('any one') in verses 39b, 41. These and some more detailed considerations lead to the following Q-version:

> Mt 5:39a (I say to you)
>> 5:39b To him who strikes you on the right cheek,
>> turn to him the other also.
>> 5:40　And if any one would sue you and take your coat,
>> let him have your cloak as well.
>> 5:42　Give to him who begs from you,
>> and him who would borrow from you do not refuse.

This Q-text can hardly be an original unit. The difference in content between the prohibition of retaliation (Mt 5:39–40 and parallel) and the exhortation to give to him who asks (Mt 5:42) leads to the conclusion that these sayings were combined at a secondary stage. Already in Q the double saying (Mt 5:39–40) stood in close relation to the command to love one's enemy (compare Mt 5:38–48 and Lk 6:27–36); but this too is to be attributed to composition. Because of their radical character Mt 5:39b–40(41) are usually considered characteristic of and so attributed to Jesus himself.

Turning now to Mt 5:38–42 in its present form and comparing it with the form of the other antitheses, we may say that Mt 5:38–39a, 'You have heard. . . . Do not resist one who is evil', is clearly distinguished from Mt 5:39b–42, first of all, in that the former is written in the second person plural, while the latter is in the second person singular. Secondly, Lk 6:29–30 provides a parallel to Mt 5:39b–42, while Mt 5:38–39a has none, so that it should be considered special Matthean material. Thirdly, it should not be overlooked that Mt 5:39b–42 can only partly be considered an illustration of the prohibition expressed in Mt 5:38–39a. Basically, only Mt 5:39b, the saying about turning the other cheek rather than striking back, provides an example of renunciation of retribution, while the statements in Mt 5:40–42 serve rather as examples of compliance and willingness. All these considerations lead us to consider Mt 5:38–39a and 5:39–42 in two separate paragraphs.

The antithesis proper (Mt 5:38–39a)

Verses 38–39a: You have heard that it was said, 'An eye for an eye and a tooth for a tooth.' (39a) But I say to you, Do not resist one who is evil.

The clause 'an eye for an eye and a tooth for a tooth' refers to texts like 'If any harm follows, then you shall give life for life, eye for eye, tooth for tooth, hand for hand, foot for foot, burn for burn, wound for wound, stripe for stripe' (Ex 21:23–25); 'When a man causes a disfigurement in his neighbour, as he has done it shall be done to him, fracture for fracture, eye for eye, tooth for tooth . . .' (Lev 24:19f.); 'Your eye shall not pity; it shall be life for life, eye for eye, tooth for tooth, hand for hand, foot for foot' (Deut 19:21). Mt 5:38 abridges the Old Testament formulations of the *jus talionis* and thus rather points out its fundamental character.

The real intention of these Old Testament texts was to restrict vengeance, not to incite to it. It should be kept in mind that the principle of 'an eye for an eye and a tooth for a tooth' was not initially a *demand* for particularly savage justice, but a *limitation* upon the custom of unrestricted revenge, which not only permitted but required an individual, a family, a clan, to take vengeance not only upon the person of the wrongdoer, but also upon all connected with him. The rule of Ex 21 was therefore a considerable advance. Matthew, however, understands it as an incitement to vengeance, so that we get a very strong antithesis in Mt 5:38–39a between the prescription of the Old Testament and the words of Jesus: the former incites to vengeance, the latter says not to resist evil at all!

In verse 39a Jesus sets his demand for renunciation of resistance against the *jus talionis*: 'Do not resist one who is evil'. There is debate whether *tōi ponērōi* should be taken as masculine or as neuter. But this question is not very important: if I do not oppose an evil man, if I undergo the evil he does to me, I refrain from opposing a form of evil (neuter). Thus both possible meanings are united: the evil done by the evil person should not be resisted.

Although similar statements can be found in rabbinical literature, the absoluteness with which retribution is here rejected is unparalleled. Jesus establishes a totally new way of thinking. Evil is not overcome so long as we fight it off with similar means. And not only the *jus talionis*, but all human legal systems are based on the principle that punishment must correspond to crime, and uphold the concepts of proportion, equivalency, and restitution. Jesus' statement puts into question all (human) law in so far as it is based on the idea of strict retribution corresponding to the wrong, but also in so far as it assumes legality as the basis for relations between fellow-men. He says: 'Do not resist one who is evil', i.e., 'do not join in the fight', or 'do not fight evil with its own means'. Indeed, evil retains its strength so long as the injured retaliate, but it loses its strength when it is absorbed by those who renounce all forms of satisfaction or revenge. The force of evil is wasted since it meets with no resistance. In this way alone can evil come to an end.

This demand is again ultimately based on the promulgation of God's eschatological intervention expressed in unlimited love and forgiveness offered to men. This same intervention makes it also possible for men to respond in terms of unlimited concern for their fellow-men. It is the proclamation of God's eschatological reign which enables men to make the transition from the righteousness of the scribes and the Pharisees (here expressed as 'an eye for an eye') to the greater righteousness of the kingdom of God ('do not resist one who is evil').

The illustrations (Mt 5:39b–42)
The structure of Mt 5:39b–42 is carefully built up: in four clauses we are given four examples of approximately the same length which illustrate Mt 5:38–39a. The first and the third, and the second and the fourth, correspond to each other in form. Although verse 42 is hardly in place between sayings about revenge and love of enemy, its annexation took place long before Matthew's redactional activity (cf. Lk 6:30).

> **Verse 39b:** But if any one strikes you on the right cheek, turn to him the other also;

> We feel uneasy about interpreting the command to turn the other cheek literally. . . . Is what this command implies always good? Is it good when applied to an oppressed group rather than an individual, or does turning the other cheek in such a situation show lack of concern for the suffering brother? Such reflections often

lead to simply ignoring this command. What help is it if it sometimes leads to evil results and if all we can say in its defense is that it is not meant literally? We can escape from this problem only if this command leaves room for the changing complexities of human situations and yet is able to help us in those situations. But are there reasons for believing that this is so?[12]

Certain aspects of the form of these sayings provide clues to the way in which this type of language functions when it is properly understood. ... The parallel syntax marks Matt 5:39b–42 as a formal unit containing a series of four parallel commands. ... Note that each of the commands deals with a specific situation and that each of the commands is extreme. ... Let us begin with the fact that these commands deal with specific situations. ... Although these commands deal with specific situations, we unconsciously assume that they have implications for many other situations as well. ... [and] establish a pattern which can be extended to other instances. ... especially the concrete situations in which he [the hearer] finds himself. ... then the hearer must recognize that the meaning of the text cannot be restricted to what it says literally. The text means *more* than it says explicitly, which gives it an indirect and allusive quality. This observation can be carried further by considering the extremeness of these commands. ... The extremeness of these commands is due in part to the situations chosen. ... It is due even more to the surprising behaviour which is commanded in these situations. ... These commands are an attack on our natural tendency to put self-protection first. ... Although these commands refer only to a few specific situations, we experience a general, fundamental attack. ... Thus a particular command is able to preside over a whole pattern of life extending far beyond its literal content. ... Thus the limits of the literal sense have been broken through. It is not 'just that' which is commanded but 'even that.' Thus the command acquires a whole field of implications to which no clear limits can be set.[13]

NB

This should be taken into account in all the following considerations.

Striking somebody on the *right* cheek was considered especially contemptuous, since it can be done only with the back of the hand; it was a double insult liable to double damages. But it is said here that the disciple should turn the other cheek, i.e. suffer the most hurting insult, rather than to answer it with denunciation or lawsuits. It has been thought that the situation in life of this saying was the persecution of the disciples and the abuses which they had to endure for the sake of being disciples. The possibility has also been considered of a reference to Isa 50:6, 'I gave my back to the smiters, and my cheeks (plural!) to those who pulled out the beard'. But such suppositions are difficult to prove.

Verse 40: and if any one would sue you and take your coat, let him have your cloak as well;

This illustration refers to the situation of the very poor (cf. Deut 24:13), more specifically to a court case in which an opponent demands the shirt-like *chitōn* or inner garment (RSV, 'coat') as pledge or compensation. In such a case the disciple should also give his cloak or outer garment. The poor man not only wore this 'coat' by day, he also slept in it at night. The cloak was therefore considered a basic necessity, and so could not be taken for debts: 'If ever you take your neighbour's garment in pledge, you shall restore it to him before the sun goes down; for that is his only covering, it is his mantle for his body; in what shall he sleep?' (Ex 22:26f.); 'And if he is a poor man, you shall not sleep in his pledge; when the sun goes down, you shall restore to him the pledge that he may sleep in his cloak and bless you' (Deut 24:12f.). Jesus, however, says: If a man sues you for your coat, which he can quite legally take from you, give him your cloak too, even though he has no legal right to take it from you.

Verses 39b–40 presuppose a particular situation by means of which it is shown that Jesus considers the law unsuitable for the regulation of relations between fellow-men. But the renunciation of resistance and rights constitutes only the negative aspect of Jesus' demand, which includes also a positive command: 'turn to him the other also – let him have your cloak as well'. Both clauses demand a radical openness also to the assailant, to whom the possibility of love should be offered. Herewith it is clear that the renunciation of one's right which Jesus asks for is at the service of a positive openness to one's fellow-man.

Therefore, the demand to renounce resistance is in reality a concretization of the command to love one's enemy. This means that the objective foundation which is explicitly mentioned in connection with the commandment to love one's enemy (cf. Mt 5:48 par.) is also the foundation of the demand to renounce resistance. It consists then ultimately in the radical concern of God's eschatological action for men as it is experienced in the proclamation and the person of Jesus. This experience explains the radical character of the demand and gives at the same time the possibility of commitment to meeting the same demand. Radical concern with the well-being of others is the real intention of Jesus' words. They should not be interpreted in anti-

Zealot terms, as if they meant, for instance, that one should not make any plans for an uprising or get involved in armed resistance in an attempt to overthrow an unjust regime. Jesus' words have no *direct* bearing on such questions. The latter should be answered, not by referring to one or another text allegedly containing Jesus' answer, but on the basis of an overall assessment of the gospel values placed in an extreme situation in which all other means have been duly tried out. Here too we should say that Jesus does not promulgate a 'law' against all use of violence.

> **Verse 41:** and if any one forces you to go one mile, go with him two miles.

The third illustration deals with an official demand. The Greek word *angareuein* underlying the verb 'to force' goes back to the Persian system of state couriers for the purpose of rapid communication throughout the empire. These couriers were empowered to 'compel' or 'conscript' other people in their service. This practice was taken over by the Roman armies: Roman soldiers could requisition civilians to carry their things or to perform other services (cf. Mk 15:21, where Roman soldiers compel Simon of Cyrene to carry Jesus' cross). It is quite understandable that this practice was hated. But Jesus says: rather than resent going one mile carrying a soldier's baggage, you should carry it two miles! In the light of our previous considerations it should be clear that this advice in no way intends to justify or condone the excesses committed by oppressive regimes!

> **Verse 42:** Give to him who begs from you, and do not refuse him who would borrow from you.

This last illustration speaks of lending as it is also recommended and commanded in the Old Testament: 'If there is among you a poor man . . . you shall open your hand to him, and lend him sufficient for his need, whatever it may be. . . . You shall open wide your hand to your brother, to the needy and to the poor, in the land' (Deut 15:7–11). Mt 5:42 seems to speak according to a rabbinical distinction, of the lending of objects which are 'asked for' or 'begged', and money which is 'borrowed'. Or perhaps we should distinguish between 'begging' which does not involve return and 'borrowing' which does. Or again, the second half of the verse may be a command not to repulse or harass a borrower: When someone has borrowed from you, do not press him to have it back (compare Lk 6:30; cf. Sir 20:15b, 'today he lends and tomorrow he asks it back; such a one is a hateful man').

It would appear that Mt 5:42 has nothing to do with the theme of

Mt 5:39b–41 – renunciation of all retribution and use of force, of insistence on one's rights, and of opposition to coercion. But it has been pointed out that, nevertheless, the saying is given a rather meaningful place in its present context: it is now the last element in an anticlimax which leads from renunciation of retribution (Mt 5:39b), by way of endurance (and more than endurance) of an unjust court action (Mt 5:40), and consent to coercion (Mt 5:41), to the readiness to lend (Mt 5:42), i.e., from an extremely hard to an – after all – bearable demand.

In the preceding illustrations it is a certain spirit which is being *N B* commended – not a regulation to be carried out literally. Should it be pointed out that when Jesus was slapped on the face, he did not turn the other cheek, but asked: 'why do you strike me?' (Jn 18:22–23; but it should not be overlooked that in Matthew and John we deal with two independent traditions and that, therefore, we should not draw excessively far-reaching conclusions from this consideration)? In the case of the coat and the cloak, the two main articles of clothing, literal following of Jesus' advice would practically lead to nudism! In the third illustration Jesus certainly does not intend to bolster the arrogance of military regimes or to rule out all forms of resistance or liberation movements. And if Mt 5:42 is understood as an exhortation to indiscriminate almsgiving, it could lead to the demoralization of many people.

> What we have here are illustrations of a principle. The illustrations are extreme, and in the one instance so much so as to approach the ridiculous; but that is deliberate. They are intended to be vivid examples of a radical demand, and it is as such that we must regard them. The demand is that a man should respond to the challenge of God in terms of a radically new approach to the business of living. This approach is illustrated by means of vivid examples of behaviour in crisis: in response to grave insult, to a lawsuit and to a military impressment. Not natural pride, not a standing on one's own rights, not even a prudential acceptance, are the proper response to these crises *now*, however much they might have been so *before*. In light of the challenge of God and of the new relationship with one's fellow man one must respond in a new way, in a way appropriate to the new situation. What the specifics of that new way are is *not* stated; these sayings are illustrations of the necessity for a new way rather than regulations for it. But the implication of these sayings is, surely, that if one approaches the crisis in this spirit, and seeks the way in terms of the reality of one's experience of God and the new relationship with one's fellow man, then that way can be found.[14]

Jesus looks forward to a world in which retribution has no longer any right to power. This is the meaning of 'do not resist one who is evil' and the following illustrations. Such a conquest of retribution presupposes people who, together with Jesus, have recognized the destructive power of the law of retribution which is accepted and practised in the world, and therefore refuse to make use of it. The demand of the fifth antithesis is based on the knowledge that the world which lives under the law of retribution lives in fact under the curse of that retribution. However, it contains also the hope that the world will ultimately be a world which is free from that curse. Jesus calls upon all his listeners – not just an elite – to be pioneers and citizens of such a world.

The sixth antithesis (Mt 5:43–48)

A detailed study of the sequence and coherence of Mt 5:43–48 and Lk 6:27–36 leads to the conclusion that on the level of the earlier tradition there is Lk 6:29–31, 27–28, 32–35, 36 and parallels in Mt 5:39–42; 7:12; 5:44, 45–47, 48, in which Lk 6:36 paralleled by Mt 5:48 constituted the conclusion of Mt 5:44–47. For further study one can start, then, from Mt 5:44–48 paralleled by Lk 6:27–28, 32–36. Mt 5:43 is generally attributed to Matthean redaction.

A careful comparison of the Matthean and Lucan versions leads to the following Q-text:

Mt 5:44	I say to you,	Lk 6:27
	Love your enemies,	
	do good to those who hate you,	
	bless those who curse you,	6:28
	pray for those who persecute you,	
5:45	so that you may be sons of the Father,	6:35c
	for he makes his sun rise on the evil (and the good),	
	and sends rain on (the just and on) the unjust.	
5:46	For if you love those who love you,	6:32
	what reward have you?	
	Do not even the tax collectors do the same?	
5:47	And if you salute only your brethren,	6:33
	what more are you doing than others?	
	Do not even the Gentiles do the same?	
5:48	Be merciful,	6:36
	even as your Father is merciful.	

It has often been stated that this text does not constitute an original unit. A tradition-critical study of Mt 5:44–48 leads to the following text as a unit and the oldest stratum of the tradition:

Mt 5:44	I say to you,	Lk 6:27
	Love your enemies,	
	(do good to those who hate you,	
	bless those who curse you,	6:28
	pray for those who persecute you),	
5:45	so that you may be sons of the Father	6:35c
	for he makes his sun shine on the evil (and the good),	
	and sends rain on (the just and) the unjust.	
5:48	Be merciful,	6:36
	even as your Father is merciful.	

Although the authenticity of this text has often been questioned, the demand to love one's enemy should certainly be attributed to Jesus himself. This demand is based on the mercy of God. How merciful God is is the object not of general religious experience but of the experience of God's concrete, merciful activity in the proclamation and practice of Jesus, more specifically an experience of God's unconditional forgiveness in Jesus' concern for sinners. Therefore, the context of Mt 5:48b (in its original form) is Jesus' proclamation of God who is radically determined to realize the salvation of man. It is an implication of Jesus' message of the eschatological reign of God. Where God turns himself so radically to men, men who experience this mercy cannot but turn themselves equally radically and mercifully to their fellow-men. The demand to love one's enemy constitutes the most radical demand of Jesus' ethics, and all his other demands should be explained on the basis of this one.

In the following paragraphs we study the text as it is now found in Matthew.

Verse 43: You have heard that it was said, 'You shall love your neighbour and hate your enemy.'

The first part of verse 43, 'You shall love your neighbour', refers back to Lev 19:18, '. . . but you shall love your neighbour as yourself'. Though the second part of the verse, 'and hate your enemy', is also dependent on 'you have heard that it was said', it is not found in the Old Testament, and is in its present form even forcefully contradicted: 'If your enemy is hungry, give him bread to eat; and if he is thirsty, give him water to drink; for you will heap coals of fire on his head, and the Lord will reward you' (Prov 25:21f.).

A number of scholars have said that, although the Old Testament nowhere states that one should hate one's enemy, Matthew is thus aptly summarizing the contemporary attitude. It is true that the Old Testament as well as Judaism drastically limited the concept of neighbour, but this is not the same as demanding hatred of enemies. At most we can speak of a warding-off of strangers, so that the translation has been proposed: 'You shall love your fellow countryman, but you need not love your enemy'. This translation is based on the following considerations. First, the pair of opposites *plēsion* (Lev 19:18)/*echthros* should be understood as 'compatriot' (only Mt 5:43 gave it the meaning 'neighbour')/one's personal enemy, one's adversary (not a national enemy). Secondly, in such a contrast in Semitic languages, the negative part is very often no more than a negation of the positive; so here: love/no love. Thirdly, the Aramaic imperfect which underlies the two Greek futures (RSV, 'shall love' and '(shall) hate') only rarely has a future significance, and we should probably understand: 'you shall love' (jussive meaning) and 'need not love' (permissive meaning). As to the alleged command to hate enemies found in the Qumran literature, the sole aim of the texts referred to is to assure the purity of this exclusive sectarian community. Thus Mt 5:43 states merely: normally one gathers from the Old Testament the obligation of love for the neighour and the non-obligation of love for the non-neighbour.

Another difference between Lev 19:18 and Mt 5:43 (beside the addition 'and hate your enemy') is that the latter omits the phrase 'as yourself', which occurs in Lev 19:18 as well as in all other citations of it in the New Testament. In these texts it is not part of the command as such, but is rather presupposed by the command: love your neighbour as you already love yourself without any need to be commanded to do so. The point of the phrase 'as yourself' is definitely not that one's love for neighbour is to be an extension of self-love of the same kind, but rather that one must have the same spontaneous loving concern for one's neighbour that one inevitably has for one's own life. If Matthew omitted the phase 'as yourself', he did not do so for theological reasons, but rather for rhetorical reasons. Retention of the phrase 'as yourself' would have disturbed the balance of the statement, and Matthew could scarcely have added 'as yourself' in the second part of the verse!

> **Verses 44–45:** But I say to you, Love your enemies and pray for those who persecute you, (45) so that you may be sons of your Father who is in heaven; for he makes his sun rise on the evil and on the good, and sends rain on the just and on the unjust.

Verse 44 constitutes a sharp contrast between the command of love for neighbour as it was currently narrowed down and Jesus' demand. In two examples (four in Lk 6:37f.) the attitude determined by the law of retribution expressed in Mt 5:43 is contradicted: one must love one's enemies and pray for one's persecutors.

In Mt 5:44 'enemies' is parallel with 'those who persecute you', while in Lk 6:27–28 the term parallels 'those who hate . . . curse . . . abuse you'. The use of the words 'evil' and 'unjust' in verse 45, and the idea of 'those who do not love you' implied in the expression 'those who love you' in verse 46, shed further light on the meaning of 'enemies'. It seems to mean: those whose opposition is expressed in direct personal ways as persecution, cursing, abuse, in short, all those who in a hostile way confront the person addressed in this verse.

What then does the command to 'love your enemies' actually mean? Some scholars base their answer on a distinction between *agapan*, which is used here and would mean 'to show respect and kindness', and *philein*, which would mean 'reciprocal, friendly love'. But the opinion that these two verbs can always be sharply differentiated is not tenable.

In the immediate context, the parallel admonition is to 'pray' for them (Mt 5:44b), but this itself requires interpretation, for how is one to pray? Should one pray that one's enemies be forgiven, or punished? But the first idea is not dealt with in this passage, and the second would be in contradiction with both the command to love them (Mt 5:44a) and the reference to God's loving concern (Mt 5:45). It has been suggested that there may be some clue in Mt 5:47 which says that even the Gentiles 'salute' their own brethren. The salute or embrace upon meeting was a visible sign of personal relationship intended to affirm someone's existence as a person and in relation to oneself. This seems to indicate that to Matthew the command to love one's enemies meant to acknowledge their presence and the bond which exists between oneself and them by virtue of sharing together in the goodness and mercy of the Father.

Verse 45 answers the question about the ultimate ground on which the demand of verse 44 is based. But before doing so it first introduces another idea: 'so that you may be sons of your Father who is in heaven'. The very original terminology of verse 45 stresses that love of enemy in reality poses the question of the relation between the Father and his sons. In fact, sonship is the goal of the relationship which is commended in verse 44. Or better, we are summoned to act in accordance with God and so to be sons of the Father, a summons which is based on the fact that God is already Father and thus makes possible the sonship of the sons. The expression 'sons of your Father who is in heaven' is unique in the New Testament, but it is found in Sir 4:10, where it refers to those who, like God (Ps 146[145]:9), care for the orphan and the widow, i.e., for the defenceless.

Hate dehumanizes fellow human beings by classifying them, for instance, as 'terrorists' or 'capitalists'. Escalating hate tends to accuse enemies of everything one is oneself prepared to do to them. Hate first kills people with words and images, after which actual killing or liquidation becomes easier. Love of enemy is not for the weak who fear their enemies. Those who fear their enemies do not know this love. It is for the free and strong who are no longer caught up in the violence of their enemies and who oppose the evil done by them without resulting to violence. Violence, on the other hand, is often inspired by fear, as is illustrated, for instance, by Jn 11:47–53 and 19:12–16 describing the attitudes of the Sanhedrin and Pilate towards Jesus. Both resorted to violence out of fear for their own position. The same is true for all violence and oppression throughout history, and very much so in our present world.

Mt 5:45b then names the origin of the divine sonship of man according to Jesus' proclamation: it is God, and God in his relation to man. God breaks through the law of retribution since he gives indiscriminately to 'the evil' and 'the good', 'the just' and 'the unjust'. Judaism too knows of God's goodness to sinners, but the fundamental character of Jesus' proclamation of God's being is unique: God breaks through the generally valid law of retribution, and not only proclaims but also practises the law of unconditional love. And those who respond to this God and are ready to practise the same unconditional love are 'sons of God'.

> **Verses 46–47:** For if you love those who love you, what reward have you? Do not even the tax collectors do the same? (47) And if you salute only your brethren, what more are you doing than others? Do not even the Gentiles do the same?

Verses 46–47 give the motivation for verse 45 (*gar*, 'for'), and at the same time develop the contrast with verse 44 in that they represent standard human behaviour: loving those from whom one receives love and greeting those by whom one is greeted. These two verses also relate the commandment to love one's enemies to the requirement for disciples to exhibit an exceeding righteousness (Mt 5:20). The true disciples' behaviour is contrasted with that of the tax collectors who do not know the God of Mt 5:45 and therefore cannot pattern their activity accordingly. The phrase 'the Gentiles' is not necessarily directed against the pagans, but rather a cliché applied to a certain type of behaviour in order to criticize such behaviour. But even these people show love where it is reciprocated. The true disciple must do better than that.

Jesus addresses the words 'what reward have you?' to a world in which everything is calculated: love for love, salute for salute, help for help. Everything is measured by a pair of scales, and nothing new is to be expected. In fact, Justin Martyr aptly paraphrases these words: 'what new do you do?' Indeed, 'do not even the tax collectors do *the same?*' It is nothing special. But it is just what is different, unusual and uncommon that receives reward (Mt 5:12; 6:1, 4, 18). Jesus now invites us to live on a totally different basis, the only one that is liberating. It may look idealistic and unrealistic, but it could turn out to be the only truly realistic line of conduct, since clearly, we get stuck in the old pattern in which we are always intent on giving a little less and getting a little more.

Verse 48: You, therefore, must be perfect, as your heavenly Father is perfect.

Verse 48 concludes the passage and, as Lk 6:36 shows, it was certainly not Matthew who placed the statement here. The use of the word 'perfect' (*teleios*; Luke has *oiktirmōn*, 'merciful') is also probably to be attributed to the pre-Matthean and here more precisely the Aramaic tradition. The word 'perfect' does not denote moral, aesthetic or other perfection. Seen in the light of its Old Testament and Jewish background (*tāmîm*, etc.), it means rather 'whole-hearted, sincere, honest, undivided'. See, e.g., Deut 18:13, 'You shall be whole-hearted (LXX: *teleios*) in your service of the Lord your God' (NEB). The meaning of 'perfect' is therefore closely related to that of 'pure in heart' in Mt 5:8. It expresses consistency (being 'all of a piece') as well as total commitment and generosity (cf. Mt 19:21, 'if you would be perfect . . .'). In Matthew's understanding, perfection is the same as the exceeding righteousness of Mt 5:20. It is not an optional 'counsel' for people who do already keep the commandments, but a must for those who want to enter the kingdom.

In the present context it can be further specified: those people are 'perfect' who perform the 'more', the 'not-the-same' of verses 46–47. They are people who relate in a way different from that of the tax collectors and Gentiles who do not know God. Their being and activities are motivated not by the law of retribution, but by God who breaks through this law. Again, the content of the word 'perfect' can further be explained in reference to God in Mt 5:45. God is perfect, undivided in as far as he gives indiscriminately and unconditionally. His perfection consists in the fact that he does not allow his being-for-man to be limited by the law of retribution, but 'makes his sun rise on the evil and on the good, and sends rain on the just and on the unjust' (Mt 5:45).

In the light of these considerations we can understand the demand to be perfect as one's heavenly Father is perfect: make your attitude correspond to that of God, who is not determined by the law of retribution, but by a love which goes beyond any law. And since God is who he is totally and unconditionally, and is totally God-for-men, men who are empowered by God must be in the totality of their being men-for-others. Such a being-for-others cannot exclude enemies and persecutors. The 'perfection' of the disciples is shown in their undifferentiating observance of the commandment of love towards friend and foe. As Matthew links the commandment of love of neighbour so closely with the new interpretation of the Law (cf. Mt 7:12; 22:40), it cannot be his intention in Mt 5:43–47 to add a further, second commandment to love the enemy, but he means thereby the limitless intensification of the commandment to love one's neighbour. The commandment to love one's enemy is the test-case of the commandment to love one's neighbour: it is its critical verification.

Verse 48 has a triple function. Firstly, it concludes the sixth antithesis. Secondly, Matthew uses 'perfect' to round off the six antitheses and to refer back to 'righteousness' in Mt 5:20. The explanation of Christian righteousness, needed for entering the kingdom, is completed. It can be summed up as being perfect as your heavenly Father is perfect. Thirdly, it summarizes the theme of the first part of the Sermon on the Mount, resuming the ideas expressed in 'the poor in spirit' (Mt 5:3), 'the pure in heart' (Mt 5:8), and 'unless your righteousness exceeds' (*perisseusei*, Mt 5:20; cf. *perisson* in Mt 5:47).

7 Almsgiving, Prayer, Fasting
(Mt 6:1–18)

Introduction

The structure of Mt 6:1–18

Mt 6:1–18 contrasts the type of piety practised by the 'hypocrites' and the piety which should be the disciples'. First we get a general principle (Mt 6:1). The following verses reprove the fact that the 'hypocrites' offer their alms (Mt 6:2–4) and their prayers (Mt 6:5–6) and conduct their fasts (Mt 6:16–18) publicly, to be noticed, and thus use these practices to enhance their self-esteem. In contrast it is demanded of the disciples that their almsgiving, prayer and fasting be done without any ulterior motive of being seen by either God or man. Their religious practices should spring from the heart in response to the *Father's* eschatological initiative of love. The spontaneous character of these practices will make them acceptable to the Father.

The three units – about alms, prayer, and fasting – are symmetrically constructed: in each case wrong and right conduct are opposed to each other by means of two clauses introduced by 'when'.

(1) 'Thus, when you give alms, sound no trumpet before you, as the hypocrites. . . .
But when you give alms, do not let your left hand know what your right hand is doing . . .' (Mt 6:2–4).

(2) 'And when you pray, you must not be like the hypocrites. . . .
But when you pray, go into your room and shut the door . . .' (Mt 6:5–6).

(3) 'And when you fast, do not look dismal, like the hypocrites. . . . But when you fast, anoint your head . . .' (Mt 6:16–18).

Each of these paragraphs contains also two refrain-like statements:

'they have their reward' (Mt 6:2, 5, 16), and 'your Father who sees in secret will reward you' (Mt 6:4, 6, 18).

But the second paragraph, which deals with prayer (Mt 6:5–6), is enlarged by three further statements about prayer:

(a) 'And in praying do not heap up empty phrases . . .' (Mt 6:7–8).

(d) 'Pray then like this: Our Father who art in heaven . . .' (Mt 6:9–13).

(c) 'For if you forgive men their trespasses, your heavenly Father . . .' (Mt 6:14–15).

Thus we get the following structure in the second paragraph about prayer (Mt 6:5–15):

First we have Jesus' admonition that the disciples should not be like the 'hypocrites' who arrange things in such a way as to get maximum publicity from their prayer practices. The disciples should pray behind closed doors.

Then follows a second admonition not to 'heap up empty phrases as the Gentiles do'. The disciples should 'not be like them', because as children of the Father they do not need to employ 'many words' (Mt 6:7–8). The terms *battalogeō* and *polulogia* are unique. Verses 7–8 may well belong to the Gentile-Christian level of the tradition (cf. 'Gentiles' instead of 'hypocrites').

Thirdly, as an example of brief prayer, we get the Lord's Prayer, which is indeed distinguished from most contemporary prayers by its brevity (Mt 6:9–13).

Finally, and emphatic in its position at the end of this paragraph on prayer, we find a saying about the necessary disposition in prayer which links up with the petition for forgiveness of the Lord's Prayer: only the disciple who is himself ready to forgive is entitled to ask the Father for forgiveness (Mt 6:14–15).

In conclusion, we may say that in Mt 6:5–15 we have a kind of 'catechism on prayer', composed of sayings of Jesus originally pronounced at different times and in different places, and used by the early Church in the instruction of the newly baptized.

The context of the Lord's Prayer in Luke (Lk 11:1–13)

In Luke, too, the Lord's Prayer occurs in the context of a catechetical instruction on prayer which, however, is not found in his Sermon on the Plain (Lk 6:20–49). The composition of this instruction is also very different from that found in Mt 6:5–15.

First we have a scene in which we find Jesus at prayer, followed by the request of an anonymous disciple, 'Lord, teach us to pray . . .' (Lk 11:1). In response to this request Jesus recites the Lord's Prayer (Lk 11:2–4).

Then follows the parable of the man who knocks at his friend's door at midnight. Whatever may have been the original meaning of this parable, in its present context it constitutes an admonition to persevere in prayer, even if it appears that the prayer is not heard (Lk 11:5–8).

Thirdly, the same admonition is repeated, this time in a series of imperatives: 'Ask, and it will be given you . . .' (Lk 11:9–10, paralleled in Mt 7:7–8).

Finally, the instruction is concluded by the picture of the father who gives good gifts to his children and the heavenly Father who will 'give the Holy Spirit to those who ask him' (Lk 11:11–13). The reference to the Holy Spirit may point to a baptismal context, which may even account for the composition of the whole of Lk 11:1–13 (cf. the alternative reading of Lk 11:2, 'May your holy spirit come down upon us and cleanse us': see below, note 15).

The differences between Mt 6:5–15 and Lk 11:1–13

In the New Testament the Lord's Prayer appears in the gospel of Matthew and the gospel of Luke. However, the contexts in which it is found in these gospels are very different. Both represent catechetical instructions, but they are directed at very different groups of people. Mt 6:5–15, on the one hand, is apparently addressed to Jewish Christians who have learned to pray in their Jewish childhood but whose prayer is in danger of becoming formalistic. Lk 11:1–13, on the other hand, is addressed to Gentile Christians for whom prayer is something new and who might easily get discouraged. But both gospels testify to the fact that about A.D. 80 the Lord's Prayer occupied a fixed place in instruction on prayer, in the Jewish-Christian as well as in the Gentile-Christian communities. Different as their situations were, they agreed that the Lord's Prayer was an indispensable model for Christian prayer.

As to the differences in the versions of the Lord's Prayer, they can hardly be attributed to the evangelists themselves, but should be traced back to the different communities to which they belonged, whose different liturgical wordings of the Lord's Prayer were transmitted to us by the evangelists.

The original form of the Lord's Prayer

Let us first compare the two versions of the Lord's Prayer:

Matthew 6:9–13	*Luke 11:2–4*
Our Father who art in heaven,	Father:
Hallowed be thy name,	Hallowed be thy name,
Thy kingdom come,	Thy kingdom come.[15]
Thy will be done,	
on earth as it is in heaven.	
Give us this day our daily bread,	Give us each day our daily bread,
And forgive us our debts,	And forgive us our sins
as we also have forgiven our debtors;	for we ourselves forgive every one who is indebted to us,
And lead us not into temptation.	And lead us not into temptation.
But deliver us from evil.	

We are struck first of all by the difference in length. The Matthean form of the prayer is longer than that of Luke at three places. Firstly, Matthew has a longer address to God: 'Our Father who art in heaven' instead of simply 'Father', or 'dear Father' (*abba*). Secondly, in the first group of petitions, Matthew adds a third petition to the two he has in common with Luke, And thirdly, at the end of the second group of petitions, Matthew adds another clause to the third petition, the antithesis, 'but deliver us from evil'. It is significant that Matthew's additional material appears at the end of the three parts of the prayer. We should also notice that Luke's version is entirely contained in the longer form of Matthew and that both share the basic structure of address, 'thou'-petitions, and 'we'-petitions.

Some biblical scholars have maintained that Matthew has preserved the more original form of the Lord's Prayer, but the majority of the commentators have argued that Luke's form of the prayer is closer to the original text than Matthew's, and as a whole their arguments do seem to be more persuasive. Firstly, they remark that the early Christians would certainly have hesitated to remove anything from the only prayer which they had received from Jesus himself. Secondly, in general, religious texts tend to become longer rather than shorter. And thirdly, the additions found in Matthew serve to round out each part of the Lord's Prayer and appear to make it more suitable for liturgical use. They do not introduce totally new ideas but bring out aspects of themes already present. On the other hand, there does not seem to be any convincing reason why Luke, or the Christian community before him, would have wanted to abridge the Lord's Prayer. The Matthean version, therefore, appears to be an expansion of the original form, and the Lucan version is closer to it with respect to *length*. However, as a more detailed discussion, especially of the second group of petitions, will show, Matthew's text is closer to the original with respect to *wording*. Following the short form according to Luke, but where there are variations of wording that of Matthew, the original text has been reconstructed as follows:

> (Dear) Father:
> Hallowed be thy name,
> Thy kingdom come,
> Give us this day our daily bread (or: our bread for tomorrow),
> And forgive us our debts, as we also forgive our debtors.
> And lead us not into temptation.

The shorter version is undoubtedly more original. Nevertheless the Lucan version seems also more strikingly 'Christian'. This is one of several instances in which Luke is apparently more faithful to the tradition but at the same time integrates it perfectly into his own theological perspective.

In this or a very similar form the Lord's Prayer should be traced back to the historical Jesus and related to his intensive expectation of the reign of God which he considered very near.

The structure of the Lord's Prayer

Since the Lucan version of the Lord's Prayer is entirely contained within Matthew's, and also since we are discussing it in the context of Matthew's Sermon on the Mount, we turn now to the latter's version to indicate its structure:

Address:	Our Father who art in heaven:
'Thou'-petitions:	Hallowed be thy name, Thy kingdom come, Thy will be done on earth as it is in heaven.
'We'-petitions:	Give us this day our daily bread, And forgive us our debts, as we also have forgiven our debtors; And lead us not into temptation, but deliver us from evil.

As the above arrangement shows, the Lord's Prayer consists of three parts: the address directs the prayer to God as Father, and the 'thou'-petitions and 'we'-petitions refer respectively to God himself and to the needs of the persons praying.

The distinction between the 'thou'-petitions and 'we'-petitions is based on a number of stylistic characteristics. The former all have the word 'thy', referring to God. The verb, which is invariably in the third person singular, is, in the Greek text, always found at the beginning of the petition. The three petitions are placed one after the other, without conjunctions. The latter set of petitions all have the words 'us' or 'our'. The verb, which is always in the second person singular, is never found at the beginning of the petitions, which are this time joined by conjunctions. These characteristics, most of which also appear in Semitic reconstructions of the Lord's Prayer, indicate that the 'thou'-petitions and 'we'-petitions form two distinct divisions of the prayer.

Exegesis of Mt 6:1–18

Mt 6:1–18 is a very carefully structured cult didache or catechesis on worship in which we pass from the discussion of a wholehearted observance of the Law (Mt 5:21–48) to that of 'inwardness' in the practice of external acts of 'piety' (Mt 6:1, literally, 'righteousness'). In the traditional contrast between being seen by men and being seen by the Lord (cf., e.g., Sir 23:19) Matthew has found the key-word which distinguishes the 'righteousness' described in Mt 5:20 from Pharisaic ethics as the 'more' which assures one of a place in the kingdom of heaven. This is done in practical terms by means of the 'three notable duties' which the early Christian tradition inherited from Judaism, which expressed this, e.g. in Tobit 12:8, 'Prayer is good when accompanied by fasting, almsgiving, and righteousness'. The general tendency of this section is reminiscent also of I Sam 16:7, 'for the Lord sees not as man sees; man looks on the outward appearance, but the Lord looks on the heart', and Rom 2:28–29, 'For he is not a real Jew who is one outwardly. . . . He is a Jew who is one inwardly, . . . His praise is not from men but from God.'

General principle (Mt 6:1)

> **Verse 1:** Beware of practising your piety before men in order to be seen by them; for then you will have no reward from your Father who is in heaven.

It has been shown that this verse is almost certainly an entirely Matthean composition. The particular way in which in the Greek text the phrase 'beware' (*prosechete*) is used is, with the exception of Lk 20:46, found in Matthew alone (cf. Mt 7:15; 10:17; 16:6, 11). The term 'righteousness' (*dikaiosunē*; RSV translates 'piety'), is used in a typically Matthean way, in line with its use in Mt 5:6, 10, 20. The expression 'to be seen by men' is also found in Mt 23:5. The reference to reward is taken from the following three paragraphs (cf. Mt 6:2, 5,

16), and is used in similar manner in Mt 10:41. Unlike the simple phrases 'your Father' (Mt 6:4, 6, 18) which is traditional, 'your Father who is in heaven' is redactional.

The verse states the general principle which governs the three following paragraphs. The disciples are warned to be *constantly* aware (suggested by the present tense of the verb) of the danger of hidden hypocrisy which is never finally resolved. 'Piety' (RSV; literally, 'righteousness') is a comprehensive term for the three practices which are mentioned in the following paragraphs: almsgiving, prayer, and fasting. It means 'religious observances' or 'works of piety'. The use of the word 'righteousness' shows that what follows is still concerned with the exceeding righteousness of Mt 5:20. Beside exceeding the righteousness of the scribes and the Pharisees in the sense illustrated in Mt 5:21–48, the disciples' righteousness should also differ from the former in avoiding ostentation. In fact, the rigorous contrast between the 'piety' of the 'hypocrites' and that of Jesus' true disciples is similar to the antithetical form of Mt 5:21–48, and the authoritative 'truly, I say to you' (Mt 6:2, 5, 16) can be compared with 'but I say to you' (Mt 5:22, 28, 32, 34, 39, 44). Just as the Law is to be understood and fulfilled in a new spirit, so the three highly prized practices of almsgiving, prayer and fasting are to be done in the right spirit. πρὸς τὸ θεαθῆναι

The warning does not refer to practising one's deeds of piety 'before men' as such, but to practising them 'to be seen by them'. The apparent inconsistency between Mt 5:16, 'Let your light so shine before men . . .', and Mt 6:1 disappears if note is taken of the motive in the two cases. In the former it is said that the disciples are to let their light (= the witness of their good deeds) shine before men for the glory of God; the latter deals with performing works of piety for self-glorification. 'To be seen' renders the Greek *theathēnai* from which the word 'theatre' is derived. The disciples are told, therefore, not to turn their religious observance into a theatrical performance or a show.

The disciples should not seek to impress men by their works of piety, otherwise (RSV translates 'for then') they will have no reward before (RSV translates 'from') their Father who is in heaven. Anyone giving alms, praying, and fasting in order to be seen by men 'has his reward', i.e., has been equitably rewarded by the approbation of men. He has what he bargained for. True piety should look toward the Father. The reward motive is only secondary. One should not practise works of piety to receive reward. Serving the Father with an eye on reward would go against the true nature of discipleship. One should practise deeds of piety without any ulterior motive 'to be seen', and the spontaneous character of one's actions will make them acceptable before the Father (cf. Mt 25:31–46, especially verses 37–39).

Almsgiving (Mt 6:2–4)

> **Verse 2:** Thus, when you give alms, sound no trumpet before you, as the hypocrites do in the synagogues and in the streets, that they may be praised by men. Truly, I say to you, they have their reward.

This is the first illustration of the principle stated in Mt 6:1. Almsgiving occupied an important place in Jewish religious life. There was an awareness, however, of the danger of ostentation and of the fact that alms could be given in such a way that they chiefly served the self-gratification of the giver and embarrassed the recipient. On this point Jesus and the best among the Jewish spiritual leaders of the time agreed.

It is known that in the synagogue the amount donated and the name of the giver were mentioned, but not whether this was ever accompanied by the sounding of trumpets. Some biblical scholars have related the idea to the sounding of trumpets during the public fasts (cf. Mt 6:16–18) in time of drought, which were accompanied by public prayer (cf. Mt 6:5–6) in the streets and possibly also by collections of alms; but the expression 'to sound the trumpet' is most probably to be understood metaphorically. The 'hypocrites' give their donations with as much 'fanfare' as possible; they give the fullest publicity to their gifts to get as much public attention as possible.

The classical Greek word *hupokritēs* originally meant an actor, without any negative connotation. It received its negative meaning only later in the Greek translation of the Old Testament, where it rendered a term which meant 'a profane person'. Although some scholars think that by Jesus' time the word had acquired the connotation of 'insincere', this is by no means certain, and it may be better to translate it as 'misguided'. In fact, there is no indication in these verses that Jesus intended to say that those who gave alms, prayed, and fasted were insincere in their practice. They did seek public approval and went to great lengths to call attention to their acts of piety, but they apparently felt that they were also pleasing God. They were 'misguided' in trying to win a double reward for their almsgiving, from men and from God. However, in the more polemical context of Matthew's composition, the word 'hypocrite' seems to have acquired that connotation of insincerity (cf. Mt 23:13, 15, 23, 25, 27, 29; cf. Mt 23:16, where the scribes and Pharisees are called 'blind guides').

Jesus says emphatically that 'they have their reward'. The Greek word *apechein*, 'to have (received)', is a commercial term which is found on receipts: 'I have received (payment)'. The conduct of the 'hypocrite' assumes the character of a transaction: he has bought public admiration; the business is concluded; he can expect no more.

Verse 3: But when you give alms, do not let your left hand know what your right hand is doing,

Unlike the almsgiving of the 'hypocrites', the disciples' must be a strictly private action. In the Greek text 'you' (*sou*) is placed emphatically at the beginning of the verse: a sharp contrast is drawn between the previous description and the practice expected from the disciples. The clause 'do not let your left hand know what your right hand is doing' has received different explanations. Some have pointed out that the Jews, like many other peoples, distinguished carefully between their two hands; the right was for positive, the left for negative activities. Others have noted that the relation of the right hand to the left is sometimes used to indicate close fellowship. The clause would then mean: 'do not even let your close friends know about your almsgiving'. In other words, if you really want to keep something a secret, you do not need any help! Finally, some scholars take the verse to mean that the left hand should not 'register' the almsgiving of the right hand, i.e., the saying would deal not only with a form of almsgiving which is kept a secret for others, but even 'for oneself', or a totally uncalculating readiness to help (cf. Mt 25:37–39). Whatever the exact meaning of the figure may be, the verse emphasizes utter secrecy, as the first part of the following sentence shows.

Verse 4: so that your alms may be in secret; and your Father who sees in secret will reward you.

The phrase 'your Father who sees in secret' is a rather awkward translation of a Semitic idiom which is to be rendered 'your Father who sees what is done in secret', in this case your secret almsgiving. The verse does not mean that a business transaction with God is to be substituted for a business transaction with men, as if Jesus were saying, 'Do not practise your almsgiving to be seen by men, rather do it to be seen by God'. Secret almsgiving, free of any motive to 'be seen' by anybody – either by men or by God – is acceptable to the Father because of its spontaneous, totally uncalculating character.

Almsgiving which seeks to receive approval – even God's approval – is hereby disqualified. All thought of measuring one's achievement should be eliminated. What is said here about almsgiving should also be applied to today's more sophisticated forms of social assistance which are often launched with considerable fanfare to let everybody know who took the initiative: 'they have their reward!'

Prayer (Mt 6:5–15)

PRAYER IN SECRET (Mt 6:5–6)

> **Verse 5:** And when you pray, you must not be like the hypocrites; for they love to stand and pray in the synagogues and at the street corners, that they may be seen by men. Truly, I say to you, they have their reward.

This is the second illustration of the general principle stated in Mt 6:1. Some have understood this saying to mean that there is to be no such thing as public prayer, but this is contradicted by the 'we'-form of the immediately following Lord's Prayer, other passages in the gospel which endorse communal prayer (cf. Mt 18:19–20), and the practice of the early Church (Acts 2:46–47).

The present statement is concerned with the tendency of people to act a part even in personal prayer. The Jews, like the Muslims today, had regular times of prayer which could be a real help for genuine devotion but also opportunities for ostentation. People could make sure that at the time of prayer they were in a crowded place, like a synagogue or a street corner, so that their piety would get maximum notice. The 'hypocrites' displayed their piety before men to collect their admiration. They 'loved' to pray at the corners of the *main* streets, i.e., the places of *greatest* visibility. They loved to be 'alone with God' surrounded by a group of admirers. Having received a certain amount of admiration for their prayer, they got what they bargained for and so 'they have their reward'.

> **Verse 6:** But when you pray, go into your room and shut the door and pray to your Father who is in secret; and your Father who sees in secret will reward you.

In the Greek text, 'you' (*su*) is again placed emphatically at the beginning of the verse: in contrast with the prayer of the 'hypocrites', your private prayer should really be private.

The Greek word *tamieion* means the small storeroom attached to the house, and the only place in the Jewish one-room house provided with a door. The formulation of the verse is indebted to Isa 26:20LXX, 'Come, my people, enter your chambers (*tamieia*), and shut your doors behind you; hide yourself for a little while until the wrath is past', where *tamieion* is used as a symbol of secrecy. In Mt 6:6 it is a figure for complete privacy, no matter whether it is found in a storeroom or on a hillside (Mt 14:23). Some scholars have emphasized the fact that the saying mentions a totally ordinary room, and not a quiet corner in the Temple or the synagogue.

The clause 'go into your room and shut the door' does not recommend silence and solitude as such, but rather the absence of admirers. It is not said either that God is present in solitude rather than in the street or the synagogue. He is everywhere; but people should 'seek' his presence rather than that of admirers.

The phrase 'your Father who is in secret' could mean that 'your Father is with you even in secret places', but the parallelism with Mt 6:4 suggests that it is praying that is in secret rather than God. A better translation may be: pray in secret to your Father, and your Father who sees your secret prayer will reward you.

Spontaneous prayer, without any motive of approval, either by men or by God, is acceptable to the Father. The reward of such prayer is not specified here, but Phil 4:7 says that genuine prayer gives 'the peace of God, which passes all understanding'. The original saying about prayer ends with Mt 6:6.

ON VERBOSITY IN PRAYING (Mt 6:7–8)

The original saying on prayer (Mt 6:5–6) is followed by a statement in which a new contrast is made, with pagan forms of prayer. On the one hand, it is clear that Mt 6:7–8 was not originally linked with Mt 6:5–6. On the other hand, Mt 6:7–8 does not necessarily introduce a prayer text. The statement offers an exhortation on the interior dispositions for prayer, but does not as such attempt to give us a model, so that after verse 8 we do not necessarily have to expect an example. It is not clear then whether Mt 6:7–8 was already an introduction to the Lord's Prayer when it was inserted here, or whether it was introduced by Matthew himself into this context to make it serve as a kind of introduction to his version of the Lord's Prayer.

Verse 7: And in praying do not heap up empty phrases as the Gentiles do; for they think that they will be heard for their many words.

The Greek word *battalogeō* translated 'heap up empty phrases' by RSV is found only here in the New Testament and is otherwise unknown before A.D. 500. Its meaning must be related to the 'many words' mentioned in the second half of the verse. It is variously translated 'babble' (JB), 'rattle on' (NAB), 'go babbling on' (NEB). The verse is certainly not criticizing the length of time devoted to prayer or perseverance in prayer. In fact, Jesus himself prayed through entire nights (Mt 14:23–25) and inculcated perseverance in prayer (Mt 7:7–11; cf. Lk 11:5–8; 18:1–8). The error of the prayer referred to is not so much in its length as such, but in the fact that by its length it seeks to exercise pressure on the deity. In the pagan world with its polytheism people were very much concerned with invoking the right deity and addressing him by the correct epithet; otherwise the prayer would be ineffective. The difficulty was usually met by 'heaping up' names and epithets in a prayer which was intended to gain a hearing from the deity by its own merits, by sheer length.

The phrase 'the Gentiles' which is also found in Mt 5:47 (cf. Mt 6:32; 18:17) does not necessarily refer to the heathens as such but rather to a certain type of behaviour. It may only be a stereotyped formula to denounce a way of life in the contemporary situation.[16]

> **Verse 8:** Do not be like them, for your Father knows what you need before you ask him.

The disciples' prayer should differ from that of the Gentiles. They should know that they are dealing with a God who is their Father and who promised 'Before they call I will answer; while they are yet speaking I will hear' (Isa 65:24). The disciples are praying to a God who has turned himself to man in unlimited love and forgiveness and who will certainly hear them. Prayer does not inform God of our needs or draw his attention to them; still less does it try to control God, to exert any pressure on him, to change his attitude by long prayers or tricks. Prayer tests man, not God. It is we who need to be changed, so that the things that are God's may be expressed in our life. It is we who need prayer, not God.

So far the Sermon on the Mount has mainly told us how *not* to pray; now it moves to a positive example of how to pray.

THE LORD'S PRAYER (Mt 6:9–13)

At the very centre of the Sermon on the Mount Matthew places the Lord's Prayer as the pattern of all prayer, as an example of a brief, sincere prayer. Jesus does not say, 'use the following words', but 'pray then like this', i.e., 'pray in the following way' or 'along these lines'.

οὕτως

The address (Mt 6:9b)
> **Verse 9b:** Our Father who art in heaven,

The very first word of the Lord's Prayer, 'our', like the following 'our bread' and 'our debts' and the repeated use of 'we' and 'us', reminds us that this is a prayer of the Christian community, a social prayer. It is appropriate, however, for private as well as public use, as long as we say it joining ourselves with the whole family of God.

In order to understand better the wealth of ideas contained in the word 'Father' in the Lord's Prayer, let us briefly look in a wider context at its meaning as a designation for God.

In the *ancient Near East* 'Father' was used to indicate that God is the creator of the world, the sovereign ruler, and protector. In ancient Egypt, the sun-god Amon-Re was called Father, but it is possible that this practice was reserved to the Pharaoh, although there is some recently discovered evidence that ordinary people could do so too. In ancient Mesopotamia, the moon-god Nanna and the sun-god Shamash were also addressed as Father.

In the *Greco-Roman world*, Zeus was referred to as 'Father of gods and men', and addressed in prayer as 'Father Zeus', designating him as divine ruler and protector, and later also as creator. The term 'Father' was also frequently used for deities like Attis, Osiris and Mithras in the mystery religions in which the promise of personal immortality was expressed in terms of becoming 'sons' of the divine 'Father'.

In the *Old Testament*, God is spoken of as 'Father' on fourteen occasions expressing his relationship to his people (cf. Deut 32:6; Isa 63:15–16; 64:7–9; Jer 3:4, 19). Many other passages describe him as creator, ruler and protector without explicitly using the word 'Father'. In this respect the Old Testament usage is parallel to that of other religions and cultures of the ancient world. But it contains also a number of distinctive features. Firstly, the title 'Father' has a connotation of God's working in history on behalf of his covenant people Israel. Secondly, God's fatherhood is primarily a reality for Israel and not so much for other people. Thirdly, as Father, God makes some moral demands: he expects Israel to respond to him with faithfulness and justice. Fourthly, the idea of God as Father is firmly embedded in a setting of monotheism. Finally, God is occasionally described as the Father of the king of Israel (cf. II Sam 7:14) and of the righteous Israelites, and who will restore the people after the exile (Jer 31:9). It should be noted, however, that there does not seem to be a single prayer in the Old Testament in which God is actually addressed as Father.

In the writings which originated in *Palestinian Judaism*, like the Book of Jubilees, the word 'Father' occurs very rarely as a designation of God. The few available passages tend to restrict the scope of God's fatherhood to those who obey his commandments, and to depict God as the Father of the individual person. The *Ahaba Rabba*, or 'Great Love', and the Litany for the New Year are two Jewish prayers in use in Jesus' time which addressed God as 'our Father, our King', and the former prayer depicted God as ruler and helper, a practice continued by the Jewish rabbis of early Christian times. But nowhere in the literature of Judaism do we find God addressed as *abba*.

So far, the *Qumran* literature has yielded only one instance in which God is called Father, in the sense of one who helps in time of need: '... but you are a father to all (the sons) of your truth ...' (1 QH 9:35). This makes Jesus' use of the word 'Father' the more striking.

Turning now to *Jesus' teaching*, and looking at the number of instances in which Jesus is quoted in the gospels as referring to God as 'Father' or 'Father in heaven', we notice a much greater number of occurrences in Matthew, and it is very likely that this evangelist was responsible for introducing the term 'Father' into some of Jesus' sayings to emphasize its importance for Jesus. If we focus on the sources of the synoptic gospels, and limit ourselves to Mark (four times 'Father') and the Q-source (eight times), it appears that Jesus referred to God as Father and used the expression 'your Father' when he was speaking to his disciples rather than to the people in general. He founded this designation not on events in the past, such as the Exodus from Egypt, but on what God was doing now and the new conditions of life which he was providing for those who responded to the proclamation of the kingdom. Strictly speaking, only those who were ready to obey God's will, especially his love-commandment and its test-case, the love of enemies, could consider God their Father, ready to forgive their sins and aware of their needs.

Entirely new was Jesus' use of the word *abba*. It is the address of the small child to its father, also used by adults as the tender, filial address to a father: 'Dear father'. No contemporary Jew would have dared to address God in this manner, but Jesus did it in all his prayers handed down to us in the gospels, except Mk 15:34; Mt 27:46, where he quoted Ps 22(21):1, 'My God, my God, why have you forsaken me?' Jesus' use of the term *abba* expressed his unique relationship to God, his unique sonship. But he also invited his disciples to repeat the word *abba* after him and thus gave them a share in his sonship (cf. Rom 8:15; Gal 4:6).

Although it is possible that Jesus did use the expression 'Father in heaven' (cf. Mk 11:25), it is more likely that the address '(dear) Father', corresponding to the Aramaic *abba*, which Jesus used in his own prayers, preserves the original beginning of the Lord's Prayer.

Matthew's longer address most probably represents an expansion of this original by the Matthean community inspired by the tendency of liturgical protocol to want to keep its distance. God was put back in heaven again and addressed as 'Our Father' by the assembled community, although Luke's 'Father' was also widespread in the early Church, as can be gathered from Rom 8:15; Gal 4:6, The adjective 'our' does not imply that Jesus' sonship and ours are identical, although the former is undoubtedly the point of departure for the latter. 'Our' introduces the possessives of the 'we'-petitions where the disciple prays for the Christian community. In fact, the individual disciples can meet God only as members of the community. Therefore, their prayer must be personal, yet never individualistic.

The second addition, 'who art in heaven (literally, in the heavens)', may be an effort to avoid the danger of familiarity – although in the patriarchal atmosphere of the ancient family that danger was much less than among ourselves – but it certainly helps to place the Father beyond all confines of nationalism. Thus the phrase 'who art in heaven' constitutes an excellent introduction to the three 'thou'-petitions which follow in Matthew's version of the Lord's Prayer. But at the same time it may also mean: God who in your own hidden way are very near to us, as is suggested by Isa 57:15, 'For thus says the high and lofty One who inhabits eternity, whose name is Holy (cf. the first petition!): "I dwell in the high and holy place, and also with him who is of a contrite and humble spirit, to revive the spirit of the humble (= poor), and to revive the heart of the contrite" '. God is both close and distant, immanent and transcendent.

The 'thou'-petitions (Mt 6:9c–10)

These three petitions which are parallel in structure and correspond to each other in content recall the first part of the Kaddish, an ancient Aramaic prayer which concluded the synagogue service and which Jesus certainly knew:

> Exalted and hallowed be his great name in the world,
> which he created according to his will.
> May he rule his kingdom
> in your lifetime and in your days,
> and in the lifetime of the whole house of Israel,
> speedily and soon.
> And to this say: Amen.

Verse 9c: Hallowed be thy name.

This clause has sometimes been understood as a formula of praise to the holy name of God or as an expression of the disciple's will to sanctify God's name, but it has the same word order and stylistic characteristics as the other 'thou'-petitions and should therefore be understood as a true request.

In the Old Testament a name is much more than an identification label. It is an expression of a person's innermost being. It tells us *who* a person is, not simply *how* he is called. This is also true of the 'name' by which God reveals who he is and will be for man (Ex 3:14) and thus summarizes his saving action in the history of his people (Ps 111[110]:9). Therefore, God's great name is mentioned in the same context as his strong hand and outstretched arm (II Chron 6:32). To announce the name of God is to make known his saving action (Isa 12:4). God's name expresses his nature, so that 'those who know your name put their trust in you' (Ps 9:10) does not mean 'those who know that your name is Yahweh', but 'those who know what you are like, what kind of a God you are, trust in you'. In fact, God's name and person are practically interchangeable: 'And the Lord will become king over all the earth; on that day the Lord will be one and his name one' (Zech 14:9).

The same is true in Judaism: 'to trust in God's name' means to trust in God himself as the source of forgiveness and salvation, and 'to bless God's name' is to bless God himself.

This background suggests that in the Lord's Prayer too the name of God signifies God himself rather than any particular name by which he is known, like Yahweh or *abba*.

The word 'hallowed' is not an adjective but is part of the passive verb form 'be hallowed' and has the same meaning as 'sanctified' or 'made holy'. Mt 6:9c asks, therefore, that God's name, or God himself, be sanctified or made holy.

Holiness, the basic meaning of which seems to be 'separateness', is especially characteristic of God, who is separate or different from everything else. The transcendent God manifests his holiness in the midst of his people by his concern for justice: he himself acts with justice and he expects his people to be holy and just. God's holiness manifests itself in glory, and 'name' and glory go together: 'glorify your name' (cf. Dan 3:43; Jn 12:28). God's name is called holy (Amos 2:7; Ez 20:39; Isa 57:15, etc.), but the verb 'sanctify' occurs only twice in connection with God's name: 'And I will sanctify my great name, which has been profaned among the nations' (Ez 36:23; RSV: I will vindicate); 'They will sanctify my name; they will sanctify the Holy One of Jacob' (Isa 29:23). In the first text it is said that *God* will sanctify his name, while the second indicates that *men* will sanctify it.

However, God's name stands for God himself (cf. Isa 29:23; Zech 14:9), and a number of Old Testament passages state that God will sanctify himself, i.e., he will manifest himself in his actions. These texts suggest that God himself is the agent in the first 'thou'-petition, which therefore asks that God may sanctify himself or manifest his holiness by decisively intervening in history. But later Jewish writers believed that God's name could be sanctified either by God himself or by men. Who then is the primary agent of 'hallowed be thy name', man or God?

Notwithstanding some evidence supporting the view that men

should sanctify God's name (cf. Isa 29:23; Jewish literature), it seems better to understand the first petition as a request that God himself may act by manifesting his holiness (cf. Ez 36:23). This interpretation does justice to the fact that we have here a real petition and to the passive verb form which is often a reverential circumlocution for divine action (compare Mt 5:4, 6, 7, 9, 19; 7:1–2, 7–8). It is also consistent with the most accepted interpretation of the second petition, to which the first is closely related. However, while insisting that God acts first, we should not forget that a considerable part of his work passes through our hands. Thus, while praying 'Hallowed be thy name', we pray to the Father to act and to make us act. Moreover, the Christian who prays for this full manifestation cannot forget that God has already begun to manifest his holiness: the Father has revealed it in his Son.

Verse 10a: Thy kingdom come,

The second petition also reminds us of the Kaddish: 'May he rule (establish) his kingdom in your lifetime and in your days'.

Although they never use the phrase 'kingdom of God', the Old Testament writers describe God as king in connection with his intervention in the Exodus (Num 23:20–24; Deut 33:2–5), and even after the establishment of a royal dynasty, Israel continued to consider God as a king whose dominion was everlasting (Ps 145[144]:13) and who would intervene in history to assert his rule over the whole world (Dan 2:44; 7:18, 22, 27).

In Judaism, God's kingship over the whole world is related to the belief that he created the world. God's rule over individual persons is also emphasized. Both ideas are found in the *Shema*, a confession of faith consisting of Deut 6:4–9; 11:13–21; Num 15:37–41. Finally, Judaism also developed the eschatological conception of the kingdom of God, referring to a time when God would assert his rule over the whole world. In the *Targum of the Prophets* Yahweh is already king in the present, but his kingdom will be fully revealed eschatologically. The political and nationalistic aspects of this eschatological kingdom are expressed in the apocryphal *Psalms of Solomon*, the *Eighteen Benedictions* and the *Assumption of Moses*.

Jesus, who used the phrase 'kingdom of God' almost exclusively in its eschatological sense, made it the central theme of his teaching. He emphasized that it was God's gift (Lk 12:32) to all who acknowledged their need for it, especially the poor (Mt 5:3; Lk 6:20) and the outcasts (Mt 9:10–13), and that it would be taken away from those who took it for granted (Mt 21:43). There is a certain (eschatological) tension in Jesus' references to the kingdom of God. On the one hand, some of his words and deeds indicate that he regarded the kingdom of God as already to some extent present in his ministry (Mt 11:2–6; 12:28) or to some extent identical with his coming: 'the kingdom of God is at hand' (Mk 1:15; Mt 4:17; 10:7). On the other hand, other words and deeds of Jesus refer to the kingdom of God as still to come in its fullness (Mk 9:1; 14:25). Some of his parables even seem to combine these two aspects. In short, Jesus regarded the kingdom of God as already to some extent present, but still to be fully realized in the future. The rule of God is already inaugurated: he has decided to realize his eschatological kingdom.

The petition 'thy kingdom come' concerns this final and full coming of the kingdom of God. It speaks of an eschatological coming which does not simply mean 'coming about', but implies also the divine action of 'bringing about' something in the future. But all this is based in the fact that the kingdom is already partially present in Jesus' ministry. Therefore, and in this sense, nobody but Jesus could have pronounced the word 'thy kingdom come' for the first time.

For Matthew the gift of divine sonship is bestowed in the eschatological kingdom. In addressing God as Father, Christians are anticipating that state which will be fully theirs at the close of time. They are looking forward to the coming of the kingdom which is already incipient in the preaching of Jesus. In the beatitudes it is stated that the poor shall inherit the kingdom of God. And so the community that prays 'your kingdom come' are the poor and the oppressed who accept Jesus' preaching of the kingdom, a kingdom prepared for his sons and daughters by the Father through Jesus (cf. Lk 22:29–30).

When the Christian community or individual Christians pronounce this second petition of the Lord's Prayer they pray for the full realization of the divine plan, rather than for the everyday growth of the kingdom in terms of an increased membership of the Church or of the growth of God's dominion in the hearts of individuals. This request is entirely directed toward God, although it also refers, of course, to the disciples gaining access to the integral salvation of their persons and the situation in which they live: 'But seek first his kingdom and his righteousness, and all these things shall be yours as well' (Mt 6:33; compare Lk 12:31 which is more radical: 'Instead, seek his kingdom, and these things shall be yours as well'). Thus, at the same time, we pray that God may help us to commit ourselves to the realization of the kingdom.

Verse 10b: Thy will be done, on earth as it is in heaven.

The third 'thou'-petition has a distinctive Matthean vocabulary. The request 'thy will be done' appears also in Matthew's version of the agony in Gethsemane (Mt 26:42; note that the prayer begins with the words 'My Father'). Absent from the Marcan parallel (Mk 14:39), it is used to fill in the actual words of the prayer. Both in Mt 6:10 and 26:42, the saying 'thy will be done' seems to be used by Matthew to fill in sequences. The prayer in Mt 26:42 almost certainly derives from the Lord's Prayer, and Matthew's Gethsemane text is interlarded with allusions to the Lord's Prayer as a Eucharistic prayer.

Are we dealing here with a request that men will do God's will, or are we asking that God will bring about his will on earth as in heaven?

The Old Testament repeatedly states that God himself accomplishes his 'will', also referred to as 'delight', 'purpose', or 'favour'. For example, 'Whatever the Lord pleases he does, in heaven and on earth' (Ps 135[134]:6). His delight and purpose is to deliver his people from oppression (Isa 46:10, 13) and to have mercy on them (Isa 49:8). But we find also texts stating that men do God's will by obeying his Law (Pss 40[39]:8; 143[142]:10).

Judaism too has two sets of affirmations. On the one hand, it is said that God accomplishes his will. While the Kaddish speaks of 'the world, which he created according to his will', the opening words of Rabbi Eliezer's prayer are 'Do thy will in heaven above'. On the other hand, it is often stated that men are expected to do God's will.

The same is true in the New Testament which speaks of God as carrying out his own will (Mt 18:14; 26:42) as well as of men doing God's will (Mt 7:21; 12:50; 21:31), but the latter may very well be a special Matthean emphasis since there is only one parallel in Mark (Mk 3:35) and none in Luke. Matthew may very well have understood 'thy will be done' in the Lord's Prayer in the latter sense. It should be noticed, however, that in the previous references God's will has different meanings. It is used in the sense of commandments to be obeyed, but also in the sense of God's plan for the universe. Because of the obvious parallelism of the three 'thou'-petitions, the latter seems to be intended in the Lord's Prayer, which therefore requests that God's will may bring about the eschatological completion of his saving plan, which is basically the same as the sanctification of his name and the establishment of his kingdom.

The present petition requests that God's will be done 'on earth as it is in heaven' (*hōs en ouranōi kai epi gēs*, literally, 'as in heaven, also upon earth'). We find a number of interesting parallels to this phrase in Mt 16:19b; 18:18, 19, but the only exact parallel in the Greek text is found in Mt 28:18, 'All authority in heaven and on earth (*en ouranōi kai epi gēs*) has been given to me'. Both phrases seem to belong to the Matthean redaction and may suggest that Jesus is the definitive expression of God's will. Jesus' presence constitutes the eschaton or the new, ultimate age.

Although some scholars have understood the phrase to mean 'both in heaven and on earth', implying that God's saving plan is still opposed in heaven as well as upon earth, and asking that God may realize his saving purpose in heaven as on earth, Jesus' own usage of the phrase 'heaven' favours the translation 'on earth as it is in heaven', which implies that God's will is already fully accomplished in heaven.

Concluding, we offer two considerations for reflection. First, the three 'thou'-petitions deal basically with the same idea: the realization of God's saving plan. But they express different aspects of this idea: God's saving plan has its origin in his innermost being (his 'name'), which expresses itself in his actual rule over the universe (his 'kingdom'), in which he realizes his work of salvation (his 'will').

Secondly, just as in the Old Testament God revealed his name in a process of liberation, the Exodus, so he revealed himself definitely in one whose name is Jesus, i.e., 'Yahweh saves', 'Yahweh is Liberator', 'for he will save his people . . .' (Mt 1:21). In the oppression of his people God saw and sees time and again his creative and saving purposes frustrated, and to restore them he identifies with the oppressed. Only those who identify with 'the cause of the poor and the needy' know God (cf. Jer 22:16). To approach him in prayer without responding to the needs of the oppressed is to nurture the vain hope that God will listen to our needs while we are deaf to those of his people. But if we try to bring about God's justice we will almost certainly be confronted by the 'justice' of the vested interests of Babylon, the archetype of all states, in which 'all shipowners grew rich from their profitable trade with her' (Rev 18:19 NAB). Nowadays, these vested interests may be referred to as 'national security', or any equivalent expression. But to implement God's will on earth as in heaven means the rejection of any other will that cannot be equated with God's. The fulfilment of God's liberating will on all levels is the mission of the Christian in the contemporary world. The Lord's Prayer is the 'priority list' of the disciple and the community.

The 'we'-petitions (Mt 6:11–13)

The three 'we'-petitions constitute the second half of the Lord's Prayer. They are distinguished from the first half by a number of stylistic characteristics mentioned above. But, like the 'thou'-petitions, the 'we'-petitions too are governed by the new relationship of sonship to the Father which the disciples have received through Jesus.

While the majority of recent Catholic scholars have agreed on the eschatological interpretation of the 'thou'-petitions, most of them shift to interpreting the first of the 'we'-petitions in terms of daily needs. They argue that the end of the third 'thou'-petition, 'on earth as it is in heaven', has brought us down to earth (note that this is valid only for the Matthean version). This argument would be convincing if all three 'we'-petitions dealt with daily needs rather than with the eschatological realization of God's purpose. However, as most scholars admit, the final petition, 'and lead us not into temptation . . .', is certainly to be interpreted eschatologically. The second 'we'-petition, 'and forgive us our debts . . .', is also probably eschatological. To interpret the first 'we'-petition in terms of daily needs would leave it isolated among all the other requests of the Lord's Prayer. But some scholars think that a good case can be made for an eschatological interpretation of the first 'we'-petition in its Matthean form (Luke's version with its present imperative and *to kath' hēmeran*, 'daily', is considered non-eschatological). Thus we would have a consistently eschatological interpretation of the Lord's Prayer.

Verse 11: Give us this day our daily bread;

In the Greek text the substantive 'bread' is found at the beginning of the clause. Bread here includes all man's (material) needs, since both the Hebrew and Aramaic equivalent mean 'that which is necessary for life'. It can mean the 'bread of life' (Jn 6:35) and is also used to speak of nourishment in the kingdom of God (Lk 14:15).

The adjective 'our' (the Greek has literally 'the bread of us') indicates that we are not praying only for our own needs and thus preserves the prayer from all egoism. We express our concern for all members of the community as well as for those who potentially belong to it, i.e., all men.

All this seems to be self-explanatory, but the real crux for the interpretation of this petition lies in the adjective which modifies 'bread', the Greek word *epiousios*. The word does not occur in literary Greek or in the popular spoken language, and its etymology is not of much help either. Four possible meanings have been suggested: (1) 'necessary for existence' (derived from *epi* and *ousia*); (2) 'for today' (equivalent to *epi tēn ousan* [*hēmeran*]); (3) 'for the coming day' (equivalent to *epi tēn iousan* [*hēmeran*]); (4) 'for the future' (equivalent to *to epion*).

Scholars who adhere to the non-eschatological interpretation of the petition favour the meanings 'necessary for existence' and 'for today'. They understand it as the Christian community's prayer for its daily needs. Those who favour the eschatological interpretation prefer 'for the coming day', and 'for the future'. They say that in their poverty the early Christians looked in the first place not for material bread, but for God's decisive intervention and the bread which would be given at the heavenly banquet: the bread of life. The latter interpretation is based on the symbolic use of food and meals in the Old Testament, Judaism, and Jesus' words and deeds.

Both in the Old Testament and in Judaism we find texts which speak of food as a gift which God provides for men according to their daily needs as expression of his providential care for his creation. But there are also passages which use the symbolism of food or meals to depict a coming time of salvation when God will manifest his rule over the universe, sometimes referred to as 'the world to come'. In Judaism, the symbolism of a meal refers entirely to the future.

Jesus too occasionally spoke of food as a sign of the Father's providential care for his creation (Mt 6:30–31; cf. 5:44–45). But most of the time he used the symbolism of food or meals in relation to his proclamation of the kingdom which God was inaugurating, sometimes to speak of its full realization in the future (Mt 8:11–12), sometimes to show that it was already partially present in his ministry, especially by having meals with tax collectors and sinners (Mt 9:10–13; 11:19). The overall emphasis is on the future aspect and suggests that the meaning of the adjective *epiousios* would be 'for the future', which is the same as 'our bread for the morrow', which is mentioned in a footnote of the RSV, and is based on Jerome's *Commentary on Matthew* 6:11: 'In the gospel according to the Hebrews, for "substantial bread" I found "mahar" which means "of the morrow", so that the sense is: our bread of the morrow, that is of the future, give us today'.

The disciples request the Father to give them the bread of the future 'this day' or 'today', which then means the short period of time before the eschatological future, and expresses the urgency of the Christian community's eschatological longing. The aorist *dos* ('give') underlines the once-and-for-all character of the petition: Give us now once-and-for-all our bread for the future.

This interpretation of the petition is based on Old Testament parallels like Ex 16:4, 'I will rain bread from heaven for you . . . a day's portion every day', and Ps 78(77):24, '. . . and he gave them bread (*arton*; RSV: 'grain') of heaven'. Both texts are talking about the manna and are referred to in the Fourth Gospel to designate Jesus as the Word which comes from the Father (Jn 6:32, 35) and the Eucharistic bread interpreted as an eschatological pledge (Jn 6:54; cf. I Cor 11:26). This petition of the Lord's Prayer has therefore been connected with the Eucharistic bread (cf. the formulation of Mk 14:22; 6:41).

This interpretation may perhaps be a surprise or even a disappointment for us. For so many people it is important that at least *one* petition in the Lord's Prayer should lead into everyday life, the petition for daily bread. Is that to be taken away from us? Isn't that an impoverishment? No, in reality, application of the petition about bread to the bread of life is a great enrichment. It would be a gross misunderstanding if one were to suppose that here there is a 'spiritualizing,' after the manner of Greek philosophy, and that there is a distinction made between 'earthly' and 'heavenly' bread. For Jesus, earthly bread and the bread of life are not antithetical. In the realm of God's kingship he viewed all earthly things as hallowed. . . . This 'hallowing of life' is most clearly illustrated by the picture of Jesus at table for a meal. The bread which he proffered when he sat at table with publicans and sinners was everyday bread, and yet it was more; it was bread of life. The bread which he broke for his disciples at the Last Supper was earthly bread, and yet it was more: his body given for many in death, the gift of a portion in the atoning power of his death. Every meal his disciples had with him was a usual eating and drinking, and yet it was more: a meal of salvation, a messianic meal, image and anticipation of the meal at the consummation. . . . It is in this sense too that the petition about 'bread for tomorrow' is intended. It does not sever everyday life and the kingdom of God from one another, but it encompasses the totality of life. It embraces everything that Jesus' disciples need. . . . It includes 'daily bread,' but it does not content itself with that. . . . One can flatly say that this petition for the bread of life makes entreaty for the hallowing of everyday life. Only when one has perceived that the petition asks for bread in the fullest sense, for the bread of life, does the antithesis between 'for tomorrow' and 'today' gain its full significance.[17]

Recently, however, this interpretation has again been questioned, and the translation 'the bread we need' has been defended (cf. the French Nouveau Testament Oecuménique: 'le pain dont nous avons besoin'). This interpretation is based on the Peshitta Bible, an early fifth-century compilation and reworking of earlier Syriac translations, and the homilies of John Chrysostom (344–407) and Theodore of Mopsuestia (350–428). Reference is also made to some rabbinic texts which indicate that the Old Testament background of the petition may be found in Ex 16:4, 'Behold, I will rain bread from Heaven for you; and the people shall go out and gather *a day's portion every day* . . .'. It is clear that the nourishment we ask from the Father is not just a piece of bread, but everything we need for the day (cf. Prov 30:8, 'give me neither poverty nor riches; feed me with the food that is needful for me'; the Hebrew text refers to the ration for one day). Moreover, 'man does not live by bread alone, but . . . by everything that proceeds out of the mouth of the Lord' (Deut 8:3), and man should learn 'that it is not the production of crops that feeds man, but that your word preserves those who trust in you' (Wis 16:26). If the spiritual bread is the most important for the evangelist, this does not allow us to forget the literal sense. It is perfectly valid to think in terms of different levels of depth. From day to day our existence depends on the Father who supports us every moment of our life. Therefore, we are invited to renew our supplication every day. More than a means to obtain what we need, this petition is an acknowledgement of our dependency. This is the meaning of 'today'. It takes men in their temporal condition, compels them to become 'poor in spirit', and tells them to rely on the heavenly Father of their existence.

> **Verse 12:** And forgive us our debts, as we also have forgiven our debtors;

The conjunctive 'and' connects this petition with the previous one: man needs bread, but also stands in need of pardon. The verb 'to forgive' (*aphienai*) has its origin in juridical language, in which it means the remission of an obligation (cf. Deut 15:2). In a religious context it means more than the remission of an exterior debt or punishment. It refers to something God alone can do: the restoration of the personal relations between God and man. The aorist *aphes* ('forgive') implies the once-and-for-all character of the forgiveness requested. Unlike Luke, where we find a present tense (*aphiomen*) in the second half of the verse, Matthew again has an aorist: *aphēkamen*. This is usually translated 'as we have forgiven', but it can equally well be rendered 'as we herewith forgive', since it is not the tense that is emphasized, but rather the singleness of the action. The two aorists of Matthew's version express the same eschatological urgency as the phrase 'today' does in the previous petition. Our declaration of pardon abolishes the past and radically commits us to the future.

The word 'debts', which is also used in the second part of the petition in Luke ('everyone who is indebted to us') and in the parable of the unforgiving servant (Mt 18:23–35), is to be preferred to Luke's 'sins'. The Greek word for debts (*ta opheilēmata*) has no religious colouring in everyday Greek, and is found only here in the New Testament as a figure for men's religious and moral failings. The underlying Aramaic term (*chôbâ*) is primarily a commercial term meaning a financial debt, but it was taken up into religious language to mean a failure toward God, possibly with emphasis on its personal character.

Prayer to God for forgiveness is already found in the Old Testament. Ps 25(24):18 says: '. . . forgive all my sins', and Sir 28:2 states: 'Forgive your neighbour the wrong he has done, and then your sins will be pardoned when you pray'. Prayer for forgiveness as such is therefore nothing new.

Like the Old Testament and Jewish writers, Jesus emphasized that forgiveness is a gift which has its source in God's love and mercy, and which man must pray for, while at the same time showing willingness to forgive others (cf. Mt 18:23–35). But unlike some Jewish writers, he refused to accept any form of calculation in setting limits to human forgiveness (cf. Mt 18:21–22) or attempting to influence God's forgiveness in a kind of business deal. Moreover, in the context of his proclamation of the kingdom of God, he announced that God's forgiveness was already a reality (Mt 9:2).

The petition of the Lord's Prayer, therefore, displays a certain newness in that the request for forgiveness is based on a new concept of the fullness of God's fatherhood and the disciples' state of sonship fully realized only when the kingdom of God has come. In view of this eschatological state we confidently approach the Father with our request for the final forgiveness of our debts. These debts will be fully apparent only at the final judgment. Until that moment we will sin frequently. And if we understand 'debts' in a wider sense – and a good case can be made for this interpretation – it may also refer to all that we are and have; our dependence on the Father for all this will also continue until the final encounter with him.

But all these reflections still leave unsolved the problem of the relationship between divine and human forgiveness, both of which are mentioned in this petition. We would express it as follows: In words and deeds Jesus proclaimed God's initiative of unconditional forgiveness which calls for men's response in their relationships to their fellow-men. If that response fails to materialize, God's initiative is, as it were, cancelled, and men fall back into their previous status, having failed to accept God's initiative. If, however, men respond to that initiative by extending unlimited forgiveness to their fellow-men (cf. Mt 18:22, 'seventy times seven'), then God's forgiveness is also a reality *for them* here and now. In the parable of the unforgiving debtor (Mt 18:23–35) it is forgiveness *already received* which makes the king as well as the fellow-servants expect the servant to forgive in his turn. This obligation which originates from God's gift (for-give-ness) becomes, however, also the condition for the continued possession of the gift.

But in what sense can sins or offences against one's fellow-man be called 'debts'? It has been pointed out that this is possible only in a community of brothers and sisters whose life is based on an exchange of fraternal love, especially in a community which is distinguished from other communities by its central commandment of fraternal love (cf. Jn 13:35), which is nothing but an extension of God's own love for them (cf. I Jn 4:7–11). It is in these terms that a Christian's sin is referred to in Mt 18:15, 'If your *brother* sins against you . . .'. The clause 'as we also have forgiven our debtors', or maybe better 'as we herewith forgive our debtors', speaks of those who under the fatherhood of God are living with us in a bond of brotherhood and anticipated eschatological sonship. The clause expected might then have been 'as we too forgive each other our debts', but the actual formulation of the second part of the petition emphasizes that both the forgiveness we ask for and the one we give to our debtors come from God.

This petition should not be understood as a bargain with God, i.e., as a reference to our own meritorious acts of forgiveness, performed in the past or promised for the future, which would prompt God to forgive us. The conjunction 'as' simply means that the forgiveness we extend to others is the counterpart of God's forgiveness, and that the seriousness of our promise equals that of our request. This is clear from the parable of the unforgiving servant (Mt 18:23–35), which shows that God's forgiveness *precedes* our forgiveness (cf. Mt 18:29), and that the latter is the *reflection* of the former (Mt 18:32–33). Moreover, God's forgiveness can become real for us only when we are willing to forgive one another (Mt 18:34–35). Few people have no enemies at all. And if we think that we have none, should not persecutors and oppressors of the poor be our 'enemies'?

Here too it seems that the meaning of 'debts' is not limited to sins only. It should be extended to include the cancellation of debts. The linking of forgiveness of sins and cancellation of debts would be in line with the regulations of the Jubilee Year (Deut 15:1–11; cf, Lk 4:18–19), which in the Septuagint is referred to as *aphesis*, the noun derived from *aphienai*, 'to forgive'. A comparison of Mt 6:12, 14–15 and Mt 18:23–35 reveals a distinctive understanding of sin and forgiveness. The key-word *aphienai* establishes an undeniable association between forgiveness and releasing someone from debts. Thus Matthew indicates that he understands the forgiveness of a personal offence as analogous to releasing someone from a financial obligation.

If people are indebted to us to the point of alienation, there cannot be true community either with each other or with God. Jesus calls us to conversion from sin in its individual, interpersonal and social levels so that we can truly be part of God's community.

The Our Father should reflect the lived experience of calling for conversion of a system built on false needs that keep people indebted to those who have the power to create needs. Instead we have made the forgiveness of debts a purely religious concept having little or nothing to do with the reality of our daily lives.[18]

Only thus do we remove the obstacles to a real community at table alluded to in the previous petition ('give us today our bread for the morrow'). In this sense the present petition is closely related to Matthew's 'parable of the last judgment' (Mt 25:31–46): 'Come, O blessed of my *Father, inherit the kingdom* prepared for you from the foundation of the world; for I was hungry and you gave me food' (Mt 25:34–35).

Verse 13: And lead us not into temptation, but deliver us from evil

The last 'we'-petition, which reminds us of Mt 26:41, 'watch and pray that you may not enter into temptation', stands out among the other petitions in that it is the only one couched in a negative form, asking that we may not be led into temptation.

The second half of the petition, which is found in Matthew alone and does not belong to the earliest form of the Lord's Prayer, expresses in a positive form the idea contained negatively in the first half, thus softening the abruptness of 'lead us not into temptation'. It does not contain anything new, but simply carries a little further the idea of not being led into temptation, by asking for a positive deliverance from what is evil.

The correct interpretation of the first half of this petition depends on our understanding of the terms 'temptation' and 'lead' as related to God. The term 'temptation' can be understood in a general, a more specific, or an eschatological sense. Firstly, as suggested by the Jewish morning and evening prayers, temptation can mean any kind of wrong-doing in everyday life. Thus we would first pray that God will forgive the sins which we have already committed (Mt 6:12), and then that he would help us to avoid any further sin.

Secondly, in a more specific sense, temptation may mean the temptation for Jesus' followers to fall away in times of suffering and persecution. This seems to be the meaning in Jesus' prayer at Gethsemane (Mk 14:38; Mt 26:41; Lk 22:40, 46), apart from the Lord's Prayer the only instance where Jesus uses the term 'temptation' to refer to a situation which the disciples would face (the wording of Lk 8:13, 'in time of temptation', is probably a late addition). Jesus repeatedly thought of this possibility, and it is not impossible that he taught his disciples to pray for God's help in avoiding this kind of temptation. However, the aorist tenses *eisenenkēis* ('lead') and *rusai* ('deliver') do not favour an interpretation of this petition in terms of daily deliverance from temptation.

Thirdly, temptation may also be understood as referring to the time of testing or tribulation which will precede and accompany God's final victory over the forces of evil (cf. 6:13b). This eschatological interpretation is supported by Rev 3:10, 'Because you have kept my word of patient endurance, I will keep you from the hour of trial (*peirasmos*, 'temptation') which is coming on the whole world, to try those who dwell upon the earth'. This interpretation becomes even more acceptable now that the Dead Sea Scrolls have given us a better knowledge of the theological views of the contemporary Jewish world. The community of Qumran expected a decisive attack of the forces of evil at the end of a period of temptation by means of persecution (1 QS 3:22–25) to which God set a time limit (1 QS 4:16–19). The early Christians had a similar outlook. The term 'temptation', therefore, refers to the temptation of the endtime (cf. Mt 24), in which Satan will shake the disciples like wheat (cf. Lk 22:31; RSV: sift). But this endtime is not like the last coach of a train one does not have to worry about if one has a seat in one of the front coaches. We are living here and now in the midst of this endtime, and therefore in the midst of this temptation. God's salvation is veiled by the cross. Can we really expect salvation from a crucified Jesus? Shouldn't we expect it rather from technological progress or one of the various efforts to build a human paradise? All this is part of the decisive temptation from which we ask God to deliver us.

This interpretation is confirmed by Matthew's addition 'but deliver us from evil (or, the evil one)', which constitutes the first attempt to interpret 'lead us not into temptation', and is the second line in a synonymous parallelism which takes the meaning of the first line a little further. Because of the parallelism with *peirasmos*, often understood as (daily) temptation, *ponērou* has equally often been translated as 'evil' (neuter). But this genitive form can also be masculine, and if *peirasmos* means the decisive trial brought about by Satan's final attack, a personal interpretation, 'the evil one', is preferable. 'The evil one' is mentioned in this same gospel (Mt 13:19, 38) as well as in Johannine and Pauline literature (Jn 17:15; I Jn 5:18; II Thess 3:3 doubtful: RSV has 'evil', but 'evil one' in footnote). A number of other passages may also be quoted for *ponēros* as 'evil one' (Mt 5:37, 39; I Jn 2:13–14; 3:12; Eph 6:16). Though one or other of these passages may be considered doubtful, as a whole, the evidence adduced is conclusive. The disciples, who have prayed for the coming of the Father's kingdom, now ask that the same Father will not allow them to perish in the struggle which will precede its full realization.

The concluding doxology, 'For yours is the kingdom and the power and the glory for ever', appears only in later manuscripts of Matthew and is patterned on I Chron 29:11–13. It does not belong to the earliest text of the Lord's Prayer.

ADDITION ON FORGIVENESS (Mt 6:14–15)

Verses 14–15: For if you forgive men their trespasses, your heavenly Father also will forgive you; (15) but if you do not forgive men their trespasses, neither will your Father forgive your trespasses.

The positive part of this statement (Mt 6:14) has a parallel in Mk 11:25, 'And whenever you stand praying, forgive, if you have anything against any one; so that your Father also who is in heaven may forgive you your trespasses'. Mk 11:26, which is the equivalent of the negative part (Mt 6:15), is rejected by modern editors on textual grounds. Together Mt 6:14 and 15 form an antithetic parallelism whose content reminds us of Mt 6:12 and makes more explicit what is already contained in that petition. Originally, these verses did not belong to the present context. Matthew inserted them here to emphasize the seriousness of Mt 6:12b; no doubt they belonged at first to another context, as can be seen from Mk 11:25 (and 26), their absence from Luke, and the very similar statement of Mt 18:35. In fact, Mt 6:14–15 express an idea which is very important to Matthew, and should be understood in the light of the parable of the unforgiving servant (Mt 18:23–35).

Readiness to forgive is the only prior condition for the disciples' prayer (Mt 6:12). It is to be limitless and applies also to one's enemies: to pray for them (Mt 5:44) presupposes that one forgives them. Prayer always includes a request for God's forgiveness and, of course, only God can forgive sins in the sense of giving an absolute and final pardon. But one cannot really ask God for forgiveness if one is not prepared to forgive (cf. Mk 11:25; Mt 18:35). The present verses extend this obligation to all men (*tois anthrōpois*, Mt 6:14a, 15a). On the other hand, Mt 5:23f. states that if a disciple has himself sinned against his brother, he is to admit his sin to his brother and ask for forgiveness; only then can he appear before God. Forgiveness, i.e., one's own willingness to forgive and a request for forgiveness when one has sinned against a brother, is the presupposition for the prayer of Jesus' disciples. Failure to forgive means that the disciple is not really forgiven by God either. Only a community which has this 'law' deeply embedded in its heart, so that it determines its actions, can live a truly Christian life.

Fasting (Mt 6:16–18)

Verse 16: And when you fast, do not look dismal, like the hypocrites, for they disfigure their faces that their fasting may be seen by men. Truly I say to you, they have their reward.

After the digression of Mt 6:7–15, inserted by Matthew after the second illustration from prayer (Mt 6:5–6), comes now the third illustration from fasting. Fasting was a regular feature of Jewish religious life and considered a sign of conversion to God. Aside from the solemn public fasts on the Day of Atonement (cf. Lev 16:29) and a few other occasions, pious Jews undertook private fasts. The Pharisees, for instance, fasted twice a week (cf. Lk 18:12), usually on Monday and Thursday. But what should have been done for God alone became for some an opportunity to display their piety. They showed up in public with a gloomy look (*skuthrōpoi*, only here and in Lk 24:17 in the New Testament), and 'disfigure (*aphanizousin*, literally, 'make disappear', 'render invisible') their faces', by leaving their beards untended and putting ashes or flour on their faces, or by letting the dirt accumulate on them. Thus they advertised that they were fasting and received a certain amount of popular admiration as their reward – their only reward. True and false fasting are already distinguished in Isa 58:5ff.

> **Verses 17–18:** But when you fast, anoint your head and wash your face, (18) that your fasting may not be seen by men but by your Father who is in secret; and your Father who sees in secret will reward you.

Although Jesus did not make his disciples fast (Mt 9:14), the early Church introduced the practice (Mt 9:15; Acts 13:1–3; 14:23). The disciples should fast 'in secret' and do everything possible to keep it a secret: they should 'anoint their heads and wash their faces', instead of strewing ashes on their heads, letting the dirt accumulate on their faces. They should appear perfectly normal, or even as if going to a feast (compare Amos 6:6; Ps 23[22]:5). Anointing one's head was an outward sign of joy. Fasting before the Father as an expression of true repentance is joy; joy at the salvation that has been given. The disciples should fast without the slightest motive to be seen by men, avoiding all side-glances towards their fellow-men. Their hidden fasting will be seen and rewarded by the Father.

Concluding this chapter, we may say that Mt 6:1–18 tries to make us

> see a deep and pervasive danger which haunts man's religious life, a danger which we have great trouble in seeing because it springs from one of our deepest needs, the need for 'reward,' which clearly includes recognition and honor. . . . The text realistically reflects the depth of man's need for such reward. Man is insecure, for the validity of his life is open to question. He must be assured that his life is worth while, and he seeks this assurance from

others. The resulting search for such approval can dominate the whole of a man's life, even his religious behavior, perhaps *especially* his religious behavior, since religion claims to deal with what has ultimate significance for man. Moreover, just because this reward is so important to us, we are afraid to let it out of our control. Therefore we search for this reward within the sphere of things and men over which we have some power, and religion becomes a tool for manipulation. Against this the text insists that the disciple must dare to live for God's reward alone. However, this seems dangerous, for, as the text says, God is 'in secret,' and over him we have no control.[19]

8 On Gathering Treasures and Anxieties *(Mt 6:19–34)*

This section is composed of four groups of sayings (Mt 6:19–21, 22–23, 24, 25–34) which are also found in Luke, though spread over six chapters. In Luke the parallels to Mt 6:19–21 and 25–33 are found together, but in reverse order, Lk 12:22–31 and 33–34. It is possible, therefore, that these two paragraphs were already connected in the Q-source, probably in the order in which they are found in Luke. Matthew may have changed this order in view of verse 33, which he uses as the climax of the whole series of sayings. Mt 6:33 places the whole section in the context of the Lord's Prayer. The disciple subordinates everything to the kingdom of God. The Lucan parallels to Mt 6:22–23 and 24 are found in different contexts, widely separated, Lk 11:34–36 and 16:13. It is worth noting that none of Luke's parallels is found in his version of the Sermon (Lk 6:20–49). The only clause that has no counterpart in Luke is the closing verse Mt 6:34. Instead Luke has: 'Fear not, little flock, for it is your Father's good pleasure to give you the kingdom' (Lk 12:32). Both Mt 6:34 and Lk 12:32 were most probably detached sayings which Matthew and Luke appended to their individual treatments of care about material things.

Already in the second part of the Lord's Prayer it has become clear that the disciples, who receive the gift of the kingdom of God and are waiting for its consummation, are not exempted from the manifold needs of this age. This theme is now taken up in a composition which strings together a number of single sayings. The passage does not gloss over the threatened character of human existence. But it makes clear that men are in no position to secure their lives by their own cares (Mt 6:19–21). If they nevertheless try to do so, they will enslave themselves to their care for security to such an extent that there is no longer room in their hearts for God (Mt 6:24). The disciples should trust in God, whom they may call Father and who will take care of them (Mt 6:25–34). It has been suggested that Matthew inserted Mt 6:19–34 because of its relation to the Our Father (Mt 6:32 is clearly reminiscent of the introduction of Matthew's catechesis on prayer, Mt 6:7-8). Mt 6:19-24 would be a commentary on the first part of the Our Father, while Mt 6:25-34 develops the second part, especially the prayer for bread.

All these sayings have been brought together under the rubric: true righteousness (Mt 5:20) must be wholly directed towards God. This applies to all aspects of human life and to every question men face. The present group of sayings confronts men with a fundamentally new attitude towards personal possessions and the satisfaction of their needs. The disciples must have a light grasp on material possessions and should not become preoccupied by worries about the things which are commonly looked at as the primary necessities of life, i.e., food and clothing. There must be no attempt to make the best of two worlds (Mt 6:24). Here too, the disciples must be 'pure in heart', i.e., singleminded, wholeheartedly devoted to God and his kingdom.

On treasures (Mt 6:19-21)

Verses 19-21: Do not lay up for yourselves treasures on earth, where moth and rust consume and where thieves break in and steal. (20) but lay up for yourselves treasures in heaven, where neither moth nor rust consumes and where thieves do not break in and steal. (21) For where your treasure is, there will your heart be also.

A link-word joins this paragraph to the preceding one – in the Greek text the term translated 'consume' in verses 19-20 is the same as the one rendered 'disfigure' in Mt 6:16 (*aphanizein*). Like the two preceding sections, Mt 5:21-48 and 6:1-18, this paragraph is cast in antithetic form. The wrong way is stated in verse 19 and the right way in verse 20, while the whole is rounded off by a general statement in verse 21.

In the ancient Near East people invested in garments, grain, gold and precious stones. The present saying stresses their perishable nature. Moths destroy garments (cf. Isa 51:8; Sir 42:13), rats and mice eat grain and thieves steal gold and precious stones. 'Rust' (*brōsis*, literally 'eating') means probably any kind of corrosion or decay, or consumption by some kind of vermin or worm. The Greek *diorussein*, rendered 'break in', means literally 'dig through', and suggests digging through the mud wall of the Palestinian house or storeroom (cf. Mt 6:6). 'Treasures on earth' are always unstable. Jas 5:1-3 is a severe condemnation of the rich based on this saying: 'Come now, you rich, weep and howl for the miseries that are coming upon you. Your riches have rotted and your garments are moth-eaten. Your gold and silver have rusted, and their rust will be evidence against you and will eat your flesh like fire. You have laid up treasure for the last days.' A saying similar to Mt 6:19ff. is also found in the *Gospel of Thomas* 76: '. . . You too, seek his unfailing and enduring treasure where no moth comes near to devour and no worm destroys'.

Some scholars believe that what underlies verse 19 is the idea that the accumulation of material wealth is caused by the desire for security, the desire to eliminate all anxiety about the future (cf. Mt 6:25–34). Man tries to obtain security by all means: insurance, investments, connections with people in power. The present saying deals explicitly with security through investments and shows that they do not really give security. The same is true of all other means not explicitly mentioned. Verse 19 would show then that so far from minimizing anxiety, the possession of material wealth becomes a source of anxiety, since it is constantly subject to decay and loss. In contrast to this, verse 20 speaks of 'treasures in heaven', i.e., treasures before God, which are exempt from decay and loss.

But other exegetes say that the important phrase in verse 19 is 'for yourselves'. The saying would then be directed not so much against gathering treasures on earth, but rather against gathering them for ourselves, hoarding them for our own enjoyment, oblivious of the needs of others. It would refer to the giving away of wealth (cf. Mt 19:21). Wealth given away is tantamount to treasures wisely preserved in conditions in which they will not lose their value. When material wealth is made the aim, then tyranny, oppression, and social injustice are the result. Jesus' disciples are to set their heart on what is permanent by making proper use of their material possessions. Various social situations will determine the best way of sharing them with the poor. It should certainly never look like scaling heaven or 'laying up treasures in heaven' by making the poor into victims of selfishly motivated charity.

To 'lay up for yourselves treasures in heaven' (verse 20) does not mean setting out to make sure of a place in heaven. It means to do what we are called to by God, i.e., to use our life to achieve the one, genuine and sincere human relation to which man is destined – the covenant relationship with God who accepts us, who knows and judges us, who gives meaning to our life and leads us to our destination.

Originally, verse 21 was most probably not linked with verses 19–20, as can be seen from the fact that the former is in the second person singular and has the singular 'treasure', while the latter are in the second person plural and have the plural 'treasures'. 'Heart' here means the soul, the self, the total identity of a person. Mt 6:21 ultimately calls for 'purity in heart' or singlemindedness with regard to possessions (cf. Mt 5:8). The emphasis is on commitment which should consist in 'seeking' the kingdom of God (cf. Mt 6:33; *Gospel of Thomas* 76).

The sound eye (Mt 6:22–23)

Verses 22–23: The eye is the lamp of the body. So, if your eye is sound, your whole body will be full of light; (23) but if your eye is not sound, your whole body will be full of darkness. If then the light in you is darkness, how great is the darkness!

Like Mt 6:19–21 (and also Mt 6:24; 7:13f.), Mt 6:22–23 has a clear structure: the main clause is studied from different points of view and its consequences are considered, after which another clause brings the passage to a decisive conclusion. At first sight it is not so clear to what extent and with what intention Matthew has introduced this particular saying in its present context. The difficulty is especially caused by the fact that it is hard to draw the line between the image and the reality intended thereby.

The simile of the single eye has gone through a long history in the tradition, in the course of which its original meaning has changed. Matthew apparently understood it as an allegory, but what exactly did it mean for him? Some exegetes believe its meaning to be that the eye shows what a person is like inwardly, and that an 'evil eye' betrays ill will and meanness (cf. Mt 20:15; RSV footnote). But Mt 6:23b indicates that more is implied.

Other scholars think that, in accordance with ancient physiology, the simile is based on the idea that the eye transmits light to the whole body or leaves it in darkness. If the body does not get its light from the eye, where will it get it? (compare Mt 5:13, the salt that becomes useless). 'If your eye is single' (*haplous*, 'single' or 'simple', rather than 'sound', corresponding to the single heart of verse 21; cf. Mt 5:8), it will admit God's light to the entire person. 'But if your eye is evil (*ponēros*, 'evil' rather than 'not sound')', it will cause darkness of heart. 'Simplicity' is an ethical attitude: straightforwardness, unselfishness and generosity (cf. Rom 12:8; II Cor 8:2, 9:11, 13). By 'evil eye' Jewish usage means envy, grudge, avarice, spite (cf. Deut 15:9; I Sam 18:9; Sir 14:8–10). In the *Testament of Issachar* 4:6 it is stated that simplicity of heart can look at life rightly, whereas evil eyes' succumb to temptation and disregard the commandments (cf. Mt 5:28; Mt 6:22–23 may have influenced the composition of Mt 5:28–29a).

The image says: The untroubled, single eye gives light to the whole body, the evil eye leaves the whole body in darkness. The reality referred to is: Simplicity of heart gives light to the whole person, whereas malice of heart leaves the whole person in darkness. But we should ask further what is meant by clearness and darkness of the eye and the whole person. Considering that the simile is now found between the sayings about gathering treasures (Mt 6:19–21) and serving two masters (Mt 6:24), the saying should be understood as a warning against greediness. One's eye, i.e., one's ethical perception, should be open to God: but through greediness it becomes troubled and leads the whole person into darkness. Repentance is authentic only when it takes hold of the whole person and all aspects of one's life.

In Jesus' preaching, however, the emphasis was different: You are blind; you are able to interpret the signs of the coming weather, but not the signs of the times (cf. Lk 12:54–56). On Jesus' level, therefore, the saying was a warning not against greediness, but against inner blindness, i.e., hardness of heart. What a fearful darkness that is ('how great is the darkness', Mt 6:23). The eye, which receives the light, here signifies metaphorically the receptiveness of man for God. The healthy eye, i.e., the honest man, can take in God. When this happens, the whole man is in the light.

On serving two masters (Mt 6:24)

Verse 24: No one can serve two masters; for either he will hate the one and love the other, or he will be devoted to the one and despise the other. You cannot serve God and mammon.

Except for Luke's use of the word 'domestic servant' (*oiketēs*), this saying is identical with Lk 16:13. Similar expressions are found in Greek literature, and also in the *Gospel of Thomas* 47a: 'It is impossible for a man to mount two horses or to stretch two bows. And it is impossible for a servant to serve two masters; otherwise, he will honour the one and treat the other contemptuously . . .'.

In Matthew, the verb 'can' (*dunasthai*) repeatedly describes the actual possibility of doing something rather than a theoretical power (Mt 3:9; 7:18; 8:2, etc.). Certainly, some people think that they can serve two masters, but that is an illusion. 'Hate' and 'love' should not be understood as emotions, but, in Old Testament manner, in the sense of a decision in favour or a rebuff (cf. Gen 29:31; Deut 21:15–17). It is a characteristic Semitic antithesis meaning that he will love one more than the other. See Mt 10:37, 'He who loves father and mother more than me is not worthy of me', compared with Lk 14:26, 'If any one comes to me and does not hate his father and mother . . . he cannot be my disciple'.

'Mammon' is derived from the Aramaic word *mammôn*, which is found in the Talmud to designate not only money, but possessions or wealth in general. In the New Testament it is found four times (Mt 6:24; Lk 16:9, 11, 13). In Lk 16:9, mammon is termed 'unrighteous'. Commenting on that text, St Jerome writes: 'And he very rightly said, "money of injustice", for all riches come from injustice. Unless one person has lost, another cannot find. Therefore I believe that the popular proverb is very true: "The rich person is either an unjust person or the heir of one".'[20]

The present saying about service without compromise confirms Mt 6:22–23. People are blind and live in darkness, because their hearts are divided, because they bet on two horses, because they want to serve both God and mammon. But the service of the latter will occupy men entirely, so that they are no longer free for the service of God and fellow-men. Wealth thoroughly enslaves men. Beyond the idea of the fragility of human security (Mt 6:19ff.), it is stated here that service to earthly treasures or dependence on wealth takes away men's freedom. Moreover, they become unfit for the service of God. The service of God *and* mammon is impossible, because both demand exclusive loyalty. The only way for the disciple is undivided loyalty to God and neighbour. True service of God and mammonism, or its modern collective form, capitalism with its many faces, are mutually exclusive.

On anxiety (Mt 6:25–33, 34)

Although Mt 6:25–33 and its parallel Lk 12:22–31 already constituted a unity in Q, it is very hard to determine what was its place in this source. Matthew's present context is certainly redactional, and the same is most probably true for the Lucan combination with Lk 12:13–21.

As a whole the text should be described as a 'warning speech', but because of its prophetic (cf. Mt 6:25, 27, 29) and eschatological elements (cf. Mt 6:33), it cannot be considered as entirely belonging to wisdom literature. It may be characterized as a prophetic warning speech which makes use of elements of wisdom argumentation.

From the point of view of tradition-history Mt 6:25–33 is not usually considered an original unit. There is agreement on the secondary character of verse 27, which interrupts the coherence and hardly fits in the context. But then verse 28a must also be considered a secondary construction intended to resume the original train of thought. Verses 25–26, 28b–30, 31–33 can be considered an original unit in the tradition and an authentic speech of Jesus.

Because of its literary character (prophetic warning speech), the intention of the text is to be sought not in the instruction about God's solicitude (verses 26, 30, 32), but in the warning not to be anxious (verse 25a) or to seek the kingdom (verse 33).

Verse 33 presupposes Jesus' proclamation of the kingdom and intends to persuade the hearers to engage themselves in this proclamation by concerning themselves with the salvation of God's reign offered in Jesus' proclamation and person. This observation is of basic importance for the interpretation of Mt 6:25–33 as a whole. The real motive and actual basis for the warning 'not to be anxious about food and clothing' (cf. verse 25a) is to be found in the proclamation of God's reign. The text is not a general warning about anxiety, but about not being anxious *because the reign of God is already proclaimed and at work*. It is a serious warning to put the emphasis where it belongs. Our present existence is supported by the promise of salvation guaranteed by God. It is a life directed toward the future. Such life does not mean dullness, irresponsibility or inactivity with regard to the future, as could mistakenly be concluded from the warning not to be anxious. Concern for the kingdom demands active commitment. It is not accidental that verse 33a is actively formulated: seek . . . !

> **Verse 25:** Therefore I tell you, do not be anxious about your life, what you shall eat (or what you shall drink), nor about your body, what you shall put on. Is not life more than food, and the body more than clothing?

Matthew and Luke preserve this saying in almost the same form. Luke's longer opening 'and he said to his disciples' was undoubtedly created by the editor himself. Matthew's additional clause 'or what you shall drink' is probably an editorial change in view of Mt 6:31; it disturbs the parallelism within verse 25, but creates a new parallelism between Mt 6:25 and 6:31. It is unlikely that the juxtaposition of 'eating' and 'drinking', found fourteen times in Luke against six times in Matthew and once in Mark, would have been changed by Luke in this context. Matthew's concluding rhetorical question has a better chance of being primitive than Luke's statement with a causal conjunction ('for').

Although the addressees are not explicitly identified, the expressions 'men of little faith' in Mt 6:30 and 'your Father' in Mt 6:32, indicate that 'therefore I tell you' is addressed to the disciples (as explicitly stated by Luke). The following saying must therefore be understood in the light of the relationship existing between the disciples and Jesus.

The term 'disciples' should not be limited here to the apostles, the leaders of the Christian community, but refers to the community as a whole. To them is addressed the evenly balanced saying:

> Do not be anxious
> about your life, what you shall eat, nor
> about your body, what you shall put on.

Is not life more than food,
and the body more than clothing?

The initial prohibition 'do not be anxious' stands out and may be considered a headline which announces the main theme of the whole passage. The verb is twice repeated in Mt 6:27–28 (parallel in Lk 12:25–26) and twice added in Mt 6:31, 34. Its meaning is therefore decisive for our understanding of the whole passage.

Some scholars who believe that the saying is addressed to the apostles alone (but see above) understand 'do not be anxious' as a prohibition of all effort to obtain food and clothing, so that they would be entirely free for the proclamation of the kingdom. But in Mt 6:26–29 the birds and the lilies are not presented as an example for human behaviour ('so do not work either . . . !), but rather as witnesses to God's loving care, which inspire men not to give up working, but rather to give up all anxious concern. In view of the loving care which God shows for creatures which cannot provide for the future by work, but especially in view of God's eschatological decision to turn towards men with unrestricted forgiveness and loving care, as proclaimed in Jesus' message, men should provide for the future without anxious concern.

It is true that the verb *merimnan* can have the meaning of 'provide for', 'care for somebody or something' (cf. Lk 10:41; Phil 2:20; I Cor 12:25). But a more specific meaning of 'being anxious about' is implied in I Cor 7:32–34, '. . . The unmarried man is anxious about the affairs of the Lord, how to please the Lord; but the married man is anxious about worldly affairs, how to please his wife . . .'. Here the verb is followed by the deliberative question 'how to please . . .'. This is also true for a verse found in the context of Lk 12:22 (parallel to Mt 6:25), namely Lk 12:11 (parallel to Mt 10:19): 'And when they bring you before the synagogues and the rulers and the authorities, do not be anxious how or what you are to answer or what you are to say'. Since in Mt 6:25 and Lk 12:22 the verb *merimnan* is also followed by deliberative questions, it seems that it associates best with the texts just mentioned. This interpretation of Mt 6:25 in terms of 'anxious concern' about the necessities of life is also supported by Sir 30:24 – 31:2,

Jealousy and anger shorten life,
and *anxiety* brings on old age too soon.
A man of cheerful and good heart
will give heed to the food he eats.

Wakefulness over wealth wastes away one's flesh,
and *anxiety* about it removes sleep.

Wakeful *anxiety* prevents slumber (MT Hebrew: 'anxiety about sustenance')
and a severe illness carries off sleep.

In a context of envy and anger, and preventing sleep, *merimnan*, concerned with sustenance in particular, refers to anxious concern. Mt 6:25 (and Lk 12:22), therefore, seems to be speaking of anxious concern about the necessities of life.

The prohibition of being anxious is followed by two clauses 'about your life (*psuchē*) ..., about your body (*sōma*)' indicating what is affected by the anxiety. It has been shown that *psuchē* with its basic meaning of 'life' is often connected with food. Similarly *sōma* is sometimes associated with clothing. *Psuchē* and *sōma* should not be understood in the Greek sense of 'body and soul' which together make up a human being. They should rather be understood in the context of Semitic anthropology, where they can have a similar meaning, each by itself referring to the whole living person. Both 'life' and 'body' have here the meaning of personal life. In Jewish context the parallel question about food and clothing referred to the most fundamental necessities of life, as can be seen, e.g., from Gen 28:20, 'If God ... will give me bread to eat and clothing to wear ...'.

The prohibition 'do not be anxious about your life, what you shall eat, nor about your body, what you shall put on' is therefore concerned with the basic needs which had often to be met under very poor circumstances. This reveals the unusual character of the prohibition, which has no real counterpart in Jewish wisdom literature. What is its motivation?

The motivation is expressed in the second half of the verse: 'Is not life more than food, and the body more than clothing?' Is this to be understood in the sense that life and body are created by God, who therefore should be trusted to give what is needed for their maintenance? Although this interpretation is possible, others must be considered as well.

Looking at the context of Mt 6:25, our attention is drawn by Mt 4:1-11 which contains several parallels to Mt 6:24, 25-33. Firstly, in both pericopes the service of God is opposed to another service, that of Satan (Mt 4:10) or of mammon (Mt 6:24). Secondly, both answer the question of food in a similar way: 'Is not life more than food?' (Mt 6:25) and 'Man shall not live by bread alone, but by every word that proceeds from the mouth of God' (Mt 4:4). The second half of this statement, which is found in Matthew alone, tells us that life means keeping the word of God. Mt 4:4 is a quotation from Deut 8:3 which sums up one of the main ideas of Deuteronomy. Deut 8 contains three key-words: life, commandments of God, and sustenance. Life is based on the keeping of the Law: 'if you will obey my commandments, . . . you may gather in your grain and your wine and your oil' (Deut 11:13ff.), one of the texts written on the phylacteries in Matthew's time. The idea that if the people keep the Law, God will provide them with sustenance, was very common among the rabbis of the first two centuries A.D.

For several reasons it has been said that Mt 6:25 can be understood in line with the popular Jewish idea that life means first of all keeping God's word, and is therefore free from anxiety. Firstly, the opposition between the keeping of God's word and anxiety is found in the synoptic tradition (Mk 4:18–19; Mt 13:22; Lk 10:41f.). Secondly, in Mt 4:4 we have an interesting parallel to Mt 6:25. Thirdly, the theme that God's commandments should be kept by the disciples in a more perfect way (Mt 5:17–48) is central to the Sermon on the Mount. Moreover, the phrases 'lay up treasures in heaven' (Mt 6:20) and 'serve God' (Mt 6:24), found in the immediate context, refer to the fulfilment of God's will.

But while the Jewish tradition considers freedom from anxiety as a consequence of keeping God's word, Mt 6:25 orders the disciple to put aside all anxiety about sustenance! And the word of God to be kept is here God's word or commandment as it is finally spoken by Jesus ('but I say to you', Mt 5:22, 28, 32, 34, 39, 44; cf. Heb 1:1). The unusual form of the prohibition expresses the eschatological character of the appeal, the foundation of which is God's eschatological initiative in the person and proclamation of Jesus. The disciple should do away with all anxiety, because 'the kingdom of heaven is at hand' (Mt 4:17). 'Do not be anxious' means to do what is necessary for God's kingdom and his righteousness (cf. Mt 6:33) in complete freedom, without fear for one's own being, one's freedom, and one's self-realization. What matters is the realization of God's kingdom and his righteousness, and all the rest will be realized and has its meaning in this framework or context.

Verses 26–30: Look at the birds of the air: they neither sow nor reap nor gather into barns, and yet your heavenly Father feeds them. Are you not of more value than they? (27) And which of you by being anxious can add one cubit to his span of life? (28) And why are you anxious about clothing? Consider the lilies of the field, how they grow; they neither toil nor spin; (29) yet I tell you, even Solomon in all his glory was not arrayed like one of these. (30) But if God so clothes the grass of the field, which today is alive and tomorrow is thrown into the oven, will he not much more clothe you, O men of little faith?

These verses are considered as one unit for the following reasons: firstly, the parallel imperatives 'look at the birds of the air' (Mt 6:26) and 'consider the lilies of the field' (Mt 6:28); secondly, the parallel conclusions *a fortiori* 'are you not of more value than they?' (Mt 6:26) and 'will he not much more clothe you?' (Mt 6:30); thirdly, an impressive number of rhetorical questions, 'are you not of more value than they?' (Mt 6:26), etc. The second and third features were very popular among the rabbis of the first two centuries A.D.

But within verses 26–30 a distinction could be made between the beginning and the end, verses 26 and 30 which, with the exception of the second half of verse 28, 'consider the lilies of the field, how they grow; they neither toil nor spin', are more poetical than the rest of the paragraph, and verses 27–29.

> **Verse 26:** Look at the birds of the air: they neither sow nor reap nor gather into barns, and yet your heavenly Father feeds them. Are you not of more value than they?

The verse begins with the familiar appeal 'look at' which is often used to direct the attention of the listeners to creation or nature as a teacher for mankind: 'look to the rock' (Isa 51:1); 'look at the earth' (Isa 51:6); 'look upon all the works of the Most High' (Sir 33:15). We are invited to observe carefully, so that we will understand the hidden meaning which we usually overlook.

Here the attention of the listener is directed to 'the birds of the air', usually understood as the free-flying birds, but because of the parallelism with 'the lilies of the field' probably to be taken in the more precise sense of the birds circling the sky. The latter are often birds of prey looking for dead bodies as food, e.g., 'and your dead body shall be food for all birds of the air' (Deut 28:26; see also I Sam 17:44, 46; Jer 7:33, etc.). Should we understand the initial words of this verse as inviting the disciples to look at such birds of prey circling in the sky, whose effort is finally rewarded with a corpse? In Lk 12:24 the phrase 'the ravens' (*korakas*) seems to suggest this interpretation.

The clause 'they neither sow nor reap nor gather into barns' represents the birds as differing notably from men and their occupations. The sequence of 'seedtime and harvest' (Gen 8:22; cf. Mt 13:3–9, 18–32, 36–43) does not concern the birds. The verbs 'sow' and 'reap', indicating the beginning and the end of the process, are most probably intended to cover the whole of the effort of men required to produce their food. The clause 'nor gather into barns' is to be understood in the same line. The elaborate structures of care in which men are involved are absent, and yet the birds' life goes on.

'And yet your heavenly Father feeds them' recalls one of the most common beliefs already found in the first page of the Bible: 'And to every beast of the earth, and to every bird of the air . . . I have given every green plant for food' (Gen 1:30). The same idea is frequently found in Judaism, e.g., 'For if I hunger, unto You will I cry, O God; and You will give to me. Birds and fish do You nourish' (*Ps. Sal.* 5:10ff.; the *Psalms of Solomon* originated from the middle of the first century B.C.).

The argument is clinched by an *a fortiori* conclusion in the form of a rhetorical question: 'Are you not of more value than they?' This conclusion is similar to those found in Jewish sources, e.g., 'if it is like that for an animal, how much less will God keep his gifts (food) from men' (*Mekilta to Exodus* 12:1). The latter text shows that God's care for the animal world is emphasized in order to establish confidence in God's providence for men themselves. Both the Old Testament and Judaism often confirm that God feeds his people, and the idea also penetrated the daily life of the early Christians, as can be seen from the 'blessing' before and the grace after the meal (cf. Mk 6:41; 14:22).

In our present verse the idea is expressed in a conclusion *a fortiori*: 'if God – as is known – feeds the birds of the air which do not produce any food, how much more will he sustain men and especially the disciples'. Mt 6:26 therefore, is a further motivation to the prohibition 'do not be anxious'.

Verses 27–28a: And which of you by being anxious can add one cubit to his span of life? (28a) And why are you anxious about clothing?

The saying about the 'span of life' has been inserted into the present context on account of the common verb 'to be anxious'. The idea of the uselessness of anxious concern is also found in a text already quoted: 'Jealousy and anger shorten life, and anxiety brings on old age too soon' (Sir 30:24). And elsewhere we read: 'For man and his portion lie before You in the balance; he cannot add to it so as to enlarge what has been prescribed by You' (*Ps. Sal.* 5:6). But while the latter saying expresses the general powerlessness of man, Mt 6:27 limits itself to the powerlessness of anxiety. Indeed, by means of a rhetorical question, the verse stresses the uselessness of anxiety. 'By being anxious' men cannot add a single hour to their lives, though, as we understand in a time in which 'stress' is a common phenomenon, they may very well shorten them. But uselessness or health reasons are not the final grounds on which Jesus condemns anxiety. He does so rather because it is a mark of lack of faith and confidence in God's providence.

It has been extensively discussed whether we should understand the verse as speaking of a 'cubit' added to one's period of life, or of a 'cubit' added to one's physical stature.

The first meaning of *hēlikia* is 'time of life', 'age', as, e.g., in Jn 9:21–23, '. . . Ask him; he is of age, he will speak for himself . . .', and Heb 11:11, 'By faith Sarah herself received power to conceive, even when she was past the age . . .'. *Pēchus*, 'cubit', 'ell', 'yard', can also have the metaphorical meaning of 'any small amount'. Thus RSV's translation 'add one cubit to his span of life' is possible and makes perfect sense. Man's 'span of life' was also a matter of concern for the people of biblical times, and popular Jewish eschatology dreamed of old age: 'for the child shall die a hundred years old' (Isa 65:20). Some rabbinic texts even give the impression that old age was considered within the reach of human efforts, especially by living a virtuous life (cf. *Meg.* 27b 28a). Against this background Mt 6:27 would mean that an extension of life, which was strongly desired and perhaps also thought to be within the reach of human efforts, cannot in any way be realized by anxious concern about it.

But *hēlikia* can also mean 'stature', 'physical size', as, e.g., in Lk 19:3, '. . . because he was small of stature', and Eph 4:13, '. . . to the measure of the stature of the fullness of Christ'. *Pēchus* would then be used in its literal meaning of 'cubit', or 'ell', a common measure to determine the height of a man (cf. I Sam 17:4). Thus the translation 'which of you by being anxious can add one cubit to his stature?' is also quite possible. It should not be said too quickly that this translation does not make sense. In contemporary Judaism it was believed that after his sin Adam lost not only his length of life but also his stature, and it was expected that in the messianic age man would have twice the height of Adam. Against such a background, Mt 6:27, understood in terms of adding a cubit to one's stature, makes good sense. The fact that 6:28b speaks of *growing* lilies may add force to this interpretation.

Compared to Lk 12:26, Mt 6:28a, 'and why are you anxious about clothing?' seems to be secondary. After the insertion of Mt 6:27, Matthew wants to get back as soon as possible to the main topic, that of anxiety about food and clothing. The word *enduma*, 'clothing', which occurs seven times in Matthew, but never in Mark and only once in Luke, may be attributed to the Matthean redaction.

Verses 28b–29: Consider the lilies of the field, how they grow; they neither toil nor spin; (29) yet I tell you, even Solomon in all his glory was not arrayed like one of these.

Matthew's longer phrase 'the lilies of the field' (compare Lk 12:27, 'the lilies') is probably intended to harmonize with 'the birds of the air' in Mt 6:26 and 'the grass of the field' in Mt 6:30.

It is not clear whether by 'the lilies of the field' are meant white lilies, purple anemones, the swordlilies of the iris family whose colour ranges from pinkish purple to violet-purple, or in general all the flowers that enliven the Galilean fields. The phrase 'how they grow' does not only mean 'how they grow up', but also 'how they grow rich', 'how they flourish'.

But why is Solomon compared to these flowers? It is possible that the comparison was inspired by the alliteration between the name Solomon and the Hebrew word for lilies. But it is also interesting to note that the Hebrew word for lilies, or its Greek equivalent *krinon*, occurs almost exclusively in a Solomonic context: four times in connection with the decoration of Solomon's Temple (cf. I Kgs 7:19, 22, 26; II Chron 4:5) and eight times in 'The Song of Songs, which is Solomon's' (Song 1:1). Solomon was believed to be the author of the Song who had described the lover as he who 'pastures his flock among the lilies' (Song 2:16; 6:2, 3), and the beloved as 'I am a rose of Sharon, a lily of the valleys. As a lily among the brambles ...' (Song 2:1, 2; compare 4:5; 7:2f.). It is possible that this association of Solomon with 'the lilies' was perceived in the gospel tradition.

The lilies grow, but 'they neither toil nor spin'. In this context the verb 'spinning' stands for the whole process necessary for preparing clothing. The laborious character of this process is expressed by the verb 'toil'. Together, 'toil' and 'spin' form a hendiadys.

But the word 'toiling' obtained a special meaning in wisdom literature, as can be seen from its frequent use in Ecclesiastes, which begins as follows: 'The words of the Preacher (Qoheleth), the son of David, king of Jerusalem (= Solomon!). Vanity of vanities, says the Preacher, vanity of vanities. All is vanity. What does a man gain by all the *toil* at which he *toils* under the sun?' (Eccl 1:1–3; cf. also 3:9; 5:15; the verb 'to toil' is used thirteen times). It may be said, therefore, that the association of Solomon and 'toiling' has its background in the Old Testament wisdom tradition. Solomon is characterized as a toiler (Eccl 2:4–10), but also as a man who has come to understand that it was all in vain (Eccl 2:11). The same critical attitude toward 'toiling' is also found in other parts of wisdom literature (e.g., Sir 11:10ff.; 31:3f.), sometimes again in a Solomonic context (Prov 23:4f.; Ps 127[126]:1). Against this background, the clause 'they neither toil nor spin' should not be understood merely as describing the lilies as distinct from Solomon and men in general – as it was the case with the clause 'they neither sow nor reap' in Mt 6:26 – but as also expressing (Solomon's self-)criticism: toiling is useless. Therefore, as far as *content* is concerned, the saying links up better with that about the powerlessness of anxiety (Mt 6:27) than with that about the birds of the air (Mt 6:26). In the wider context of Mt 6:25–33, the saying criticizes anxious concern in so far as it consists of strenuous toiling, but not every effort to assure the necessities of life.

The phrase 'yet I tell you' emphasizes the following statement that 'even Solomon in all his glory was not arrayed like one of these' (Mt 6:29). God promised to Solomon: 'I give you also what you have not asked, both riches and honour (*doxa* = glory)' (I Kgs 3:13). *Doxa*, 'glory', can also indicate royal garments: 'On the third day . . . Esther put on her royal robes and arrayed herself with her glory' (Est 5:1LXX, which has *doxa* and the aorist middle form *periebaleto*, 'arrayed', in common with Mt 6:29). In light of the latter text, it may be preferable to translate Mt 6:29 'yet I tell you, even Solomon in all his glory did not dress like one of these', emphasizing his toiling. In view of the attempts of some circles to identify Solomon with the 'King of glory' of Ps 24(23):7–10, exemplified by *Midrash Ps* 24:7 in which Solomon identifies himself with the King of glory, for which Solomon was criticized by some rabbis, we may submit that this same criticism is also at work in the New Testament, in which Solomon is mentioned only three times, always to his disadvantage (Mt 6:29; 12:42 and parallel; Acts 7:47ff.).

> **Verse 30:** But if God so clothes the grass of the field, which today is alive and tomorrow is thrown into the oven, will he not much more clothe you, O men of little faith?

Matthew's phrase 'the grass (plants) *of the field*' is a traditional Semitic one, meaning the wild plants (in Luke, 'in the field' is opposed to 'into the oven'). The phrase is often used as a symbol of man's mortality: 'All flesh is grass, and all its beauty is like the flower of the field' (Isa 40:6; cf. Isa 37:27; 51:12), quoted in I Pet 1:24 as 'All flesh is like grass and all its glory like the flower of grass'. This is also found in the Psalms (Pss 37[36]:2; 102[101]:4, 11; 103[102]:15; 129[128]:6) and in Jas 1:9–11, '. . . because like the flower of the grass he (the rich) will pass away'. The same is also suggested by the use of the pair of words 'today' and 'tomorrow', in the sense of 'now' and 'in a very short time' (cf. Jos 22:18; Isa 22:13 quoted in I Cor 15:32), which are sometimes applied to the transitory character of human life (I Macc 2:63; Jas 4:13f.). This picture is completed by the use of the phrase 'oven', which is often used as a symbol of quick destruction of human life (Hos 7:7; Mal 4:1[3:19]; Isa 31:9). Strictly speaking, the first two lines of Mt 6:30 describe only the fate of the grass, but the vocabulary used was familiar to the early Christians and suggested to them the shortness and sudden end of human life.

But the clause 'will he not much more clothe you?' gives a new direction to the train of thought: the moral of the comparison is not 'these things pass, and so must we', but 'if God shows so much loving concern for the flowers, brief though their span of life is, how much more will he care for you?' This leads us back to the idea of God's providence for the least of his creatures, as expressed in Mt 6:26. Though less widespread than the thought that God feeds the animals and man, the idea that God clothes nature as well as man is found several times (Gen 3:21; Deut 29:5). The most interesting parallel is Ez 16:7ff.: 'Live, and grow up like a plant of the field. . . . I clothed you also with embroidered cloth and shod you with leather, I swathed you in fine linen and covered you with silk.'

The characterization 'O men of little faith' has its background in rabbinic literature where it is always used for members of the Jewish community itself, and thus refers to the lack of faith of the faithful themselves, often in a context of food. For example, Rabbi Eliezer ben Hyrcanus (about A.D. 100) said: 'Whoever has a piece of bread in his basket and says, "what shall I eat tomorrow?" belongs only to them who are little in faith'.

In the gospel tradition too, the phrase 'men of little faith' is used only for members of the community, the disciples who are found lacking in faith; and sometimes also in a context of food: 'And they discussed it among themselves, saying, "We brought no bread." But Jesus, aware of this, said, "O men of little faith, why do you discuss among yourselves the fact that you have no bread?" ' (Mt 16:7f.).

In view of the previous two paragraphs, 'O men of little faith' can be understood as the concluding phrase of the whole passage Mt 6:25–30, which began with the anxious question as to what they were to eat. In fact, the present imperative 'do not be anxious' suggests that the disciples are anxious and should no longer be so: 'cease to be anxious'. Mt 6:25–30, then, is addressed to the Christian community in a situation of anxiety and lack of faith.

Summing up, we may say that we have in Mt 6:25–30 not a uniform teaching, but a juxtaposition of divergent outlooks on life arranged in chiastic order. The first and the last sayings (Mt 6:26 and 30) tell the worried listeners to have confidence in God's loving care and goodness for man. But between these utterances we find three verses (Mt 6:27–29) criticizing the uselessness of anxious concern and toil. Both outlooks present their arguments and contribute to the issue 'do not be anxious'. But whatever the differences of origin and outlook of these passages may be, they are now brought together and subordinated to the eschatological outlook of the whole.

Verses 31–33: Therefore do not be anxious, saying, 'What shall we eat?' or 'What shall we drink?' or 'What shall we wear?' (32) For the Gentiles seek all these things; and your heavenly Father knows that you need them all. (33) But seek first his kingdom and his righteousness, and all these things shall be yours as well.

In these verses Matthew and Luke differ considerably. A good number of scholars think that while Matthew has preserved almost intact the traditional form of the first part of the pericope (Mt 6:25–30; Lk 12:22–28), Luke is closer to the traditional version of the last verses (Lk 12:29–31; Mt 6:31–33).

Matthew seems to have made many changes in the last three verses of the pericope. Verse 31 has been almost entirely rewritten. The phrase 'therefore do not (*mē oun*)' assures a smoother transition. Mt 6:29–31 is more closely connected with the preceding context by the imperative, 'do not be anxious' (not found in Lk 12:29). The verb 'to be anxious' – added once more together with the whole of verse 34 – now dominates the whole pericope. Matthew may have avoided 'do not seek (demand) what you are to eat' (cf. Lk 12:29), because he felt that it contradicted Mt 6:11, 'Give us this day our daily bread'. The prohibition 'nor be of anxious mind' (= do not be overdemanding) is replaced by a third deliberative question: 'What shall we wear?' This change harmonizes the verse with the preceding context, more precisely with 'what you shall put on' (Mt 6:25) and 'Why are you anxious about clothing?' (Mt 6:28). The same idea may be found in Mt 6:19: 'Do not lay up for yourselves treasures (riches which often consisted in garments) on earth, where moth and rust consume . . .'. Although verse 31 is an almost perfect parallel to the first half of verse 25, it is not a mere repetition. With its aorist *merimnēsēte* ('do not be anxious'), verse 31 has the force of a categorical prohibition, and the transition to direct speech, 'What shall we eat . . .', lends more vivacity to the text.

The series of questions mentioned in verse 31 is summed up in verses 32–33 by the thrice-repeated phrase 'all these'. In verse 32a, the phrase 'Gentiles' is not directed against the heathens, but is rather a cliché applied to certain types of behaviour in order to criticize such behaviour. 'The Gentiles seek all these things', then, should be understood as a denunciation of a certain way of life in the contemporary situation (cf. Mt 5:47; 6:7).

Verse 32b too seems to be concerned with the present life: 'and your heavenly Father knows that you need them all'. This sentence gives a foundation to the prohibition not to be anxious: 'for' (*gar*, not translated by RSV, JB, NAB). The loving knowledge of the Father is opposed to the anxious questions of the disciples (in the Greek text, the verb 'knows' is placed at the beginning of the sentence). God's knowledge is not just a theoretical knowledge, but expresses the whole of God's loving care for the disciples, which in the context of the

Sermon on the Mount is the present care of the Father (cf. Mt 5:45; 7:11). But most interesting is the parallelism between Mt 6:31–34 and 6:7–11:

Mt 6:7–11	*Mt 6:31–34*
And in praying do not heap up empty phrases	Therefore do not be anxious, saying, 'What shall we eat?' or 'What shall we drink?' or 'What shall we wear?'
as *the Gentiles* do; for they think that they will be heard for their many words. Do not be like them, *for your Father knows* what *you need* before you ask him. *Pray* then like this: Our Father . . . *Thy kingdom* come, *Thy will* be done on earth as it is in heaven. *Give us* . . . our daily bread	For *the Gentiles* seek all these things;
	(*for*) *your* heavenly *Father knows* that *you need* them all.
	But *seek*
	first *his kingdom* and *his righteousness*;
	and all these things shall be yours (= *shall be given* to you) as well. Therefore do not be anxious about
this day.	*tomorrow.*

Matthew, who is responsible for the composition of Mt 6:7–15 out of previously scattered material, is also responsible for its insertion into Mt 6:1–18, and the parallelism between Mt 6:7–11 and Mt 6:31–34 has probably also been created by Matthew himself. The parallelism suggests that Matthew understood the verb 'to seek' in verses 31–33 in the sense of praying, asking or demanding, as he does again in the saying '*Ask*, and it will be given you; *seek*, and you will find' (Mt 7:7). Both Mt 6:9 and 6:33 encourage the disciples to ask (first) for the kingdom of the Father, and for his 'will' or 'his righteousness'. Then both texts speak of daily sustenance. Matthew is certainly thinking here of the present, as can be seen from the additional verse 34.

But how can this interpretation be reconciled with the eschatological character of verse 33: 'seek first his kingdom and his righteousness'? Here we should pay close attention to two editorial changes introduced by Matthew.

Firstly, we should note that by means of the insertion of the adverb 'first' Matthew changes the exclusive character of the demand (cf. Lk 12:31) into a question of priority: 'seek first the kingdom of God before all these things'. Such an alteration occurs more often in Matthew and has been considered especially characteristic for Mt 5 – 7, 18 – 19: radical demands are adjusted in an attempt to give them significance for daily life.

Secondly, the object of the exhortation is: his kingdom *and his righteousness*, 'his' in both cases referring to 'your Father' in verse 32b. The noun 'righteousness', found in Matthew seven times, five of them in the Sermon on the Mount, indicates the uprightness of man before God, the whole of true conduct of life according to God's will. It has this meaning in Mt 5:20 and 6:1 and, notwithstanding the fact that here in Mt 6:33 '*his* righteousness', i.e., the Father's righteousness, is mentioned, it has still the same meaning of uprightness of human life, but with special reference to the Father as the norm of this righteousness. God's will is decisive for the righteousness of the disciples (compare Mt 6:10 and Mt 6:33 in the above parallelism!).

As to the relation of the righteousness of the Christian life and the coming kingdom of God, 'righteousness' and 'kingdom' should not be considered as condition and consequence respectively. The 'righteousness' in Mt 6:33 is not a condition but rather a first fulfilment of the eschatological kingdom of the Father.

But what about the relation between the still expected kingdom of the Father and the already present messianic righteousness in the life of the Christian community? We should say that just as in the Lord's Prayer Mt 6:10b ('on earth . . .') should be interpreted as an application of Mt 6:10a ('thy kingdom come . . .'), expressing how the expected kingdom of the Father should already be realized 'on earth', here and now, so Matthew's addition of 'righteousness' to 'kingdom' applies the meaning of that future kingdom to the present life of the Christian community. Mt 6:33a could, therefore, be paraphrased as follows: 'But seek first his kingdom, that is to say here and now his righteousness'. This righteousness, which should 'exceed that of the scribes and the Pharisees' (Mt 5:20), should be the realization of God's will in an upright life according to Jesus' final interpretation of that will, a life according to 'every word that proceeds from the mouth of God' (Mt 4:4) i.e., God's *final* word in Jesus. And so, notwithstanding Matthew's attention to the present situation of the Christian community, the radical demands not to be anxious about food, drink and clothing, retain an eschatological and revelatory character. With Jesus the final revelation of God's word and will has taken place. The radical demands of Mt 6:25–33 reveal that the critical moment has arrived for a decision for or against a life according to the words of Jesus. However, to seek first God's kingdom does not cut the disciples off from the world, but transforms and inspires their life, and gives it a particular Christian style. In practical terms, one seeks the kingdom of God by practising righteousness in everyday life (see Mt 25:31–46).

> **Verse 34:** Therefore do not be anxious about tomorrow, for tomorrow will be anxious for itself. Let the day's own trouble be sufficient for the day.

This verse has no parallel in Luke. It may have been originally spoken in a different context or may even have been composed by Matthew himself, although in the latter case we would expect a closer agreement with the previous verses. It is indeed the case that though 'do not be anxious' forms a link with the preceding verses, the thought is different, and the attempt to square Mt 6:34 with the trust in the fatherly providence of God expressed in Mt 6:25–33 has repeatedly been regarded as wasted labour.

The Greek word translated by RSV 'trouble' means 'evil' (*kakia*), i.e., material evil or calamities, a sense which the word never has elsewhere in the New Testament. Elsewhere it always means 'moral evil' (cf. Acts 8:22).

We may have here a traditional proverb comparable to 'Do not boast about tomorrow, for you do not know what a day may bring forth' (Prov 27:1). We could also refer to Jas 4:13f.: 'Come now, you who say, "Today or tomorrow we will go into such and such a town and spend a year there and trade and get gain"; whereas you do not know about tomorrow. What is your life? For you are a mist that appears for a little and then vanishes.' As far as Matthew's composition is concerned, we are not dealing here just with a practical wisdom saying: it is trusting faith in the Father and the seeking of his kingdom that free men from anxiety about tomorrow. In the life of the true disciple there is no room for anxious concern for tomorrow, 'for tomorrow will be anxious (= will take care) for itself'. Fear for tomorrow makes people slaves of mammon (cf. Mt 6:24). Can one live without anxiety for the next day when today one has little to eat or is unemployed? This statement does not claim that poverty and misery are good and does not offer cheap consolation. But it does intend to eliminate the reign of the fear and discouragement which make people incapable of solidarity.

> How 'Franciscan' this whole passage is! . . . The sheer simplicity of this faith challenges and perplexes us. 'Into our modern world,' says Johannes Weiss, 'with its hurry and its striving, with its desperate struggle for existence, this song about freedom from care comes ringing like a strain from the lost Paradise.' We cannot

help asking: what has it to say to us who are daily engrossed in the fight to make ends meet, or must we regretfully dismiss it as another Utopian precept? Before we do that, let us note one or two things. To begin with, life in the Galilee of Jesus' day was no economic idyll. . . . Next, common sense should tell us that Jesus is not here bidding his disciples quit work and wait for God to put bread in their mouths and clothes on their backs. . . . Thirdly, what Jesus condemns here is not a wise forethought for the future but nervous anxiety about it. Did he not elsewhere bid men reckon and count the cost? . . . But the main point to remember is that here, as often, he is putting his truth in an extreme, almost one-sided, way. What he is stating is a principle of living. And the principle is surely this, that, taking reasonable care, we are to face life trustingly, accepting each day fresh from God, and leaving the unknown future in his hands. Who will say that we do not need this teaching? We who take out insurance policies to cover almost every contingency – we who are so concerned about getting a livelihood that we have forgotten the art of living – do need to be told to trust God more. True, every now and then history throws up men who really live as Jesus advises. Francis of Assisi was one. . . . The rest of us need the challenge of this Franciscan Christianity – need to be told to put our faith in God and go forward trustingly.[21]

9 On Judging Others and the Joy of Prayer *(Mt 7:1–12)*

This section groups together a number of sayings without much logical or real relationship. Some scholars have suggested that the connecting theme is that the disciple must act as one who hopes to receive mercy himself, or that the disciple also faces the coming judgment. But any attempt at discerning a principle of arrangement which may have guided the redactor here involves a number of subjective elements. We may probably say that Mt 7:1–12 consists of four paragraphs (Mt 7:1–5, 6, 7–11, 12) which deal with injunctions on various themes, but one does not seem to lead to the other, or to require the paragraph which follows for its own completion. Except for Mt 7:6, these paragraphs have parallels in Luke, but spread over several chapters (Lk 6:37–38, 41–42; 11:9–13; 6:31).

On judging *(Mt 7:1–5)*

Verses 1–5 form a unity. First comes a general statement or recommendation (Mt 7:1); then an explanation in two parallel members which contain a theological and eschatological justification (Mt 7:2); and finally the counsel is illustrated by the example of the speck and the log (Mt 7:3–5). The present place of these verses in the Sermon on the Mount seems to be the original one. Its ideas agree well with the whole Sermon, especially with Mt 5:21–48 dealing with greater righteousness, and with Mt 6:1–18 which stigmatizes hypocrisy. Moreover, the Lucan parallel is found in the Sermon on the Plain (cf. Lk 6:37–42).

> **Verses 1–2:** Judge not, that you be not judged. (2) For with the judgment you pronounce you will be judged, and the measure you give will be the measure you get.

Comparison with the parallel Lucan passage, Lk 6:37–38(39–40) often leads to the conclusion that Matthew has considerably abbreviated his source and has thereby changed the meaning of the saying. In

Mt 7:1–2 Matthew would have omitted almost two-thirds of the corresponding material in Luke (Lk 6:37–38) and entirely omitted two Lucan verses (Lk 6:39–40). But is this so certain? It is indeed possible that the 'extra' in Luke is more original, but, on the other hand, that 'extra' expresses typically Lucan concerns. It would seem better, therefore, not to be too definite on this point.

Mt 7:1–2	*Lk 6:37–40*
(1) Judge not, that you be not judged. (2) For with the judgment you pronounce you will be judged,	(37) Judge not, and you will not be judged; condemn not, and you will not be condemned; forgive, and you will be forgiven; (38) give, and it will be given to you; good measure, pressed down, shaken together, running over, will be put into your lap.
and the measure you give will be the measure you get.	For the measure you give will be the measure you get back. (39) He also told them a parable: 'Can a blind man lead a blind man? Will they not both fall into a pit? (40) A disciple is not above his teacher, but every one when he is fully taught will be like his teacher.
(3) Why do you see the speck	(41) Why do you see the speck. . . .

The 'omissions' in Mt 7:2 result in joining the saying 'and the measure you give will be the measure you get' to the initial injunction, 'judge not', thus determining the sense in which this injunction is to be understood. This effect is reinforced by adding a similar clause which may well be of Matthew's making: 'for with the judgment you pronounce you will be judged', thus easing the transition from the thought of judgment (Mt 7:1) to the metaphor of the measure (Mt 7:2b). The latter accords better with the clause 'give, and it will be given to you', with which it is combined in Lk 6:38. On may wonder whether Matthew's arrangement has not watered down the impact of Mt 7:1, which demands not that we judge others generously but that we do not act as judges at all. Unlike the sectarians of Qumran, who are to judge the sons of darkness carefully and punish them accordingly, the disciple is not to judge, whether severely or generously, but to forgive (cf. Lk 6:37). In Mt 18:15 it is spelt out how an absolute prohibition is to work in the practical life of the Church (cf. also Mt 7:6).

Men like to see themselves in the role of judges, but thereby place themselves above their brothers. This does not suit them well because, when it comes to debt, all men are in the same situation before God. One should avoid judging, i.e., one should not attempt to deprive God of the authority of (final) judgment. The passive form of the verb, 'that you may not be judged', is a thinly veiled allusion to divine judgment. However, the ultimate foundation and action principle is not judgment, which appears here as a consequence of our judging, but rather the eschatological proclamation of salvation which makes this demand possible (cf. Mt 18:35 for the demand of forgiveness).

Mt 7:1f. forbids anything that condemns a brother or casts suspicion on him, and expects that he will be treated by the standard of mercy. The statement is founded on the sentence about the right measure (Mt 7:2b), which appears also in Mk 4:24, and therefore probably at one time existed independently and was used in various contexts. Mk 4:24 applies it to the new knowledge that is continually given to anyone who listens to Jesus' words; Lk 6:38 speaks of the reward for generosity; and Mt 7:2 applies it to the judgment by which anyone who judges will be judged. As elsewhere (cf. Mt 5:7; 6:14f.; 25:31ff.), Jesus makes use of the Jewish doctrine of the two measures of mercy and judgment, but he completely transforms it. If we judge and condemn others, we exclude ourselves from God's mercy offered to us in Jesus' eschatological proclamation, and we place ourselves again under the Law which will condemn us. The parable of the unforgiving servant (Mt 18:23–35) is an adequate illustration of this text.

Jesus asks us not to judge and thereby rejects all ready-made judgments. But he asks more: to understand others. This is well illustrated in the pericope of Jesus and the adulterous woman (Jn 8:3–11) which ends with the words, 'Neither do I condemn you' (Jn 8:11b). Although in a somewhat different context, the next paragraph of the Fourth Gospel relates another statement of Jesus concerning judging: 'You judge according to the flesh (= with human judgments, in a human way), I judge no one' (Jn 8:15). From this and other statements it appears that judging other people is something typically human. God is not eager to judge (Jn 3:17; 5:22). People, on the other hand, seem to like to judge others. 'Judge not' refers to the sphere of the divine. And people who take Jesus' demand seriously make the divine visible in this world. They are anything but moralists. They do not address the demand 'judge not' to others but practise it themselves.

Especially in the area of religion people often judge and condemn one another. There is no lack of examples of accusations and court cases, not so much before a non-Christian judge (cf. I Cor 6:1–6) as *within one's own Church*. But it may be doubted whether the whole approach is by that fact itself more just and compassionate.

> **Verses 3–5:** Why do you see the speck that is in your brother's eye, but do not notice the log that is in your own eye? (4) Or how can you say to your brother, 'Let me take the speck out of your eye,' when there is the log in your own eye? (5) You hypocrite, first take the log out of your own eye, and then you will see clearly to take the speck out of your brother's eye.

The metaphor of the speck and the log is another concrete illustration of the recommendation 'judge not', and by the omission of the sayings found in Lk 6:39–40, Matthew brings this metaphor into closer relation with it. The statement is also found in Lk 6:41f., and in the *Gospel of Thomas* 26, 'Jesus said, "You see the mote in your brother's eye, but you do not see the beam in your own eye. When you cast the beam out of your own eye, then you will see clearly to cast the mote from your brother's eye".' The metaphor was originally addressed to the Pharisees (the word 'hypocrite' is never applied elsewhere to the disciples), but is transformed by Matthew into a parable for the disciples.

Verse 4 adds no new information, but nevertheless adds to the force of the words by repetition with a subtle change. Matthew's phrase 'Look! The log in your eye!' (not so well rendered by RSV) represents the moment in which the 'brother' discovers the log, or the moment of the hearer's embarrassing discovery of what every one can see but him. In fact, the contrast between the speck and the log is repeated three times (Mt 7:3, 4, 5), and thus the hearer is not allowed to lose sight of this extreme contrast for a moment.

The role of judge is not only unsuitable for men, but also puts them in imminent danger of becoming blind. They become hypocrites. These verses expose the behaviour of all who give themselves airs about improving their fellow-men. They make clear that such people, however astutely they may observe their fellow-men, are blind and biased as far as they themselves are concerned. They act superiorly towards their brothers and are thus prevented from considering themselves realistically. The spirit of judging others makes us blind to our own situation.

Verse 5 introduces two new ideas. 'First take the log out of your own eye.' Nothing in verses 1–4 permitted us to suppose that one could deliver oneself from one's 'log'. Secondly, it seems that after serious self-criticism one would be allowed to criticize and judge others. This appears to contradict the preceding verses and especially Mt 7:1a, 'judge not'. Two solutions are suggested. First, we could consider it as an inadequate continuation of verses 1–4, more or less in the spirit of Luke's text where the preceding verses (Lk 6:39–40) seem to suggest an interpretation of this saying in terms of a warning against the blindness of a would-be guide, rather than as an injunction to a disciple to practise self-criticism. But we could also propose an ironical interpretation of the text, which would make it homogeneous with the whole pericope: since you will never be able to get entirely rid of your 'log', never attempt to remove the 'speck' in your brother's eye. Removing the 'log' from your own eye will take a lifetime!

On profaning the holy (Mt 7:6)

Verse 6: Do not give dogs what is holy; and do not throw your pearls before swine, lest they trample them under foot and turn to attack you.

First a note on the text of this verse. 'Holy' is an adequate translation of the Greek word *hagion*, but it has been suggested that the latter is a mistranslation of an Aramaic word meaning a 'ring' (of gold). This would give a perfect parallelism: 'Do not give *rings* to dogs; and do not throw your *pearls* before swine'. It has then further been suggested that the saying should read: 'Do not give earrings to dogs or pearl necklaces to pigs'. Thus formulated the saying reminds us of Prov 11:22, 'Like a gold ring in a swine's snout is a beautiful woman without discretion'. As a whole Mt 7:6 constitutes a perfect example of a chiasmus or inverted symmetrical construction: 'Do not give to *dogs* . . . do not throw . . . before *swine*; lest they (i.e., the swine) trample them under-foot, and (the dogs) turn to attack you'. The saying is also found in the *Gospel of Thomas* 93: 'Do not give what is holy to dogs, lest they throw them on the dung-heap. Do not throw the pearls to swine, lest they grind it [to bits]'.

Nothing similar is found in Luke. It is possible that he did not appreciate the thought expressed in these images and that thinking of his Gentile readers he left it out. But we must also reckon with the possibility that Matthew introduced the saying here in order to correct the absolute character of the prohibition 'judge not'. This care for nuances, this way of correcting a statement by a complementary sentence is very characteristic of Matthew. But it cannot be denied that it is rather difficult to situate this verse in the context of the Sermon on the Mount.

In the Old Testament and in rabbinic literature dogs were considered to be among the wild beasts (cf. Ex 22:31), and pigs to be unclean (cf. Lev 11:7). In Henoch 89:42 the enemies of Israel are depicted as dogs (= Philistines), foxes, and wild boars (= Edomites). The Gentiles were called 'dogs' and 'swine', not as being non-Jews, but as being enemies of Israel and Israel's God. We may also point to Mt 15:22ff., the healing of the daughter of the Canaanite woman, where Jesus himself is quoted as saying: 'It is not fair to take the children's bread and throw it to the dogs' (Mt 15:26), undoubtedly using here a term blunted by repeated use. Later on, 'dog' refers to the enemies of the Christian community, e.g., Phil 3:2, 'Look out for the dogs, look out for the evil-workers, look out for those who mutilate the flesh'. The term may even refer to unfaithful Christians as in II Pet 2:22, 'It has happened to them according to the true proverb, The dog turns back to his own vomit, and the sow is washed only to wallow in the mire'. This is a reminiscence of Prov 26:11, 'Like a dog that returns to its vomit is a fool that repeats his folly'. All these sayings sound much harsher to us than they did in their original setting, where the use of popular proverbs of this kind was commonplace.

As to Matthew's understanding of this motif, which is also found in apocalyptic and in the Dead Sea Scrolls, three possibilities have chiefly been proposed. Firstly, it has been suggested that we have here a bit of cautionary *gemara*,[22] a passage which insists on discriminatory caution following on the prohibition of judging in Mt 7:1-5. Certainly one should not judge, but one should not act without discernment either, handing over the gospel to the misunderstanding and hostility of irresponsible people. In Matthew, this statement is probably speaking not of Gentiles as such but of outsiders of any kind. Originally most probably shaped by a Jewish-Christian community and intended as an attack on the Gentile mission, it was no longer understood in this way by Matthew (cf. Mt 28:19), as can be seen from the context in which he put it.

Secondly, some scholars have held this verse to be an 'ecclesiastical' addition directed against Gentiles, which would explain why Luke would have omitted it, if he knew it.

Thirdly, a few scholars understand the statement as merely ironical. But this is rather unlikely because of the deliberate character of the verse.

Fourthly, some have understood the statement in close relationship to the theme of judging (cf. Mt 7:1-5; I Cor 6:1-6). A community in which people bring each other before non-Christian judges gives up something precious and holy, namely their mutual brotherhood, by throwing it before people who do not understand or appreciate it.

The reference to violence in the last part of the verse has sometimes been understood quite literally and taken to be an allusion to persecution. However, the verbs 'trample' and 'attack' should not be taken too literally. They illustrate two ways of refusing the truth. Prov 9:7 says in a more or less parallel context: 'He who corrects a scoffer gets himself abuse, and he who reproves a wicked man incurs injury'.

Taking all the previous considerations into account, it seems best to understand the verse in its present context as a directive for the missionary work of the disciples. As such it can be related to Jesus' command in the Mission Discourse, 'And if any one will not receive you or listen to your words, shake off the dust from your feet as you leave that house or town' (Mt 10:14). If we take into account the parable of the pearl (Mt 13:45f., which has the words 'pearl' and 'to seek' in common with Mt 7:6, 7), the phrases 'what is holy' and 'pearls' seem to refer to the message of the kingdom. Mt 7:6 is then a warning against irresponsible proclamation of the gospel to people who do not show any readiness to receive it. The proclamation of the gospel requires tact and empathy. It will certainly meet with persecution, but this should not be brought about by our own lack of judgment or inability to assess the situation. We have neither the right nor the power to force the gospel on anyone.

> Every attempt to impose the gospel by force, to run after people and proselytize them, to use our own resources to arrange the salvation of other people, is both futile and dangerous. . . . Our easy trafficking with the word of cheap grace simply bores the world to disgust, so that in the end it turns against those who try to force on it what it does not want. Thus a strict limit is placed upon the activities of the disciples . . . . Their restless energy which refuses to recognize any limit to their activity, the zeal which refuses to take note of resistance, springs from a confusion of the gospel with victorious ideology. An ideology requires fanatics, who neither know nor notice opposition, and it is certainly a potent force. But the Word of God in its weakness takes the risk of meeting the scorn of men and being rejected. There are hearts which are hardened and doors which are closed to the Word. The Word recognizes opposition when it meets it, and is prepared to suffer it. It is a hard lesson, but a true one, that the gospel, unlike an ideology, reckons with impossibilities. The Word is weaker than any ideology, and this means that with only the gospel at their command the witnesses are weaker than the propagandists of an opinion. But although they are weak, they are ready to suffer with the Word and so are free from that morbid restlessness which is so characteristic of fanaticism.[23]

Trust in God's goodness: prayer of petition (Mt 7:7–11)

The question concerning the connection between this paragraph and

the preceding one(s) is not easy to answer. The present setting of
Mt 7:7–11 may have been partly determined by the formal link-word
connection 'to give' in Mt 7:6 and 7. Mt 7:7–11 is parallel to
Lk 11:9–13, which belongs to Luke's context of the Lord's Prayer
(Lk 11:1–13). It follows the parable of the importunate friend
(Lk 11:5–8), which seems to be a better context than Matthew's.

> **Verses 7–8:** Ask, and it will be given you; seek, and you will
> find; knock, and it will be opened to you. (8) For every one
> who asks receives, and he who seeks finds, and to him who
> knocks it will be opened.

The force of the present imperatives ('ask', 'see', 'knock') in verse 7 is
iterative. The disciples are never to be weary of asking, seeking and
knocking. The passive mood, 'will be given, will be opened', is a
reverential circumlocution for divine action, and means: God will give
you, God will open to you. The parallelism requires that the finding is
also granted by God. The verb 'ask' (*aitein*) implies a request in prayer.
The situation in life of the clause 'ask and it will be given you' has been
defined as 'beggars' wisdom'. The saying intends to strengthen the
certainty of gaining a hearing. The sequence 'seek ... find' occurs
repeatedly in the gospel (Mt 7:7–8; 12:43; 13:45–46; 18:12–13;
26:59–60). The present passage recalls Jer 29:12–14, 'Then you will
call upon me and come and pray to me, and I will hear you. You will
seek me and find me; when you seek me with all your heart, I will be
found by you, says the Lord . . . .' In rabbinic literature, knocking on a
door and having it opened is associated with study of the Law and
prayer for God's mercy. The three verbs refer to the same reality:
prayer is explained as seeking and knocking. The threefold emphasis
intends to exclude all doubt.

Verse 8 repeats the three injunctions in the form of general truths,
thus again emphasizing the certainty of being heard: 'every one who
asks receives ...'. However, this should not be understood as an
unfailing magic ritual. The fact that the seekers are assured of finding
does not mean that they can control God. We should not lose sight of
the nature of this asking described in the preceding sections of the
Sermon on the Mount and summed up in the Lord's Prayer.

> **Verses 9–11:** Or what man of you, if his son asks him for
> bread, will give him a stone? (10) Or if he asks for a fish, will
> give him a serpent? (11) If you then, who are evil, know how
> to give good gifts to your children, how much more will your
> Father who is in heaven give good things to those who ask
> him!

The situations supposed in verses 9–10 are definitely absurd. Anyone to whom these questions were addressed would deny them emphatically: 'Of course not!' It has been pointed out that Jesus prefers to use this kind of question in disputes with opponents or in addressing the crowds (Mt 12:11; Lk 15:4, etc.). A comparison with Lk 11:11–12 shows that Luke abandons the double parallelism of bread–stone, fish–snake, and substitutes fish–snake, egg–scorpion. The original image is probably based on the fact that some eel-shaped fish resemble snakes and a round piece of bread looks like a stone. Bread and fish were the daily food of simple people. The substitution of an egg and a scorpion destroys the image, but results in a gradation. Unfortunately, today many so-called 'Christian' countries are producing serpents instead of fish by selling weapons to countries suffering from hunger and by keeping down the prices of raw materials. Likewise, credit given by international banking institutions often has a strangling effect on poorer countries.

Verse 11 is the conclusion of Jesus' argument from minor to major: 'If you then, who are evil, . . . how much more will your Father . . .'. It has been pointed out that elsewhere the condemnation 'who are evil' (*ponēroi ontes*) is addressed not to the disciples but to the Pharisees (Mt 12:34). Moreover, it is noted that in Mt 7:11b, it does not say 'he will give *you*', but 'he will give *to those who ask him*', so that 'those who ask' are contrasted with 'you who are evil'. These considerations have led to the conclusion that we have here a polemical saying of Jesus, originally addressed to the Pharisees, but transformed by Matthew into a saying for the disciples. But the same is true in Luke, and therefore this secondary application does not originate from Matthew himself. Moreover, the apparent accusation 'you who are evil' is used here to give more relief to the *a fortiori* argument: although you are evil, you prove yourselves good to your children; with how much more reason will God be good to his children! The saying does not intend to affirm the intrinsic malice of the listeners, but to give full emphasis to God's goodness. It is very doubtful, therefore, whether a polemic origin should be attributed to this saying.

The present saying simply presupposes that men are evil. It should be understood in the light of man's relationship to God, who alone is truly good (Mt 19:17). But at the same time it is presupposed that the love of an earthly father for his children reflects in some way the love of the Father 'from whom every family (*patria*, literally 'fatherhood') in heaven and on earth is named' (Eph 3:14–15). God bestows on his children the gifts of the time of salvation with more than fatherly love. According to Isa 52:7, alluded to in Rom 3:8 and cited in Rom 10:15, the 'good things' (*agatha*) are the gifts of the time of salvation (cf. also Heb 9:11; 10:1); here in Mt 7:11, the 'good things' probably include everything mentioned in the Lord's Prayer. Instead of 'good things', Lk 11:13 has 'the Holy Spirit', the eschatological gift of salvation *par excellence*.

'The golden rule' (Mt 7:12)

> **Verse 12:** So whatever you wish that men should do to you, do so to them; for this is the law and the prophets.

Since the sixteenth century this saying has been called the 'golden rule'. It is a basic summary of human ethics which in its negative form, 'do not do to anyone what you would not like others to do to you', is already found in Buddhism and Confucianism. In Greek literature the idea is found in Homer's *Odyssey* and in Herodotus' *History*, and the so-called 'golden rule' is stated in negative form in Isocrates' *Nicocles* 61: 'Whatever angers you when you suffer it at the hand of others, do not do it to others'.

In Greek-speaking Judaism, the 'golden rule' is found in its negative form in Tobit 4:15, 'And what you hate, do not do to any one'. In Sir 31(34):15, we read: 'Judge your neighbour's feelings by your own, and in every matter be thoughtful'. Beside these two biblical passages there is also an important text in the Hellenistic Jewish *Letter of Aristeas* 207: 'If you want that no evil befall you, but that you share in all that is good, do the same to your subjects'. This passage shows that the 'golden rule' was sometimes understood as the sum of wisdom.

Rabbi Hillel (about 20 B.C.) summarized the Torah as follows: 'Whatever is not pleasing to you do not do to anyone else; this is the whole law and the rest is commentary; go and study' (*Sabbath* 31a). Hillel relates the 'golden rule' to the command of love of neighbour.

In Jesus' message too, love of neighbour (together with love of God) appears as the sum of the whole Law (Mk 12:28–34; Mt 22:34–40). Only Matthew adds: 'on these two commandments depend all the law and the prophets' (Mt 22:40). Similarly, he adds in Mt 7:12, 'for this is the law and the prophets' (compare Lk 6:31, 'And as you wish that men would do to you, do so to them'). This is undoubtedly the clue to Matthew's understanding of the 'golden rule': the 'golden rule' and the great commandment are identical, i.e., they represent the same demand.

By means of the addition 'for this is the law and the prophets' Matthew also brackets the 'golden rule' with Mt 5:17, 'think not that I have come to abolish the law and the prophets'. According to some scholars, Matthew took the 'golden rule' out of the context of love of enemy (cf. Lk 6:31) to place it here at the end of the exposition on the greater righteousness (Mt 5:21 – 7:11) to conclude and epitomize the latter. This is said to be the meaning of 'so' (*oun*). Mt 7:12 should then be separated from Mt 7:7–11 and presented as a summary of the whole Sermon on the Mount so far (as is done in NEB and JB, but not in RSV): the instructions given between Mt 5:20 and 7:12 are the contents of the Law and the prophets.

But the importance attributed to this conclusion has been questioned, because it would seem to relegate Mt 5:3–16 and 7:13–27 to the role of prologue and epilogue respectively. The importance of the material in these two sections would not allow this. Moreover, it is said that Mt 7:12 can in no way be considered a summation of the body of the Sermon on the Mount, especially Mt 6 which seems to emphasize one's relation to God (rather than to one's fellow-man). However, it should be noted that the rather abstract formulation of the rule receives its concrete contents only from the context in which it is inserted. The 'golden rule' demands that one make the good of the other person one's action principle. But as such it cannot make possible or motivate love of enemy (cf. Lk 6:31). This can be derived only from Jesus' promise of God's decisive eschatological intervention on behalf of men. In this context the 'golden rule' is not so much a summation of Jesus' ethical demands, as a bridge which leads men to turn themselves radically toward their fellow-men, as this demand results from the message of God's eschatological action and expresses itself in practice in the love of enemy and the waiving of one's own rights. This means then that the good of one's fellow-man is not an autonomous principle of action within Jesus' ethics. The radical concern for one's fellow-man is rather a principle derived from the eschatological proclamation of the kingdom which constitutes the decisive principle of action and bestows on the concern for one's fellow-man its radical dimension which receives its orientation from God's concern for men. Only in this context can 'the law and the prophets' be fulfilled.

10   The Disciple in the Face of Judgment (Mt 7:13–27)

The paragraphs of the last section of the Sermon on the Mount are rather loosely related to each other. They are collected according to one viewpoint: the expectation of the end and the prospect of judgment. The first paragraph contains the call to 'enter by the narrow gate' (Mt 7:13–14). Secondly, we have a warning against 'false prophets', which should be understood in the light of the end (Mt 7:15–20). Thirdly, there is a paragraph which speaks of the true criterion of the disciple at judgment (Mt 7:21–23). Fourthly, the whole discourse ends with the parable of the building of the house (Mt 7:24–27). The first and the fourth pericope are addressed to all, the second and third to false prophets.

The first three paragraphs are kept together by means of the verb 'to enter' which occurs in verses 13 and 21, and the decision between 'destruction' and 'life' to which the listeners are called (cf. Mt 7:13, 14, 19, 22, 23). All three paragraphs deal with determination in the face of divine judgment.

The verb 'to do' (*poiein*, translated in different ways by RSV) is one of the key-words of this section. It appears nine times, sometimes more than once in the same verse (Mt 7:17, 18 [in some manuscripts *enenkein*], 19, 21, 22, 24, 26). At the end of his programmatic discourse Jesus lays stress on doing the will of the Father as he has explained it in this Sermon.

The narrow gate (Mt 7:13–14)

Verses 13–14: Enter by the narrow gate; for the gate is wide and the way is easy, that leads to destruction, and those who enter by it are many. (14) For the gate is narrow and the way is hard, that leads to life, and those who find it are few.

It is unlikely that this saying is to be related to Mt 7:12. Matthew's version is very different from its Lucan parallel, Lk 13:23–24: 'And someone said to him, "Lord, will those who are saved be few?" and he said to them, "Strive to enter by the narrow door; for many, I tell you, will seek to enter and will not be able"'. Luke's version is found in a different context and at a much later stage of the narrative, as Jesus journeys to Jerusalem (cf. Lk 9:51 – 19:27). The abruptly introduced question, 'Lord, will those who are saved be few?', provides an artificial setting, but the saying itself (Lk 13:24) seems to have been preserved in a more primitive form than in Matthew.

Matthew does not speak of one gate (*pulē*), but of two roads, supposing also two gates. However, some see in 'gate' and 'way' synonymous metaphors which are not to be interrelated but which stand next to each other supplementing and strengthening each other. In Luke one single door (*thura*) gives admission to a banquet hall; this door is narrow and will soon be locked (cf. Lk 13:25). Therefore, one should try one's best to enter on time. In Matthew we do not have the door to a hall but the gate which gives admission to a city, an image that corresponds to that of the road. Matthew's text may be the result of a combination of the common theme of the two roads and the saying on the narrow gate. The latter image probably does not mean a gate which is so narrow that one could hardly enter, but rather a gate which is unknown to a great number of people, as the end of Mt 7:14 seems to indicate.

Mt 7:13–14 and its Lucan parallel (Lk 13:24) have been recognized as an original saying of Jesus about striving to enter (the kingdom) by the narrow gate. This saying seems to have been expanded in the Christian tradition by the addition of features from Jewish exhortation. While the imagery of the gate seems to have been very rare in Judaism, that of the two ways and the idea of ways leading to 'life' and 'destruction' respectively occur frequently. 'Thus says the Lord: Behold, I set before you the way of life and the way of death' (Jer 21:8). 'For the Lord knows the way of the righteous, but the way of the wicked will perish' (Ps 1:6). 'And see if there be any wicked way in me, and lead me in the way everlasting' (Ps 139[138]:24). 'Better is a poor man who walks in his integrity than a rich man who is perverse in his ways. . . . He who walks in integrity will be delivered, but he who is perverse in his ways will fall into a pit' (Prov 28:6, 18). The two-ways schema symbolizes man's ethical decision between good and evil. The idea, deriving ultimately from Deut 30:15, 19, became a commonplace of Jewish catechesis which left its mark on the early Church (cf. *Didache* 1; *Epist. Barn.* 18–20). The terms 'destruction' and 'life' are not characteristic of Jesus; we would rather expect expressions like 'entering' or 'failing to enter' the kingdom.

The less common image of the gate may have its setting in the Temple liturgy. 'Open to me the gates of righteousness, that I may enter through them and give thanks to the Lord. This is the gate of the Lord, the righteous shall enter through it' (Ps 118[117]:19–20; cf. Ps 24[23]:7–10, where the Lord himself enters the Temple. In Mt 5:8 there was already an allusion to Ps 24[23]:3–5 and the Temple liturgy). The comparison of entrance into the kingdom to a city gate, the gate of the eschatological Jerusalem is quite common in apocalyptic usage (cf. Rev 22:14, '. . . that they may enter the city by the gates').

In this saying Matthew emphasizes that if the disciples wish to be saved they must have the courage to cut themselves off from the mass of people who follow the 'wide road', and tread the 'hard way' found by only a few. In Luke, some nameless person asked the question, 'Lord, will those who are saved be few?' Jesus replied with the exhortation to strive earnestly, because many will lack perseverance (Lk 13:23–24). It is a serious summons to become a follower, with emphasis on the high stake demanded.

What do the narrow gate and the hard way refer to? Matthew has probably combined the image of the gate with that of the way. In this combination the 'way' is found at the end and is thereby emphasized. In the context of the Sermon on the Mount, then, the way and the gate refer to the totality of discipleship and the better righteousness without which the disciples 'will never *enter* the kingdom of heaven' (Mt 5:20). Only thus can one obtain eschatological 'life' in the kingdom of God. In fact, 'life' and 'kingdom of God' are interchangeable.

The clause 'those who find it are few' is not an absolute statement about the number of those who will be saved (cf. Lk 13:23–24, where Jesus refuses a direct answer to the question whether those who are saved will be few). It should not be understood as a 'grim and even pessimistic saying' (W. Trilling). It is rather an urgent request to follow the hard road which leads to life. Neither Jesus nor Matthew is thinking in terms of divine predestination or God's dooming 'many' to hell. The use of the term 'find' (cf. 'seek' in Lk 13:24) supports the idea expressed in Mt 7:7–11, that the giving to those who ask and the opening of the door to those who knock are always divine *gifts* whose undeserved nature is underlined by the mention of 'few'. In realistic earnestness Jesus states how easily men can go to their destruction.

Warning against false prophets (Mt 7:15–20)

This pericope is a Matthean composition. Verse 15 is redactional. Verse 16a, 'you will know them by their fruits', is a transition composed by the redactor to introduce the traditional logion found in verse 16b, 'are grapes gathered from thorns, or figs from thistles?' (derived from Q; cf. Lk 6:44). Verse 17 is a development added by the evangelist. Verse 18 is derived from Q (cf. Lk 6:43), while verse 19, already found in Mt 3:10b, is again used here to introduce the motif of judgment. The conclusion, verse 20, which literally repeats verse 16a, is also redactional. The redactional activity in this pericope is of decisive importance. It consists mainly of connecting in an original manner the theme of the false prophets with the motif of the tree and its fruit.

Verse 15: Beware of false prophets, who come to you in sheep's clothing but inwardly are ravenous wolves.

Typical of Matthew's catechesis, the verb *prosechein*, 'to beware', always expresses a warning against deviations or perversions of the religious life; it is characteristic of Matthew's ecclesial concern (Mt 6:1; 10:17; 16:6ff.).

The warning against false prophets relates this verse to Mt 7:22, '. . . did we not *prophesy* in your name?' Since in Lk 13:26f. we do not find a counterpart for this question, we should probably attribute the discussion about false prophecy to Matthew himself.

The word *pseudoprophētēs* ('false prophet') occurs three times in Matthew (Mt 7:15; 24:11, 24), once in Mark and once in Luke (Mk 13:22; Lk 6:26). While in Mt 24:24 it is traditional (cf. Mk 13:22), its mention in Mt 7:15 and 24:11 is redactional. It appears only in the great Matthean discourses, the Sermon on the Mount (Mt 7:15) and the Eschatological Discourse (Mt 24:11, 24). In all three instances the context is paraenetic, and it is clear that the false prophets constitute a problem which concerns the existence of the disciples after Easter, not that of the earthly Jesus. Matthew tackles the problem in the perspective of the discernment of spirits. He intends to give his community a criterion which will enable it to distinguish good and bad spirits (*epigignōskein*, Mt 7:16, 20).

Why is this so urgent? Mt 7:15 suggests an answer: the false prophets are not readily recognizable, they are disguised as sheep, i.e., they appear as members of the Christian community, and possibly believe they really are (cf. Mt 7:22). Matthew may even intend a vivid depiction of how the false prophets awaken trust by wearing the prophet's clothing, sheepskin, and thus enter the fold; only afterwards do they reveal themselves as the wolves that they are. They constantly invoke the Lord Jesus (Mt 7:21) and claim to act in his name (Mt 7:21–22). This is confirmed by the use of the term 'false prophets' in Mt 24, so that we may say that the false prophets announced and denounced by Matthew's Jesus are Christians, members of the post-Easter community. *Probaton*, 'sheep', is a favourite term of Matthew's, used eight times for the faithful or, alternatively, the Christian community. Matthew is definitely dealing with a contemporary problem in his community.

He qualifies the false prophets as externally identical to the faithful. They are 'faithful' with a rich spiritual life, probably charismatics: they confess the Lord publicly (Mt 7:21), have the gift of prophecy (Mt 7:22; 24:23, 26) and perform exorcisms and miracles (Mt 7:22; 24:24). Matthew does not condemn these charismatic riches as such, but he says that they are misleading (*pseudo-*) and lead astray those who trust in them (*planan*, 'lead astray', Mt 24:11, 24). In reality the false prophets are ravenous wolves, i.e., they are enemies of the flock, the people of God, and threaten to destroy it (cf. Mt 10:16; Jn 10:12 and especially Acts 20:29). The fruit of the activity of false prophets is the destruction of the community. In today's Christian communities, too, there are wolves, i.e., people who oppress others, subject the poor to injustice and destroy life.

> **Verses 16–18:** You will know them by their fruits. Are grapes gathered from thorns, or figs from thistles? (17) So, every sound tree bears good fruit, but the bad tree bears evil fruit. (18) A sound tree cannot bear evil fruit, nor can a bad tree bear good fruit.

As already said, verse 16a is a clause composed by the redactor to introduce the traditional logion found in verse 16b. Together with verse 20 it forms an inclusion, enclosing sayings which illustrate it. The phrase 'you will know' may have to be understood as a command: the disciple may be forbidden to judge (Mt 7:1), but he is ordered to inspect fruits! Matthew uses the verb *epigignōskein*, which is an intensive form of the verb *gignōskein*: to know them as they really are. Verse 16b illustrates this principle of fruit inspection. Grapes and figs were among the most prized fruits of Palestine. The illustration is in the form of a question requiring a negative answer. The statement is axiomatic. In verse 17, the illustration becomes a wisdom saying which, with Semitic redundancy, is repeated in a more emphatic form in verse 18: the simple assertion of verse 17 is replaced by the phrase 'cannot'.

An interesting parallel is found in Jas 3:11–12, 'Does a spring pour forth from the same opening fresh water and brackish? Can a fig tree, my brethren, yield olives, or a grapevine figs? No more can salt water yield fresh.' And the *Gospel of Thomas* 45 states: 'Grapes are not harvested from thorns, nor are figs gathered from thistles, for they do not produce fruit. A good man brings forth good from his storehouse; an evil man brings forth evil things from his evil storehouse, which is in the heart, and says evil things. For out of the abundance of the heart he brings forth evil things.' The latter text should be compared with Lk 6:43–45.

The criterion which makes it possible to manifest the error of false prophecy is presented by way of an image; a sound tree bears good fruit, but a bad tree evil fruit; the conduct of a false prophet will correspond to his error. But what is meant by fruit, to bear fruit, and a sound tree?

It has been pointed out that the main accent of Matthew's reformulation of this Q tradition is ethical. In fact, the real Matthean parallel to Lk 6:43–45 is not Mt 7:15–20 but Mt 12:33–35, which is addressed to the Pharisees, 'Either make the tree good, and its fruit good; or make the tree bad, and its fruit bad; for the tree is known by its fruit . . .'. In Mt 7:15–20, the evangelist introduces a variant of the motif which he applies unilaterally to false prophets (cf. Mt 7:16a and 'them' in Mt 7:20), and gives it an ethical emphasis (note the plural 'fruits', the partial replacement of *kalon*, 'beautiful', by *agathon*, 'good', and *sapron*, 'bad' or 'rotten', by *ponērous*, 'evil', in contrast to Mt 12:33). Anyone who does not bear fruit or bears bad fruit is one who transgresses the will of God. However, we should not understand this criterion in a restrictive way and introduce into the text distinctions unknown to biblical anthropology. Just as the nature of the fruit cannot be dissociated from the quality of the tree, so the ethical conduct of a man expresses what he is fundamentally. Therefore, to say of false prophets that they bear evil fruit does not only mean that they behave in a wrong way, it is also a global condemnation of both their teaching and their acts. In the final analysis, in Matthew's eyes, the false prophets are in irreducible opposition to the will of God as it is expressed in the Sermon on the Mount. The criterion for the discernment of spirits is obedience to the will of God as defined in the Sermon. The false prophets are charismatic heretics, and Matthew attacks them, choosing the theme of obedience because this is the fundamental issue. They transgress the will of God in that they do not acknowledge the authority of the Law as it is 'fulfilled' in Christ.

Verse 19: Every tree that does not bear good fruit is cut down and thrown into the fire.

The verse is a quotation from the conclusion of John the Baptist's address (Mt 3:10b; Lk 3:9b). By means of the image of fire it refers to God's judgment. In Mt 3:7–10 it makes perfect sense, since in this passage everyone is required to bear fruit. The presence of the same saying in the present context indicates that only at God's final judgment will it be fully clear which initiatives in the Church were truly initiated by genuine prophets. However, the reference to God's judgment concerns not only the false prophets, but also the individual disciple. All men are subject to judgment, and from all God will require fruits. In the Greek, the verb translated as 'to *bear* fruit', is *poiein* which means 'to do, to make'. This key-word is constantly emphasized by the evangelist: it is found fifteen times in the Sermon on the Mount. Convictions and dispositions are not sufficient.

Verse 20: Thus you will know them by their fruits.

This verse, which repeats Mt 7:16a, enables us to make an important point: placed here at the conclusion of the Sermon on the Mount, it is not alluding to 'spiritual' works. True prophets will be recognized not by the miracles they perform, but by the works or fruits constantly mentioned in these chapters: the works of 'righteousness' (Mt 5:20) and love (Mt 5:43–48). Mt 7:20 announces verses 21–23 which have exactly this meaning: they take issue with the prophets-wonderworkers who are 'evildoers' (cf. Mt 7:23).

The illusion of false religiosity (Mt 7:21–23)

Verses 21–23 are derived from the Q-source. In so far as it can still be discerned, Matthew's redactional activity appears on a double level. On the one hand, Matthew has gathered in a single pericope two traditional sayings (Mt 7:21 and 22–23) which Luke uses in different contexts (Lk 6:46; 13:25–27). The two sayings are held together by means of the key-phrase 'say to me, "Lord, Lord"' (Mt 7:21, 22). One can notice a certain shift in meaning between verse 21, which condemns religious verbalism, and verses 22–23, which attack certain charismatics. As a whole, verses 21–23 reflect the situation of the Matthean community. On the other hand, Matthew has re-interpreted these sayings, as his terminology shows. In verse 21, the expressions 'to enter the kingdom of heaven', and 'the will of my Father who is in heaven' are to be attributed to the evangelist, who thus transforms the saying into a statement about entrance into the kingdom. It is impossible to establish with certainty the form which verses 22–23 had in the Q-source. Nevertheless, Matthew's attempt at actualization is perceptible: Jesus' words are no longer addressed to the Jews (cf. Lk 13:26), but applied to the community (cf. the invocation 'Lord' and the reference to charisms). The term *eprophēteusamen* is to be attributed to Matthew. The exact citation of the end of Ps 6:9aLXX, *hoi ergazomenoi tēn anomian* (RSV: Ps 6:8, 'evildoers'), allows him to introduce the concept of *anomia*, literally 'lawlessness' (cf. Lk 13:27, *adikia*, 'unrighteousness, iniquity'). In short, Matthew's redactional intervention in this pericope is very important.

On the redactional level there is continuity between Mt 7:15–20 and 21–23: both pericopes deal with false prophets. Firstly, Matthew uses link-words to connect the two pericopes: the phrase 'false prophets' of verse 15 is taken up again in the redactional 'did we not prophesy?' of verse 22; the verb *poiein*, 'to do' (translated 'to bear' in verses 17, 18, 19) occurs in Mt 7:17, 18, 19, 21, 22. Secondly, the thematic homogeneity is unquestionable: the theme of the 'fruit' corresponds to that of the fulfilment of God's will, and in both cases it is the transgression of this norm which is condemned; moreover, the theme of judgment introduced by the redactor at verse 19 announces the great eschatological scene of verses 21–23.

Verse 21: Not every one who says to me, 'Lord, Lord,' shall enter the kingdom of heaven, but he who does the will of my Father who is in heaven.

This verse is based on the antithesis 'say–do' and has the characteristics of a prophetic saying. 'Not every one who says' is a Semitic way of saying 'it is not people who say'. In order to interpret this verse correctly the exact meaning of the invocation 'Lord, Lord' should be determined. Applied to Jesus, 'Lord' (*kurios*) in Matthew is both redactional and confessional, and is used to attribute authority and exalted status to him. In Mt 7:22 it is found in the context of the final judgment, and in the parable of the ten bridesmaids (Mt 25:11) it occurs again in a way which recalls the final judgment (Mt 25:37, 44). It is therefore a title addressed to the risen Christ, a title which implies faith in his coming to judge all men, and a confession of faith in Christ the Lord. The situation in life of this invocation is the liturgy, the prayer of the community. Matthew seems here to be continuing his catechesis on prayer (cf. Mt 6:5–15; 7:7–11).

The discourse on the efficacy of prayer may have led to interpretations which were not in conformity with the spirit of the gospel and merited the reproach of Isaiah, 'this people draw near with their mouth, and honour me with their lips, while their hearts are far from me' (Isa 29:13; cf. Amos 5:21). But beyond this particular context the verse also has a more general import: the confession of faith itself may be ambiguous or worthless if one considers it a personal privilege, a right or an advantage on which one can pride oneself. The false prophets are described here as people animated by an intense piety in which the invocation of the Lord occupies a central place.

The antithesis is not only between 'say' and 'do', but between two religious attitudes, two types of faith.

. . . 'say' and 'do' – this does not mean the ordinary contrast between word and deed, but two different relations between man and God . . . the man who says 'Lord, Lord' – means the man who puts forward a claim on the ground that he has said 'it,' . . . the doer – is the man of humble obedience. The first is the one who justifies himself through his confession, and the second, the doer, the obedient man who builds his life on the grace of God.[24]

'He who does the will of my Father in heaven' is privileged. The latter phrase is a typically Matthean expression derived from Jewish piety. Matthew emphasizes, however, that God's will is compassionate: Mt 9:13 and 12:7 cite Hos 6:6, 'For I desire steadfast love (mercy) and not sacrifice'. Mt 7:21 speaks of the will of the Father which *we* must accomplish in our life, and not the will which God exercises in the context of his saving plan, as in the Lord's Prayer (Mt 6:10b), 'for whoever does the will of my Father in heaven is my brother, and sister, and mother' (Mt 12:50).

The new people of God comprises those who do the will of the Father in heaven. While for the rabbis the will of the Father is revealed in the Torah, for Matthew it is Jesus who truly reveals the will of the Father, both in his exegesis of the Torah (Mt 19:3–9) and in his own pronouncements (Mt 18:14). Those who do the will of the Father are, therefore, those who hear Jesus' words and do them.

In Mt 7:21 Jesus speaks for the first time emphatically about '*my* Father' (cf. Mt 10:32f.; 12:50), thus expressing a uniquely close relationship between himself as Son and God as his Father (compare Mt 11:27). This does not exclude, however, God's being also the Father of the disciples, and even of all men (Mt 5:16, 45, 48). He takes care of them (Mt 6:25ff.) and they can pray to him with confidence (Mt 6:9). But this gift of 'sonship' (Mt 5:45) expects men's response, which is given in doing the will of the Father.

Verse 21, therefore, resumes the fundamental teaching on prayer which has already emphasized the necessary link between prayer and conduct. After the Lord's Prayer (Mt 6:9–13) (and related to it by 'for') occurs an exhortation to forgiveness (Mt 6:14–15). The pericope on the efficacy of prayer (Mt 7:7–11) was related to the 'golden rule' (Mt 7:12) by 'so'. The present verse, however, reinforces and radicalizes this connection: even the most typically Christian prayer cannot save if it is not accompanied by the concrete accomplishment of the will of the Father who wants mercy. It is not sufficient to say 'Lord, Lord' to enter the kingdom of heaven. 'To enter the kingdom of heaven' means to participate in it definitively by God's favourable final verdict.

Verses 22–23: On that day many will say to me, 'Lord, Lord, did we not prophesy in your name, and cast out demons in your name, and do many mighty works in your name?' (23)

And then will I declare to them, 'I never knew you; depart from me, you evildoers.'

In these verses the thought passes from everyday life (Mt 7:21) to the day of judgment: 'that day' (Mt 7:22; cf. 10:15; 11:22–24). Matthew makes use of the image of the 'day of Yahweh' (cf. Joel 2:1; Amos 5:18–20). The setting refers to the great scene of Mt 25:31–46: in both instances the parties concerned object to the sentence of the Lord, the supreme judge. The features of the Lord-judge are suggested here by the absolute character of the sentence without appeal and by the verb *homologēsō*, 'I will declare', which is used for an official declaration in the strict sense. In the early Church the word was used for the confession of faith (cf. Acts 24:14; Rom 10:9, 10). It can also be translated as 'to declare freely and openly'. The rejection by the judge Jesus reveals who a man really is.

The sentence is expressed in two propositions, the second of which, a citation of Ps 6:9(8)a, 'depart from me', translates into the form of a commandment what has been said in the first. The sentence proper is found in the declaration 'I never knew you', which in Old Testament style (cf. Isa 1:3; Hos 5:4) excludes all association and communion (compare Mt 25:12, 'Truly, I say to you, I do not know you'). The verb 'know' has here a typically Semitic meaning: it does not refer to a purely intellectual knowledge which may leave one indifferent, but to the acknowledgment of people as one's friends. It may therefore be translated 'you have never really been my friends'.

Verse 22 evokes the charisms to which the accused refer in vain before the eschatological judge: prophecy, exorcisms and miraculous healing. The false prophets do not appeal to their knowledge, and so we are not dealing with Gnostics; they do not appeal to their faith, and so the conflict has nothing to do with that mentioned in the letter of James. The false prophets appeal to their charisms: they practise a kind of enthusiastic piety and know themselves filled with the Spirit to such an extent that they feel that the preaching of the earthly Jesus loses its importance for them.

The sentence is addressed to people who have acted 'in the name' of Jesus. The triple emphatic repetition of 'in your name' is intentional. It refers to people who consider themselves particularly authorized to use the name of Jesus. They have prophesied in his name by claiming his authority to do so; they have cast out demons in his name by using that name as the formula of exorcism and they have been able to perform miracles in his name, i.e., through his power. The works which they claim are authentic miracles. One might think, then, that the Lord condemns not just ordinary charismatics, but disciples who enjoyed authority in the Church and were endowed with apostolic powers (cf. Mt 10:7–8). Not without some malice Thomas Aquinas applied this to prelates: 'Et sic etiam aliquando prelatus male vivens potest et miracula facere', 'and so sometimes even a bad-living prelate can also perform miracles'.

Matthew is not criticizing the value of charismatic gifts, the invocation of the Lord, prophecy, exorcism or miraculous healing as such. The dominant theme of his criticism is obedience to the will of God: only those who do the will of the Father as Jesus announces it will enter the kingdom of heaven (Mt 7:21). The false prophets will be rejected at the final judgment because of their *anomia*, literally 'lawlessness'. This is a term proper to Matthew (cf. Mt 13:41; 23:28; 24:12). It is hard to believe that the *anomia* of which the false prophets are accused consists only in a lack of religious devotion, a guilty indifference regarding the exigencies of the Christian life. The charisms which Matthew acknowledges can hardly be reconciled with such an interpretation. It is more probable that the enthusiastic piety which emphasized the actual presence of the risen Christ attested by the manifestations in the Spirit was accompanied by a relativization or even abolition of the normative value of the Law. The word of the glorified Lord passed on by inspired prophets gained the upper hand over the preaching of the earthly Jesus and especially over his sovereign reinterpretation of the Law. The conflict, then, does not only concern the Law as such, but has Christological roots.

The *anomia* of the false prophets consists in a lack of love, as can be seen from Mt 7:12 where the 'golden rule' sums up the whole Law, and Mt 24:12, where *anomia* (RSV: 'wickedness') is opposed to love. The sin of the charismatics, then, consisted in doing their works without practising love (compare I Cor 13:1–2). This is certainly one of the grave dangers which threaten the Church. Its most official representatives – and Matthew asserts that they will be 'many' – might fail to be recognized by Christ as authentic disciples.

> To those who believed their religious obligation in the world could be fulfilled by observances of rituals and norms with no concern for the oppressed, he said, 'None of those who cry out, "Lord, Lord," will enter the kingdom of God, but only the one who does the will of my Father in heaven' (Matt. 7:21). To those who find their salvation in a personalistic religion divorced from concern about conditions in their world that created and sustained the cry of the poor, to those who pride themselves on prophesying in his name and exorcising demons by his power Jesus says, 'I never knew you' (Matt. 7:23). Jesus cannot *know* those who claim membership in his kingdom if they do not incorporate now on

earth, in their prayer and ministry, the effort to realize the signs of the kingdom. . . .[25]

Hearers and doers of the word (Mt 7:24–27)

At the end of the Sermon on the Mount, and parallel with the antithesis of 'saying and doing', occurs a twofold parable about the correspondence of 'hearing and doing', which was already found in the Q-source (cf. Lk 6:47–49), but which Matthew has provided with his own emphases. Firstly, he retains the eschatological perspective of the preceding pericopes by means of the future introduction 'every one . . . will be like' (Mt 7:24; compare Lk 6:48, 'he is like'). Secondly, in verses 24 and 26 Matthew added 'these' (words of mine) in order to relate the parable to the words of the Sermon on the Mount. Thirdly, in both parts of the parable he has added a qualifying adjective: the first man is 'wise' or 'sensible' (Mt 7:24), the second is 'foolish' or a 'moron' (Mt 7:26, *mōros*). This contrast corresponds to that found in the parable of the ten bridesmaids (Mt 25:1–13) where the same adjectives 'wise' and 'foolish' occur (Mt 25:2–4, 9).

Mt 7:24–27 has clear affinities with the Old Testament Book of Proverbs and may in fact be called a wisdom speech. The form, language, imagery, contents, and function of the passage are typically sapiential. Moreover, it epitomizes the pervasive wisdom antithesis, the doctrine of the two ways. However, all these features are subordinated to the eschatological outlook of the proclamation: The wise man is the one who has grasped the eschatological situation.

Matthew and Luke give a different picture of the building of the house.

In Matthew the contrast is between a house built on rock and one built on sand, and the causes of destruction are heavy rain, which brings torrents of water beating against the house, and a violent wind. These conditions are typically Palestinian: the heavy winter rains are always accompanied by a gale and often by thunder and lightning. As a result, floods of water rush along the *wadi*-beds (a *wadi* is a watercourse which is dry except after heavy rain); the 'sand' on which the house was built is the floor of such a *wadi*, and the man who built there was asking for trouble. Luke has changed the details so that the parable might be more readily understood by his non-Palestinian readers. He is not concerned with the situation of the house, but describes whether or not it was given a sound foundation – the wise man 'dug deep.' The flooding is not caused by torrential rain but by an overflowing river. With a few simple strokes he has given the parable a more general coloring;

but, from a literary point of view, he has not improved on it. Matthew's version, with its balanced parallelism, its rhythm and its local color, is manifestly a faithful rendering of the Aramaic original spoken by the Lord. However, Luke's variations, readily understandable, have not at all affected the meaning of the parable.[26]

In short, Matthew and Luke were apparently more concerned to repeat the parable in a form which their readers would be able to understand than to retain the precise wording.

> **Verses 24–25:** Every one then who hears these words of mine and does them will be like a wise man who built his house upon the rock; (25) and the rain fell, and the floods came and the winds blew and beat upon that house, but it did not fall, because it had been founded on the rock.

By means of 'then' (*oun*) the following parable is closely related to the previous concluding warnings of the Sermon on the Mount. However, this parable is the conclusion of the whole Sermon and not just of the previous section starting with Mt 7:13. By the emphatic use of the word 'mine', Matthew has laid more stress on the fact that everything depends on obeying *Jesus'* words. They take the place of the Torah. In contemporary Judaism, it was said, 'The person who hears the words of the *Torah* and does good works builds on firm ground'. In Mt 7:24 we have 'Every one who hears these words of *mine*'. It is not sufficient to listen to these words; one must do them. To 'hear' seems to have, here as elsewhere, the emphatic meaning of 'receive, welcome the word' (cf. Mt 10:14; 11:5, 15; 13:16, 19, 20).

Jas 1:22, considered in the immediate context of verses 21–25, clarifies the meaning of 'hearing and doing'. After the recommendation to receive the word with docility (verse 21), the author insists that this is not sufficient; it has to be put into practice: 'But be doers of the word, and not hearers only, deceiving yourselves' (verse 22). Then follows the comparison with the man who observes himself in a mirror: 'For if any one is a hearer of the word and not a doer, he is like a man who observes his natural face in a mirror . . .' (verses 23–24). And then the conclusion: 'But he who looks into the perfect law, the law of liberty, and perseveres, being no hearer that forgets but a doer that acts, he shall be blessed in his doing' (verse 25). To 'do a word' is a typically Semitic expression. But while rabbinic literature usually speaks of 'studying and doing', the gospel insists on 'hearing and doing'. In the synoptic tradition, the verb 'do' has an absolute meaning, to the extent of being practically the only term used to describe the attitude of the man who accomplishes God's commandments.

The parable of the two houses with its strictly symmetrical structure is a model of its kind. Some authors maintain that we have here two parables, but others have rightly stated that one cannot speak of a double parable because there is only one image, unlike, e.g., the parables of the mustard seed and of the leaven (Mt 13:31–32, 33). Mt 7:24–27 is a single parable arranged in the form of antithetic parallelism. This antithetic parallelism develops in a dramatic and almost rhythmic progression which reaches its summit in the description of the storm, and its outcome in the result: salvation or catastrophe. The underlying idea is the same in both cases: in order to overcome the trial and survive one must put into practice Jesus' words. The 'rock' or solid ground are the words of Jesus, his teaching on the greater righteousness (Mt 5:20) as it is proclaimed in the Sermon on the Mount. As contrasted with those who hear the word but do not draw any conclusions for their life (Mt 13:19–22), the seed 'sown on good soil . . . is he who hears the word and understands it; he indeed bears fruit . . .' (Mt 13:23; cf. 7:16–20).

The image has been well chosen: a house remains stable by itself unlike, for instance, a tent. The Palestinian house had no foundations: its solidity depended entirely on the soil on which it was built. In the parable it is tested by a violent storm accompanied by heavy winds and rains. Especially among the prophets, the storm is an image evoking God's intervention in history. Ez 13:11–15 und Isa 28:16–17 are particularly close to Matthew. Ezekiel announces a 'deluge of rain' and 'stormy wind' which will cause the destruction of the protective wall erected by the false prophets (cf. also Ez 38:22). Isaiah says that only the building constructed on the sure foundation-stone laid in Zion will resist the onset of the deluge.

In the light of this Old Testament background, the violence of the storm emphasized by the gospel takes on a precise meaning: it is the intervention by which God will test the solidity of our life. And since there is no allusion whatsoever to a particular historical event, this trial should be interpreted as an allusion to the final judgment (cf. Mt 7:22–23), which explains the future tense 'will be like', i.e., 'will be rendered effectively similar to', at the beginning of the parable. Some scholars have suggested that Matthew refers here to the final judgment in terms of a 'second deluge'. In fact, elsewhere, Matthew compares the end of the world to a universal deluge (Mt 24:37–39).

Verses 26–27: And every one who hears these words of mine and does not do them will be like a foolish man who built his house upon the sand; (27) and the rain fell, and the floods

came, and the winds blew and beat against that house, and it
fell; and great was the fall of it.

In light of the previous comments these verses are easily understood.
He 'who built his house upon the sand', i.e., hears the words of Jesus
without doing them, cannot expect that it will survive the coming
storm. However, to put too much stress on the description of the storm
would displace the emphasis of the parable, to the extent of understanding it as an image of the suddenness of the final judgment, which
seems to be absent from Mt 7:24–27. Other elements define the
eschatological perspective more precisely: the construction of the
parable draws one's attention not so much to the storm itself but to
what results from it. In the first case, the house did not collapse because
it was built upon the rock . . . in the second case the house collapsed,
'and great was the fall of it'. The latter clause is a proverbial expression
which means a complete collapse.

The house (*oikia*) is not only the building but also the community
of people it houses. We are familiar with expressions like 'the royal
house', i.e., the royal family. Scripture speaks in a similar way. Paul
writes to the Corinthians: I did baptize also the household (= *oikos*,
house', i.e., the royal family. Scripture speaks in a similar way. Paul
writes to the Corinthians: 'I did baptize also the household (= *oikos*,
the leaders of the Church at Philippi Paul and Silas say: 'Believe in the
Lord Jesus, and you will be saved, you and your household' (= *oikos*,
house; Acts 16:31).

As a whole the parable intends to answer the question: who will
resist in the final trial? The answer is simple: he who built his 'house' on
the rock, i.e., he who has not only listened but also put into practice the
teaching of Jesus.

However much 'doing' Jesus' words may be marked by
eschatological expectation, it rests on us as a necessity in this earthly
life, it is a moral conduct to be practised in this world. The disciples are
sent into this world to reflect the loving and saving will of the Father
(Mt 5:13–16). The verbs 'to hear' and 'to do' are all in the present
tense.

But this does not imply a mere pragmatism, for the 'doing' is
always oriented towards the future: '. . . shall enter the kingdom of
heaven. . . . On that day many will say to me. . . . And then will I
declare to them . . .'. (Mt 7:21–23). It is totally dominated by the will
of God, which will be fully accomplished only at the end. The tension
towards God's future gives dynamism to all Christian activity.

11 Matthew's concluding remarks *(Mt 7:28–29)*

Verse 28: And when Jesus finished these sayings, the crowds were astonished at his teaching,

While Mk 1:21–22 speaks of the people listening to Jesus in the synagogue of Capernaum who were 'astonished at his teaching', . Mt 7:28–29 serves as the conclusion of the Sermon on the Mount to which the 'crowds' have listened with approval (cf. Mt 7:29). Matthew's verses have been redactionally revised.

The first half of verse 28 is a regularly recurring editorial formula in Matthew (in the Greek: *kai egeneto hote etelesen ho Iēsous*, literally repeated in Mt 11:1; 13:53; 19:1; 26:1). It draws attention to and marks the close of the five great discourses which are characteristic of Matthew's gospel. Many scholars think that this quintet derives from the five books of the Torah and that it refers to Jesus as a new Moses. This idea would be supported by still another feature: the concluding parable of the Sermon (Mt 7:24–27) with its antithetical parallelism faces men with an alternative, and invites them to act like a 'wise man'. Similarly, at the end of the Pentateuch, the Law of Moses, men are confronted with the alternative of life or death (cf. Deut 30:15–19). This conclusion of the Pentateuch corresponds to the conclusion of the Sermon on the Mount. It should also be noted that nowhere at the end of the five discourses is the concluding formula as momentous as here.

The verse begins with a Semitism, literally, 'And it happened that when . . .', thereby acquiring a definitely significant and solemn character. As in Mt 7:24, 26, the evangelist uses the phrase 'these words (of mine)', in the Greek (*mou*) *tous logous toutous*, in order to make clear that it was the words of the Sermon on the Mount at which the crowds were astonished (literally, 'they were beside themselves'). Matthew is not speaking of simple astonishment at an unusual message, but rather of being beside oneself about the authority which speaks from Jesus' words. The listeners are deeply moved. The Sermon on the Mount is referred to as *didachē* ('teaching') in keeping with Matthew's image of Jesus as 'teacher' (Mt 23:8).

Verse 29: for he taught them as one who had authority, and not as their scribes.

Jesus is distinguished from the scribes by means of the authority (*exousia*) with which he teaches. His authority is from God (Mt 21:23–27). The authority of Jesus, like Jesus himself, is of divine derivation; in it, God's authority graciously manifests itself. The crowds therefore follow the teaching of Jesus, who possesses an authority which they could not find in 'their scribes', the latter phrase expressing a conscious contrast between those who listen to Jesus and the Jews.

It has been pointed out that this reference to the authority of Jesus should not be misunderstood as if he were dogmatic in his statements while the scribes by contrast were not. In fact, the latter posed as the guardians of an infallible tradition. The real difference was that Jesus spoke with the authority or assurance of first-hand knowledge: 'But I say to you . . .'. He does not speak as one who merely explains or passes on the tradition. He has received 'all authority in heaven and on earth' (Mt 28:18). The authority of Jesus is that of the Son who purely and ultimately proclaims the will of the heavenly Father (Mt 7:21, 24, 26).

The Sermon on the Mount is directly addressed to the disciples. But, as we learn from verse 28, the crowds should also be included in the audience. They too are invited to discipleship. They may be beside themselves about Jesus' teaching, but the latter requires the risk to *live* according to the Sermon on the Mount. 'Every one' is called to such conduct (Mt 7:24). All nations should be taught to observe what Jesus has commanded the disciples to do (Mt 28:19–20).

The 'authority' of which Matthew speaks is nothing but Jesus' power (*exousia*, compare Mt 7:29 and 8:9; 9:6, 8). The astonishment of the disciples and the crowds indicates that they were confronted with somebody who was different from what they saw at first sight. They constantly asked themselves who he was, and they found the answer only after the resurrection. Only then did they really see and hear everything.

12 The practicability of the Sermon on the Mount

State of the question

A number of questions and problems have occupied the mind of any committed Christian reading the Sermon on the Mount from the first to the twentieth century. And they occupy us today. After reading Mt 5 – 7 one will inevitably ask questions like: How can anybody, even the most committed Christian, even a saint, practise these demands? It is quite obvious that no one in his right mind can say of these demands what the young man said referring to the ten commandments: 'All these I have observed' (Mt 19:20). But if they are no more than a utopian dream, a dream of a kingdom of God to be realized in the future, and even then only by an elite, why bother preaching them to the rank-and-file Christian who has to make a living in this world? Are they not an ideal that founders on the realities of everyday life?

These and similar questions have been raised since the beginning of Christianity. Two points should be noted in this connection. Firstly, all issues which arose in the course of the history of the interpretation of the Sermon on the Mount were ultimately related to the question of its practicability. Secondly, the many answers given in the course of the centuries were often coloured by fundamental options concerning what was believed to be the essence of Christianity. Thus Gnostics and anti-Gnostics, Scholastic theologians and the founders of the Reformation, liberal Protestants and the adherents of so-called consistent eschatology, all more or less decided on the overall meaning of the Sermon on the Mount even before coming to grips with any detailed exegesis of these chapters of Matthew's gospel.

Some answers

Especially since the Middle Ages, the question of the practicability of the Sermon on the Mount has received numerous answers.

(1)   The Catholic Church, or more precisely Scholastic theologians, distinguished between the commandments binding on all Christians and the 'evangelical counsels' intended only for those who strive towards perfection, in practice those who withdraw from the world and join the religious life. But, as we have seen, the Sermon on the Mount is not addressed merely to an elite (cf. Mt 5:1–2; 7:28–29). Jesus' message is directed to everyone. No one can be a true disciple and settle for anything less than 'all that I have commanded you' (Mt 28:20). In fact, before the advent of Scholasticism, practically all great Church Fathers, like John Chrysostom (344–407) and Augustine (354–430; most probably the first to speak of Mt 5 – 7 as the 'Sermon on the Mount'), held that the Sermon, though first of all addressed to the disciples, was also intended for all men. Therefore it was relevant and applicable to all Christians, not only to an elite.

(2)   In opposition to Scholastic theology, Martin Luther (1483–1546) spoke of 'two kingdoms'. This doctrine distinguishes between what the disciple of Jesus is obliged to do in virtue of his office, e.g., as judge or chief of police, and what is required of him in his private, personal life. One must act in these different realms of life according to their appropriate rules; e.g., as chief of police one must enforce law and order, imprison robbers, etc. But the same person should refuse to avenge any wrong suffered in his private life. But there is not the slightest indication in the Sermon on the Mount that Jesus (or Matthew) distinguished between a realm where his words would be binding and another realm where they would not.

(3)   The left wing of the Reformation, and all the movements down to the present which understand the Sermon on the Mount as a realizable social programme, are right in insisting that its demands are meant to be fulfilled. However, the whole of Jesus' message is based on the call to faith, a faith which can only grow in freedom. The difficulty of enforcing Jesus' demands by legislation leads either to anarchism, as with Leo Tolstoy (1828–1910), or, for those who insist on established order, to a totalitarian system.

(4)   Albert Schweitzer (1875–1965) understood the Sermon on the Mount as an 'interim-ethic'. Jesus' demands, which were intended to be followed literally, were rooted in his conviction that the end of the world was near, and could be practised only by people who had the same outlook. In the short 'interim' remaining, there was no room for any thought of civil order or reform of society, but only for leading a life pleasing to God. However, the motive of imminence postulated by Schweitzer plays a strikingly small role in Jesus' actual instructions.

What is said, e.g., of marriage is less determined by the expectation of the end than Paul's considerations on the matter are in I Cor 7.

(5)   On the other hand, Wilhelm Herrmann (1846–1922), and to some extent also his disciple Rudolf Bultmann (1884–1977), interpreted Jesus' words as a call to a new way of life and of looking at the world, irrespective of whether his demands were actually practicable or not. Although this approach makes the important point that Jesus' demands reach far beyond what is actually translated in actions (cf. Mt 5:21–22, 27–28), it fails to recognize that the Sermon on the Mount insists on hearing *and doing* (Mt 7:24–27).

(6)   Then there is the answer of Lutheran orthodoxy which says that the Sermon on the Mount cannot be fulfilled and that Jesus knew it. He pronounced it in order to confront men with the fact that they are sinners and radically incapable of living up to God's expectation and that only Jesus' death on the cross can solve their problem. In a mitigated form this approach was also advocated by Romano Guardini: the Sermon on the Mount is the breakthrough of the new age, but Jesus' death shows how little it was accepted, while at the same time being the only way by which men can be reconciled with God. While this view may provide an interesting context for the interpretation of the antitheses (Mt 5:21–48), the Sermon on the Mount does not make any allusion to Jesus' atoning death. But it does require certain attitudes and corresponding actions.

Is the Sermon on the Mount a law?

For all their obvious differences, most of the answers surveyed above have one conviction in common: they consider the Sermon on the Mount as a law. But is it a law in the sense in which we call, e.g., the ten commandments a law? Three considerations are in order.

(1)   As far as its *form* is concerned, the Sermon on the Mount will not be understood by anybody who considers it as a book of law in the technical sense, as a code. The concrete, paradoxical, at times even ironical formulation is very different from that of a book of law.

(2)   The *spirit* of the Sermon on the Mount is very different from that of a code of law, which is always directed at the minimum and, as it were, has its feet on the floor. Jesus, however, aims at the maximum and points at the ceiling, but at a ceiling with an open roof.

(3)   The Sermon on the Mount manifests a *dynamism* which is missing in

a code of law; it is the ethic of the kingdom which is always coming. It eliminates the distinction between what is obligatory and what is free, and does not allow men the feeling of having done enough or something special. But this also means that the Sermon always calls for free men's free initiative and faces them with the task of creative responsibility. In this sense it does not issue *directives*, but points in a *direction*.

In the Sermon on the Mount we are confronted with the New Testament praxis of the kingdom of God vis-a-vis the ethics of the world. It is striking that Catholic moralists have often taken away the impact of the Sermon on the Mount by means of the distinction between command and counsel, thus neutralizing the entire utopian-critical force of the Sermon. This led to two categories of Christians: second-rate Christians for whom ethical demands suffice, and other Christians who in addition to this follow the counsels, i.e., in fact, the core itself of New Testament ethics. Other theologians, who do not accept the distinction between command and counsel, speak of 'disposition', as if the Sermon on the Mount were not speaking of concrete acts, of a praxis which can change the face of the earth. But the Sermon on the Mount shows us that Christian ethics has its own source of inspiration. In this sense ethical 'non-conformism' belongs to the essence of the 'imitation of Jesus'.

The Sermon on the Mount cannot be formulated in legalistic terms; neither can it be expressed in a distinction between command and counsel or in an ethics of disposition. It may not be turned into the ethics of an elite, or deprived of its evangelically-binding ethical force. As an evangelical, utopian-critical stimulus, the Sermon is valid for all Christians and for all times, not just a counsel which one is free to follow or not.

> The Sermon on the Mount is certainly not meant to be a *stricter legal ethic*. It has occasionally been described in a misleading way as the 'law of Christ.' But the Sermon on the Mount deals with the very things which cannot be the object of legal regulation. Talk of 'more abundant justice' or of 'perfection' does not mean a quantitative increase in requirements. . . . His message is anything but a sum of precepts. Imitating him does not mean carrying out a number of regulations. There are good reasons why the Sermon on the Mount should open with promises of happiness for the unhappy. The gift, the present, grace, are prior to the norm, the demand, the directive: everyone is called, to everyone salvation is offered, without any prior achievements. And the directives themselves are the consequences of his message of God's kingdom.[27]

It is unmistakably clear from the Sermon on the Mount that the decisive directive for the disciple of Christ is that of the goal commandments, which are 'commandments' of beatitude, the Good News, grace, and the kingdom of God which draws near with power. The goal commandments . . . are no less serious than the fulfilment commandments (limitative commandments) of the Decalogue; they are absolutely normative in their seriousness. However, the word 'norm' attains a new, analogous meaning here. It looks to a dynamic propulsion, an initiated movement, an organized action toward clearly defined goals.[28]

The practicability of the Sermon on the Mount

Attempts have been made in many ways to weaken or restrict the meaning of the Sermon on the Mount: it is a dream of the future, it does not apply to all realms of life. The common starting point of all these attempts is clear: we ordinary human beings cannot and, therefore, do not have to live up to these demands. We have sensed the tension between Jesus' demands and those of the world and have found a way out, but only via the capitulation, 'that is the way it is', or 'that is the way we are'. But it is possible to opt for another starting point, to say: one man, Jesus, was able to realize this, and he wanted others to live the Sermon on the Mount together with him.

A practicable way will be found only if we realize that the Sermon on the Mount is part of a greater reality: the proclamation of the gospel, the account of God's saving action in Jesus. It tells us that he has come to set people free, to lift them out of their sin, their weakness, their despair, in order to open a new future for them. Immediately after the Sermon on the Mount, the sick are cured, evil spirits are expelled, fear is overcome, isolation is broken through (Mt 8:1 – 9:34).

The Sermon on the Mount was (and should always be) preceded by the proclamation of the gospel (Mt 4:17); it was (and should always be) preceded by conversion, by being overwhelmed by the good news that God has turned himself definitively to men in unrestricted forgiveness and love. That Matthew begins his Sermon on the Mount with the beatitudes, which are primarily proclamation, shows his awareness that only God's promise of grace and mercy, which of course evokes right conduct on the part of men, can stand at the beginning.

The Sermon on the Mount is not an abstract doctrine, as it were, a chapter of Jesus' ethics. It is not a theory but a message, the message of the reign of God which opposes itself to the kingdom of the world and calls for imitation. We should never lose sight of this context.

Neither should we lose sight of the 'context' of the one who proclaims this message. Jesus *is* the authority of the Sermon on the Mount. Without him it would only be a merely utopian philosophy, but with him it becomes a message of promise and a demand from God who speaks in and through Jesus.

In this twofold context we should listen to the difficult words of the Sermon. They do not say: This is what you have to realize with your own resources. Thus understood, the Sermon on the Mount would be experienced as a crushing burden. But the Sermon says: You are saved by Jesus, and therefore things can start changing, you can adopt new priorities in your life. Thus understood, the Sermon calls us to join Jesus on the mountain. It is not a complete compendium of Christian discipleship, but it contains signs and examples of what is implied in the breakthrough of the kingdom of God. If we live with Jesus and are being transformed by the Spirit, things will start happening. The Sermon on the Mount does not give a total picture, but a picture which is clear enough to suggest what the totality is supposed to be like.

The only way in which the Sermon on the Mount can be practised is in the trust and obedience of faith. In fact, the passages of the Sermon in which we clearly recognize Jesus' own voice constitute a summons to faith, an invitation to a total trust which considers the 'Father' as the centre, and experiences the whole of life as a gift. At the same time, Jesus' words are also a summons to a way of life, but to a way of life which is always based on joy (cf. Mt 5:12; 6:17). This is a life not without trial and error, without struggle, without failure, but also not without 'miracles'. We know, however, that there are things in this world which we will never be able to rectify fully. This should inspire us to humility, but it should not make us powerless or passive.

At this stage it may be good to ask ourselves what we really mean by practicability. Do we mean to ask whether an 'ordinary Christian' can keep all these 'commandments and laws'? If we mean it in this way, we should realize that we do not completely keep the ten commandments either. Even if we manage to do rather well for most of them, we know that we fail in some respects.

Moreover and more importantly, the Sermon on the Mount is not a collection of commandments or laws. It is not a law in the ordinary sense of the word and does not allow us to judge people by standards of merit, still less to classify them as good and bad. Neither is it the rule of a society to be realized right here and now, and to make it function as well as possible. It is rather the expression of the (hidden) dynamism of the kingdom of God which progresses to the extent to which the demands of Jesus are accepted and obeyed with more love. The central question is ultimately: do we really give priority to 'seeking the kingdom of God' in all decisions of our life? Or, in other words, are we willing to gravitate towards the one goal: the realization of God's reign on earth, and to do this in complete trust in God whom Jesus calls 'his Father' and invites us to call 'our Father'.

By formulating the question of practicability in this way we escape the narrow-minded examination of all kinds of prescriptions but do not minimize the seriousness of the question. Are we really able radically to ask ourselves in every decision whether we are staying in line with 'seeking the kingdom of God and his righteousness'? The answer will certainly be that we cannot do it on our own.

Therefore it is also good to remind ourselves of the fact that the Sermon on the Mount is addressed not to an individual but to a community. It is addressed to a group of people who are ready to listen to Jesus' words and to accept them. The question then becomes: as a group, can we time and again try to commit ourselves to the priorities of the kingdom? Can we do it, and especially, do we *want* it? We are reminded here of Jesus' question to the man at the pool of Bethzatha: 'Do you want to be healed?' (Jn 5:6). Are we ready as 'sons (and daughters) of God' to take part in the realization of a kingdom of justice and peace, including suffering persecution for the sake of justice (cf. Mt 5:9–12)?

Indeed, the proclamation and realization of the kingdom of God gain their sharpness only within the horizon of the question about justice – the justice of God, of men, and of the world. The beatitudes turn the so-called justice of the world upside-down. The antitheses should be read in the same perspective: they tell us not to insist on our own rights and refer us to unlimited concern for the good of others. They do not allow us to close ourselves to others while hiding behind the law. Are we willing to live in this way?

But where do we get the strength to keep on trying? This question is dealt with towards the end of the Sermon on the Mount; 'Ask, and it will be given you; seek, and you will find . . .' (Mt 7:7–11; the verbs are in the plural, addressed to a community), and even clearer in the Lucan parallel, Lk 11:9–13, with its powerful conclusion: 'how much more will the heavenly Father give the Holy Spirit to those who ask him' (Lk 11:13b).

Notes

1. I. Hermann, *Encounter with the New Testament. An Invitation* (New York: P. J. Kenedy and Sons, 1965), pp. 116–17.
2. This question is further discussed under Mt 5:38–42.
3. W. Brueggemann, *The Land. Place as Gift, Promise and Challenge in Biblical Faith* (Philadelphia: Fortress Press, 1977), pp. 174–5.
4. W. Brueggemann, *ibid.*, pp. 193–4.
5. C. E. Carlston, *The Parables of the Triple Tradition* (Philadelphia: Fortress Press, 1975), p. 49.
6. R. Pregeant, *Christology Beyond Dogma. Matthew's Christ in Process Hermeneutic* (Philadelphia: Fortress Press, 1978), p. 72. The word in square brackets is mine.
7. Mk 13:31 and parallels; Rev 20:11; 21:1; Heb 12:26 (cf. Hag 2:6); II Pet 3:10–13 (cf. Isa 65:17; 66:22); see also Heb 1:11f. (cf. Ps 101:26ff.LXX).
8. *Pal. Sanhedrin* 20c, *Exodus Rabbah* 6,2. Cf. H. L. Strack and P. Billerbeck, *Kommentar zum Neuen Testament aus Talmud und Midrasch* I (Munich: C. H. Beck, 1922), p. 244.
9. J. P. Meier, *Law and History in Matthew's Gospel. A Redactional Study of Mt 5:17–48* (Analecta Biblica 71; Rome: Biblical Institute Press, 1976), p. 52.
10. J. P. Meier, *ibid.*, pp. 123–4.
11. The distinction between *haggadah* (narrative) and *halachah* (conduct) is further discussed in H. Hendrickx, *The Infancy Narratives* (revised ed.; London: Geoffrey Chapman, 1984), p. 6.
12. R. C. Tannehill, *The Sword of His Mouth* (Philadelphia: Fortress Press, 1975/Sheffield: JSOT Press, 1983), pp. 67–8.
13. R. C. Tannehill, *ibid.*, pp. 67–72 *passim*.
14. N. Perrin, *Rediscovering the Teaching of Jesus* (New Testament Library; London: SCM Press, 1967), pp. 147–8.
15. Another reading is attested by Gregory of Nyssa, Maximus of Turin and two cursive manuscripts (700, 162): 'May your spirit come down upon us and cleanse us'. A. Harnack and B. H. Streeter thought it to be original in Luke, and A. R. C. Leaney argued that 'this form may be derived from the Lord himself' (*A Commentary on the Gospel according to St Luke* [2nd ed.; London: A. & C. Black, 1966], p. 68). But most scholars

consider the manuscript evidence too scanty to regard this reading as original. The thought of this variant is in harmony with Luke's subsequent stress on the giving of the Spirit (Lk 11:13). It may well have originated in liturgical usage (cf. 1 QH 3:21), a post-Lucan clarification that subsequently gained liturgical status as part of the Lord's Prayer understood as an initiation prayer over baptismal candidates. It is a witness to the Church's liturgical freedom and its boldness in revising even the words of Jesus.

16. See Chapter Eight for the remarkable parallelism between Mt 6:7ff. and Mt 6:31–34.

17. J. Jeremias, *The Lord's Prayer* (Philadelphia: Fortress Press, 1964), pp. 25–6.

18. M. H. Crosby, *Thy Will Be Done. Praying the Our Father as Subversive Activity* (New York: Orbis Books, 1977/London: Sheed and Ward, 1979), pp. 140–1.

19. R. C. Tannehill, *The Sword of His Mouth*, pp. 85–6.

20. Jerome, *Letter* 120: J. P. Migne, *Patrologiae cursus . . . Series Latina* 22, col. 984; translation in J. Miranda, *Marx and the Bible* (Maryknoll, N.Y.: Orbis Books, 1974/London: SCM Press, 1977), p. 15.

21. A. M. Hunter, *Design for Life. An Exposition of the Sermon on the Mount* (revised ed.; London: SCM Press, 1965), pp. 83–5 *passim*.

    Our reflections on Mt 6:25–33 are very much indebted to M. F. Olsthoorn, *The Jewish Background and the Synoptic Setting of Mt 6,25–33 and Lk 12,22–31* (Jerusalem: Franciscan Printing Press, 1975).

22. *Gemara* (original meaning: 'completion'): commentary on the Mishnah, a codification of decisions of great Jewish teachers.

23. D. Bonhoeffer, *The Cost of Discipleship* (revised ed.: New York: Macmillan Publishing Co., Inc., 1963), pp. 206–7.

24. D. Bonhoeffer, *ibid.*, p. 215.

25. M. H. Crosby, *Thy Will Be Done*, p. 67.

26. W. J. Harrington, *The Gospel according to St Luke. A Commentary* (Westminster, Md.: Newman Press, 1967/London: Geoffrey Chapman, 1968), pp. 114–5.

27. H. Küng, *On Being a Christian* (Garden City, N.Y.: Doubleday, 1976/London: Collins, 1977), p. 244.

28. B. Haering, 'The Normative Value of the Sermon on the Mount', *The Catholic Biblical Quarterly* 29 (1967), 380.

For Further Reading

Barclay, W., *The Old Law and the New Law* (Edinburgh: The Saint Andrew Press/Philadelphia: The Westminster Press, 1972).

Bligh, J., *The Sermon on the Mount. A Discussion on Mt 5 – 7* (Slough: St Paul Publications, 1975).

Crosby, M., *Spirituality of the Beatitudes. Matthew's Challenge for First World Christians* (Maryknoll, N.Y.: Orbis Books, 1981).

Fischer, F. L., *The Sermon on the Mount* (Nashville, Tenn.: Broadman Press, 1976).

Hunter, A. M., *Design for Life. An Exposition of the Sermon on the Mount* (revised ed.; London: SCM Press, 1965)/*A Pattern for Life* (Philadelphia: The Westminster Press, 1965).

Jeremias, J., *The Sermon on the Mount* (Facet Books; Philadelphia: Fortress Press, 1963).

McArthur, H. K., *Understanding the Sermon on the Mount* (Westport, Conn.: Greenwood Press, 1978).

Stott, J. R. W., *Christian Counter-Culture: The Message of the Sermon on the Mount* (The Bible Speaks Today; Downers Grove, Ill./Leicester: Inter-Varsity Press, 1978).

Thurneysen, E., *The Sermon on the Mount* (Chime Paperbacks; Richmond, Va.: John Knox Press, 1964/London: SPCK, 1965).

General Bibliography

1. On the Sermon on the Mount in general

Berner, U., *Die Bergpredigt: Rezeption und Auslegung im 20. Jahrhundert* (Göttinger theologische Arbeiten 12; Göttingen: Vandenhoeck & Ruprecht, 1979).

Betz, H. D. 'The Sermon on the Mount. Its Literary Genre and Function', *Journal of Religion* 59 (1979), 285–97.

Beyschlag, K., 'Zur Geschichte der Bergpredigt in der Alte Kirche', *Zeitschrift für Theologie und Kirche* 74 (1977), 291–322.

Böcher, O., Jacobs, M., and Hild, H. (eds), *Die Bergpredigt im Leben der Christenheit* (Bensheimer Hefte 56; Göttingen: Vandenhoeck & Ruprecht, 1980).

Böcher, O., 'Die Bergpredigt, Lebensgesetz der Urchristenheit', *ibid.*, pp. 7–16.

Boerwinkel, F., *Meer dan het gewone over Jezus en zijn bergrede* (Amboboeken; Baarn: Uitgeverij Ambo, 1977).

Boice, J. M., *The Sermon on the Mount* (Grand Rapids: Zondervan, 1972).

Bonhoeffer, D., *The Cost of Discipleship* (revised ed.; London: SCM Press, 1959/Macmillan Paperbacks; New York: Macmillan Publishing Co., Inc., 1963).

Bonnard, P., 'Le sermon sur la montagne' in *Anamnesis. Recherches sur le Nouveau Testament* (Geneva/Lausanne/Neuchâtel: Revue de Théologie et Philosophie, 1980), pp. 81–92.

Bornkamm, G., 'The History of the Exposition of the Sermon on the Mount' in *Jesus of Nazareth* (trans. I. and F. McLushey with J. M. Robinson; New York: Harper and Row/London: Hodder and Stoughton, 1960), pp. 221–5.

Bornkamm, G., 'Der Aufbau der Bergpredigt', *New Testament Studies* 24 (1977–78), 419–32.

Bouttier, M., 'Hésiode et le Sermon sur la Montagne', *New Testament Studies* 25 (1978–79), 129–30.

Büchele, H., 'Bergpredigt und Gewaltsfreiheit', *Reformatio* 31 (1982), 14–23.

Burchard, C., 'Versuch, das Thema der Bergpredigt zu finden' in *Jesus Christus in Historie und Theologie* (ed. G. Strecker; Tübingen: J. C. B. Mohr, 1975), pp. 408–32.

Carson, D. A., *The Sermon on the Mount. An Evangelical Exposition of Matthew 5 – 7* (Grand Rapids: Baker, 1978).

Catchpole, D., 'The Sermon on the Mount in Today's World', *Theologia Evangelica* 14 (1981), 4–11.

Collins, R. F., 'Christian Personalism and the Sermon on the Mount', *Andover Newton Quarterly* 10 (1969), 19–30.

Davies, W. D., *The Setting of the Sermon on the Mount* (London/New York: Cambridge University Press, 1964).

Davies, W. D., *The Sermon on the Mount* (London/New York: Cambridge University Press, 1966).

Descamps, A., 'Le Discours sur la montagne. Esquisse de théologie biblique', *Revue Théologique de Louvain* 12 (1981), 5–39.

Dibelius, M., 'Die Bergpredigt' in *Botschaft und Geschichte* I (Tübingen: J. C. B. Mohr, 1953), pp. 80–174.

Driver, J., *Kingdom Citizens* (Scottdale, Pa.: Herald Press, 1980).

Du Buit, M., *En tous les temps Jésus-Christ*, Tome 3: *Sermon sur la Montagne* (Mulhouse: Salvator, 1977).

Egger, W., 'Faktoren der Textkonstitution in der Bergpredigt', *Laurentianum* 19 (1978), 177–98.

Ellis, P. F., 'Matthew, his Mind and his Message. The Sermon on the Mount – The Authority of Jesus "in Word" – Mt 5:1 – 7:29', *The Bible Today* no. 69 (February 1974), 1483–91.

Feuillet, A., 'Die beiden Aspekte der Gerechtigkeit in der Bergpredigt', *Internationale Katholische Zeitschrift/Communio* 7 (1978), 108–15.

Ford, J. M., 'Reflections on W. D. Davies *The Setting of the Sermon on the Mount*', *Biblica* 48 (1967) 623–8.

Gollwitzer, H., 'Bergpredigt und Zwei-Reiche-Lehre' in *Nachfolge und Bergpredigt* (ed. J. Moltmann; Kaiser Traktate 65; Munich: Chr. Kaiser, 1981), pp. 89–120.

Goppelt, L., *Die Bergpredigt und die Wirklichkeit dieser Welt* (Stuttgart: Calwer Verlag, 1968).

Grant, R. M., 'The Sermon on the Mount in Early Christianity', *Semeia* 12 (1978), 215–31.

Grayston, K., 'Sermon on the Mount' in *The Interpreter's Dictionary of the Bible* VI (ed, G. A. Buttrick; New York: Abingdon Press, 1962), pp. 279–289.

Greenwood, D., 'Moral Obligation in the Sermon on the Mount', *Theological Studies* 31 (1970), 301–9.

Gründel, J., 'Die Bergpredigt als Orientierung für unser Handeln. Zum Erneuerung der Moraltheologie "aus der Lehre der Schrift"' in *Die Bergpredigt. Utopische Vision oder Handlungsanweisung?* (ed. R. Schnackenburg; Patmos-Paperback; Düsseldorf: Patmos, 1982), pp. 81–112.

Guelich, R. A., *The Sermon on the Mount. A Foundation for Understanding* (Waco, Tex.: Word Books, 1982).

Günther, H., 'Die Gerechtigkeit des Himmelreiches in der Bergpredigt', *Kerygma und Dogma* 17 (1971), 113–26.

Häring, B., 'The Normative Value of the Sermon on the Mount', *The Catholic Biblical Quarterly* 29 (1967), 375–85.

Hamaide, J., *Le discours sur la montagne: charte de vie* (Paris: Le Centurion, 1973).

Hanssen, O., 'Zum Verständnis der Bergpredigt' in *Der Ruf Jesu und die Antwort der Gemeinde* (ed. E. Lohse; Göttingen: Vandenhoeck & Ruprecht, 1970), pp. 94–111.

Hawkins, R. A., 'Covenant Relations of the Sermon on the Mount', *Restoration Quarterly* 12 (1969), 1–9.

Hickling, C. J. A., 'Conflicting Motives in the Redaction of Matthew: Some Considerations on the Sermon on the Mount and Matthew 18:15–20' in *Studia Evangelica* VII (ed. E. A. Livingstone; Texte und Untersuchungen 126; Berlin: Akademie-Verlag, 1982), pp. 247–60.

Hild, H., 'Die Bergpredigt, Wegweisung in unserer Zeit' in *Die Bergpredigt im Leben der Christenheit* (ed. O. Bocher *et al.*; Bensheimer Hefte 56; Göttingen: Vandenhoeck & Ruprecht, 1980), pp. 41–55.

Hochgrebe, V. (ed.), *Provokation Bergpredigt* (Stuttgart: Kreuz, 1982).

Hoerber, R. G., 'Implications of the Imperative in the Sermon on the Mount', *Concordia Journal* 7 (1981), 100–3.

Hoffmann, P., 'Die Stellung der Bergpredigt im Matthäus-evangelium. Auslegung der Bergpredigt I', *Bibel und Leben* 10 (1969), 57–65.

Jacobs, M., 'Die Bergpredigt in der Geschichte der Kirche' in *Die Bergpredigt im Leben der Christenheit* (ed. O. Bocher *et al.*; Bensheimer Hefte 56; Göttingen: Vandenhoeck & Ruprecht, 1980), pp. 17–40.

Keck, L. E., 'The Sermon on the Mount' in *Jesus and Man's Hope* II (ed. D. G. Miller and D. Y. Hadidian; A Perspective Book; Pittsburgh: Pittsburgh Theological Seminary, 1971), pp. 311–22.

Kertelge, K. 'Die Bergpredigt als Thema heutiger Verkündigung' in *Das Evangelium auf dem Weg zum Menschen* (ed. O. Koch *et al.*; Frankfurt am Main: J. Knecht, 1973), pp. 25–34.

Kingsbury, J. D., 'Preaching the Sermon on the Mount', *The Bible Today* no. 80 (November 1975), 504–9.

Kissinger, W. S., *The Sermon on the Mount. A History of Interpretation and Bibliography* (Metuchen, N.J.: The Scarecrow Press, Inc., 1975).

Knörzer, W., *Die Bergpredigt. Modell einer neuen Welt* (Stuttgart: KBW Verlag, 1970).

Krause, C., 'The Sermon on the Mount in Ecumenical Thought since World War II', *Lutheran World* 15 (1969), 52–9.

Kümmel, W. G., 'Jesusforschung seit 1965. IV. Bergpredigt – Gleichnisse – Wunderberichte (Mit Nachträgen) (Schluss)', *Theologische Rundschau* 43 (1978), 233–65.

Kürzinger, J., 'Zur Komposition der Bergpredigt nach Matthäus', *Biblica* 40 (1959), 569–89.

Lachs, S. T., 'Some Textual Observations on the Sermon on the Mount', *Jewish Quarterly Review* 69 (1978), 98–111.

Lamberigts, S., *De Bergrede. Grondwet van het Kristendom* (Louvain: Davidsfonds, 1977).

Lamberigts, S., 'Jesus en de Tora volgens de Bergrede', *Getuigenis* 25 (1981), 55–9.

Lambrecht, J., *Maar ik zeg u. De programmatische rede van Jezus* (Louvain: ACCO, 1982).

Lambrecht, J., 'Ik ben gekomen om te vervullen', *Emmaüs* 14 (1983), 11–15.

Lamote, J., *De Bergrede. Grond van elke kritiek, opgave tot echtheid* (Antwerp: Patmos, 1972).

Lapide, P., 'Die Bergpredigt, Theorie und Praxis', *Zeitschrift für evangelische Ethik* 17 (1973), 369–72.

Lapide, P., *Die Bergpredigt – Utopie oder Programm?* (Mainz: Matthias-Grünewald, 1982).

Lerle, E., 'Realizierbare Forderungen der Bergpredigt?', *Kerygma und Dogma* 16 (1970), 32–40.

Luck, U., *Die Vollkommenheitsforderung der Bergpredigt. Ein aktuelles Kapitel der Theologie des Matthäus* (Munich: Chr. Kaiser, 1968).

Luz, U., 'Die Bergpredigt im Spiegel ihrer Wirkungsgeschichte' in *Nachfolge und Bergpredigt* (ed. J. Moltmann; Kaiser Traktate 65; Munich: Chr. Kaiser, 1981), pp. 37–72.

McEleney, N. J., 'The Principles of the Sermon on the Mount', *The Catholic Biblical Quarterly* 41 (1979), 552–70.

Marquardt, G., 'Die Bergpredigt des Mt-Ev. Eine meisterlich disponierte komposition des Evangelisten', *Bibel und Kirche* 13 (1958), 81–4.

Moltmann, J. (ed.), *Nachfolge und Bergpredigt* (Kaiser Traktate 65; Munich: Chr. Kaiser, 1981).

Neirynck, F., 'The Sermon on the Mount in the Gospel Synopsis', *Ephemerides Theologicae Lovanienses* 52 (1976), 350–7.

Nielsen, J. T., et al., 'De Bergrede', *Schrift* no. 12 (December 1970), 203–37.

Noordegraaf, A., *De bergrede* (Apeldoorn: Willem de Zwijgerstichting, 1982).

Noordmans, O., 'De achtergrond van de bergrede' in *Verzamelde Werken* II: *Dogmatische Peilingen: Rondom Schrift en Belijdenis* (Kampen: J. H. Kok, 1979), pp. 36–56.

Pathrapankal, J., 'Aspects of Discipleship in the Sermon on the Mount', *Jeevadhara* 10 (56; March-April 1980), 148–58.

Peacock, H. F., 'The Text of the Sermon on the Mount', *Review and Expositor* 53 (1956), 9–23.

Phillips, J. A., *The Sermon on the Mount* (Melbourne: The Central Catholic Library, 1965).

Pokorný, P., *Der Kern der Bergpredigt* (Hamburg: Herbert Reich Evangelischer Verlag, 1969).

Pokorný, P., 'The Core of the Sermon on the Mount' in *Studia Evangelica* VI (Berlin: Akademie-Verlag, 1973), pp. 429–33.

Ragaz, I., *Die Bergpredigt Jesu* (Stundenbücher 102; Hamburg: Furche Verlag, 1971).

Reuter, H.-R., 'Bergpredigt und politische Vernunft' in *Die Bergpredigt. Utopische Vision oder Handlungsanweisung?* (ed. R. Schnackenburg; Patmos-Paperback; Düsseldorf: Patmos, 1982), pp. 60–80.

Ridez, L., *Die Bergpredigt. Mensch sein nach Jesus* (Glaubens-Seminar 1; Cologne: Benzinger Verlag, 1979).

Riga, P. J., *Be Sons of Your Father* (Staten Island, N.Y.: Alba House, 1969).

Roberts, J. H., 'The Sermon on the Mount and the Idea of Liberty', *Neotestamentica* 1 (1967), 9–15.

Sabourin, L., *Il discorso della montagna nel Vangelo di Matteo* (Marino: Edizioni 'Fede et Arte', 1976).

Schäfer, P., 'Die Torah der messianischen Zeit', *Zeitschrift für die neutestamentliche Wissenschaft* 65 (1974), 27–42.

Schmall, G., 'Gültigkeit und Verbindlichkeit der Bergpredigt', *Bibel und Leben* 14 (1973), 180–7.

Schnackenburg, R., 'The Challenge of the Sermon on the Mount' in *Present and Future. Modern Aspects of New Testament Theology* (Notre Dame, Ind.: University Press of Notre Dame, 1966), pp. 21–43.

Schnackenburg, R., 'Jewish Moral Teaching and Jesus' Moral Demands. The Sermon on the Mount' in *The Moral Teaching of the New Testament* (2nd revised ed.; London: Burns and Oates, 1965/New York: Herder and Herder, 1967), pp. 56–89.

Schnackenburg, R. (ed.), *Die Bergpredigt. Utopische Vision oder Handlungsanweisung?* (Patmos-Paperback; Schriften der Katholischen Akademie in Bayern 107; Düsseldorf: Patmos, 1982).

Schnackenburg, R., 'Die Bergpredigt', *ibid.*, pp. 13–59.

Schneider, G., *Botschaft der Bergpredigt* (Die Botschaft Gottes – Neutestamentliche Reihe, 20; Leipzig: St. Benno-Verlag, 1973).

Schneider, J. W., 'De Bergrede', *Verbum* 25 (1958), 400–5, 456–60.

Schrage, W., 'Aspekte heutiger Bergpredigt-Interpretation', *Der Evangelische Erzieher* 34 (1982), 387–98.

Schubert, K., 'The Sermon on the Mount and the Qumran Texts' in *The Scrolls and the New Testament* (ed. K. Stendahl; New York: Harper and Row, 1957/London; SCM Press, 1958), pp. 118–28.

Schürmann, H., 'Die Warnung des Lukas vor der Falschlehre der "Predigt am Berge" Lk 6, 20–49', *Biblische Zeitschrift* 10 (1966), 57–81.

Schweizer, E., *Die Bergpredigt* (Kleine Vandenhoeck-Reihe 1481; Göttingen: Vandenhoeck & Ruprecht, 1982).

Shinn, R. L., *The Sermon on the Mount. A Layman's Guide to Jesus' Most Famous Sermon* (Festival Books; Nashville: Abingdon Press, 1979).

Skibbe, E. M., 'Pentateuchal Themes in the Sermon on the Mount', *Lutheran Quarterly* 20 (1968), 44–51.

Soares Prabhu, G. M., 'The Dharma of Jesus: An Interpretation of the Sermon on the Mount', *BibleBhashyam* 6 (1980), 358–81.

Stegemann, W., 'Plädoyer für die Aktualisierung der Bergpredigt' in *Zur Rettung des Feuers. Solidaritätsschrift für Kuno Füssel* (Münster: Christen für den Sozialismus, 1981), pp. 22–30.

Stöger, A., *Die Bergpredigt. Eine Botschaft von Hoffnung und Frieden* (Klosterneuburg: Österreichisches Katholisches Bibelwerk, 1982).

Stuhlmacher, P., 'Jesu vollkommenes Gesetz der Freiheit. Zum Verständnis der Bergpredigt', *Zeitschrift für Theologie und Kirche* 79 (1982), 283–322.

Thielicke, H., *Das Leben kann noch einmal beginnen. Ein Gang durch die Bergpredigt* (Thielicke-Taschenbücher; Stuttgart: Quelle-Verlag, (1980).

Tigcheler, J., *De Bergrede. Matteüs* (Verklaring van een Bijbelgedeelte; Kampen: J. H. Kok, n.d.).

Tuttle, G. A., 'The Sermon on the Mount. Its Wisdom Affinities and Their Relation to Its Structure', *Journal of the Evangelical Theological Society* 20 (1977), 213–30.

Vaganay, L., 'L'absence du Sermon de la montagne chez Marc', *Revue Biblique* 58 (1951), 5–46.

Vaganay, L., 'Existe-t-il chez Marc quelques traces du Sermon sur la montagne?', *New Testament Studies* 1 (1954–55), 192–200.

Wolbert, W., 'Bergpredigt und Gewaltlosigkeit', *Theologie und Philosophie* 57 (1982), 498–525.

Wrege, H.-T., *Die Überlieferungsgeschichte der Bergpredigt* (Tübingen: J. C. B. Mohr, 1968).

Zee, W. R. van der, *Uit de bergrede* (The Hague: Boekencentrum, 1975).

2. The Beatitudes (Mt 5:3–12)

Agourides, S., 'La tradition des béatitudes chez Matthieu et Luc' in *Mélanges bibliques en hommage au R.P. Béda Rigaux* (ed. A. Descamps and A. de Halleux; Gembloux: Éditions J. Duculot, 1970), pp. 9–27.

Bammel, E., '*ptōchos*, etc.' in *Theological Dictionary of the New Testament* VI (ed. G. Kittel and E. Friedrich; Grand Rapids: Eerdmans/London: SCM Press, 1968), pp. 885–915.

Barclay, W., *The Beatitudes and the Lord's Prayer for Everyman* (New York: Harper and Row, 1968; includes *The Plain Man Looks at the Beatitudes*, London: Fontana, 1963).

Bergant, D., '"Blest are the Not-so-Poor". Admonitions for the Middle Class', *The Bible Today* no. 101 (March 1979), 1962–68.

Bertrangs, A., *Les Béatitudes* (Études religieuses 753; Brussels: La Pensée Catholique, 1962).

Best, E., 'Matthew V, 3', *New Testament Studies* 7 (1960–61), 255–8.

Betz, H. D., 'Die Makarismen der Bergpredigt (Matthäus 5, 3–12). Beobachtungen zur literarischen Form und theologischen Bedeutung', *Zeitschrift für Theologie und Kirche* 75 (1978), 3–19.

Bleichert, G., 'Die Seligpreisungen. Eine meditative Erschliessung', *Geist und Leben* 51 (1978), 326–37.

Böhl, F., 'Die Demut als höchste der Tugenden. Bemerkungen zu Mt 5, 3.5', *Biblische Zeitschrift* 20 (1976), 217–23.

Braumann, G., 'Zum traditionsgeschichtlichen Problem der Seligpreisungen Mt V, 3–12', *Novum Testamentum* 4 (1960), 253–60.

Brown, M. P., 'Matthew as EIRENOPOIOS', *Irish Biblical Studies* 4 (1982), 66–81.

Brown, R. E., 'The Beatitudes according to Luke' in *New Testament Essays* (Milwaukee: Bruce Publishing Company/London: Geoffrey Chapman, 1965), pp. 265–71.

Brueggemann, W., 'Blessed are the Meek' in *The Land. Place as Gift, Promise and Challenge in Biblical Faith* (Overtures to Biblical Theology; Philadelphia: Fortress Press, 1977), pp. 167–83.

Carré, A.-M., *L'Homme des Béatitudes* (Paris: Éditions du Cerf, 1962).

Carré, A.-M., 'Quand Jésus invite au bonheur', *Fêtes et Saisons* no. 300 (December 1975).

Chevignard, B. M., 'Bienheureux vous qui êtes pauvres', *Lumière et Vie* 7 (no. 39; 1958), 53–60.

Coppens, J., 'Les Béatitudes – Miscellanées Bibliques 74', *Ephemerides Theologicae Lovanienses* 50 (1974), 256–60.

Dodd, C. H., 'The Beatitudes: a form-critical Study' in *More New Testament Studies* (Manchester: University Press/Grand Rapids: Eerdmans, 1968), pp. 1–10.

Dodd, C. H., 'New Testament Translation Problems I', *The Bible Translator* 27 (1976), 301–11.

Dumbrell, W. J., 'The Logic of the Role of the Law in Matthew V, 1–20', *Novum Testamentum* 23 (1981), 1–21.

Dupont, J., *Les Béatitudes*. I: *Le Problème Littéraire. Les deux versions du Sermon sur la montagne et des Béatitudes* (new ed.; Louvain: Nauwelaerts, 1958).

Dupont, J., *Les Béatitudes*. II: *La Bonne Nouvelle* (Collection 'Études Bibliques'; new ed.; Paris: Éditions J. Gabalda, 1969).

Dupont, J., *Les Béatitudes*. III: *Les Évangelistes* (Collection 'Études Bibliques'; Paris: Éditions J. Gabalda, 1973).

Dupont, J., 'Introduction aux Béatitudes', *Nouvelle Revue Théologique* 98 (1976), 97–108.

Dupont, J., *Le message des béatitudes* (Cahiers Évangile – Évangile et Vie; Paris: Éditions du Cerf, 1978).

Dussel, E., 'The Kingdom of God and the Poor', *International Review of Mission* 68 (270, 1979), 115–30.

Faber van der Meulen, H. E., 'De christologische relevantie van de zaligsprekingen bij Matteüs' in *De knechtgestalte van Christus. Festschrift H. N. Ridderbos* (Kampen: H. J. Kok, 1978), pp. 47–53.

Flusser, D., 'Some Notes to the Beatitudes (Matthew 5:3–12, Luke 6:20–26)', *Immanuel* 8 (1978), 37–47.

Frankemölle, H., 'Die Makarismen (Mt 5, 1–12; Lk 6, 20–23). Motive und Umfang der redaktionellen Komposition', *Biblische Zeitschrift* 15 (1971), 52–75.

George, A., 'Heureux les coeurs purs! Ils verront Dieu! (Matth 5.8)', *Bible et Vie Chrétienne* 13 (1956), 74–9.

Grimm, W., 'Die Hoffnung der Armen. Zu den Seligpreisungen Jesu', *Theologische Beiträge* 11 (1980), 100–13.

Guelich, R. A., 'The Matthean Beatitudes: "Entrance-Requirements" or Eschatological Blessings?', *Journal of Biblical Literature* 95 (1976), 415–34.

Hauck, F., and Bertram, G., '*makarios*, etc.' in *Theological Dictionary of the New Testament* IV (ed. G. Kittel; Grand Rapids: Eerdmans/London: SCM Press, 1967), pp. 362–70.

Heider, J., 'The Beatitudes for Contemporary Adult Christians', *Lumen Vitae* 27 (1972), 489–500.

Heinrich, R., 'Gott, rücksichtlos der Gott der Armen. Leben mit Matthäus 5, Vers 3' in *Nachfolge und Bergpredigt* (ed. J. Moltmann; Kaiser Traktate 65; Munich: Chr. Kaiser, 1981), pp. 73–88.

Hinnebusch, P., 'The Messianic Meaning of the Beatitudes', *The Bible Today* no. 59 (March 1972), 707–17.

Hoffmann, P., '"Selig sind die Armen . . ." Auslegung der Bergpredigt II (Mt 5:3–16)', *Bibel und Leben* 10 (1969), 111–22.

Hoyt, T., 'The Poor/Rich Theme in the Beatitudes', *Journal of Religious Thought* 37 (1980), 31–41.

Jacob, G., 'Die Proklamation der messianische Gemeinde. Zur Auslegung der Makarismen in der Bergpredigt', *Theologische Versuche* 12 (1981), 47–75.

Jacquemin, P.-E., 'Les béatitudes selon saint Matthieu. Mt 5.1–12a', *Assemblées du Seigneur* 66 (1973), 50–63.

Jones, D. C., 'Who are the poor?', *Presbyterion* 3 (1977), 62–72.

Kieffer, R., 'Wisdom and Blessing in the Beatitudes of St Matthew and St Luke' in *Studia Evangelica* VI (Berlin: Akademie-Verlag, 1973), pp. 291–95.

Kieffer, R., 'Weisheit und Segen als Grundmotive der Seligpreisungen bei Matthäus und Lukas' in *Theologie aus dem Norden* (Studien zum Neuen Testament und seiner Umwelt, Ser. A.2; ed. A. Fuchs; Linz: SNTU, 1976), pp. 29–43.

Lamberigts, S., 'De Zaligsprekingen. Belofte en levensweg', *Collationes* 5 (1975), 203–25.

Lapide, P., and Weiszäcker, C. F. von, *Die Seligpreisungen. Ein Glaubensgespräch* (Stuttgart/Munich: Calwer Verlag/Kösel-Verlag, 1980).

Lawlor, G. L., *The Beatitudes Today* (Grand Rapids: Baker, 1974).

Légasse, S., 'Les pauvres en esprit et les "volontaires" de Qumran', *New Testament Studies* 8 (1961–62), 336–45.

Légasse, S., 'Pauvreté et salut dans le Nouveau Testament', *Revue Théologique de Louvain* 4 (1973), 162–72.

Légasse, S., *Les Pauvres en Esprit* (Lectio Divina 78; Paris: Éditions du Cerf, 1974).

Lotz, J., *Eure Freude wird gross sein. Die acht Seligkeiten als Weg in die Tiefe* (Freiburg/Basel/Vienna: Herder, 1977).

McEleney, N. J., 'The Beatitudes of the Sermon on the Mount/Plain', *The Catholic Biblical Quarterly* 43 (1981), 1–13.

Mánek, J., 'On the Mount—On the Plain (Mt V, 1—Lk VI, 17)', *Novum Testamentum* 9 (1967), 124–31.

May, J., 'Fehlt dem Christentum ein Verhältnis zur Natur? Eine Analyse der Seligprisungen (Mt 5, 2–12) und der Feuerpredigt des Buddha (Samy 35, 28)', *Una Sancta* 34 (1979), 159–71.

Michaelis, C., 'Die π-Alliteration der Subjektsworte der ersten 4 Seligpreisungen in Mt V, 3–6 und ihre Bedeutung für der Aufbau der Seligpreisungen bei Mt, Lk und in Q', *Novum Testamentum* 10 (1968), 148–61.

Morlot, F., '"Heureux les pauvres": béatitude ou conseil?', *La Vie Consacrée* 11 (1975), 46–55.

Newman, B. M., Jr, 'Translating "the Kingdom of God" and "the Kingdom of Heaven" in the New Testament', *The Bible Translator* 235 (1974), 401–4.

Newman, B. M., Jr, 'Some Translational Notes on the Beatitudes. Matthew 5.1–12', *The Bible Translator* 26 (1975), 106–20.

Queffelec, H. (ed.), 'Béatitudes', *Journal de la Vie—Aujourd'hui la Bible* no. 129 (March 1973).

Reicke, B., 'The New Testament Conception of Reward' in *Aux Sources de la Tradition Chrétienne. Mélanges offerts à M. Maurice Goguel* (Bibliothèque Théologique; Neuchâtel: Delachaux & Niestlé, 1950), pp. 195–206.

Reiling, J., 'The Use of *PSEUDOPROPHETES* in the Septuagint, Philo and Josephus', *Novum Testamentum* 13 (1971), 147–56.

Riga, P. J., 'Reflections on the Beatitudes', *The Bible Today* no. 39 (December 1968), 2731–9.

Ru, G. de, 'The Conception of Reward in the Teaching of Jesus', *Novum Testamentum* 8 (1966), 202–22.

Satake, A., 'Das Leiden der Jünger "um meinetwillen"', *Zeitschrift für die neutestamentliche Wissenschaft* 67 (1976), 4–19.

Schnackenburg, R., 'Die Seligpreisungen der Friedenstifter (Mt 5, 9) im matthäischen Kontext', *Biblische Zeitschrift* 26 (1982), 161–78.

Schottroff, L., 'Die Seligpreisungen' in *Zur Rettung des Feuers. Solidaritätsschrift für Kuno Füssel* (Münster: Christen fur den Sozialismus, 1981), pp. 14–20.

Schreiner, G., 'De acht zaligheden', *Verbum* 32 (1965), 271–85.

Schwarz, G., 'Lukas 6, 22a, 23b, 26. Emendation, Rückübersetzung, Interpretation', *Zeitschrift für die neutestamentliche Wissenschaft* 66 (1975), 269–74.

Schwarz, G., '"Ihnen gehort das Himmelreich"? (Matthäus V, 3)', *New Testament Studies* 23 (1976–77), 341–3.

Schweizer, E., 'Formgeschichtliches zu den Seligpreisungen Jesu', *New Testament Studies* 19 (1972–73), 121–6.

Sicari, A. M., 'Bevrijding en zaligsprekingen', *Communio* 5 (1980), 81–104.

Spicq, C., 'Bénignité, mansuétude, douceur, clémence', *Revue Biblique* 54 (1974), 324–32.

Stock, A., 'Beatitudes: Two Versions' in *Kingdom of Heaven. The Good Tidings of the Gospel* (New York: Herder and Herder, 1964), pp. 41–56.

Stock, A., 'Beatitudes: Eschatological Original', *ibid.*, pp. 57–73.

Strecker, G., 'Die Makarismen der Bergpredigt', *New Testament Studies* 17 (1970–71), 255–75.

Trilling, W., 'Heilsverheissung und Lebenslehre des Jüngers (Mt 5:3–12)' in *Christusverkündigung in den synoptischen Evangelien* (Munich: Kösel-Verlag, 1969), pp. 64–85.

Truhlar, K., 'The Earthly Cast of the Beatitudes', *Concilium* 39 (*The Gift of Joy*; ed. C. Duquoc; New York: Paulist Press, 1968), 33–43/'The Beatitudes and the Kingdom', *Concilium* 39 (IX. 4; *Christian Life and Eschatalogy*; ed. C. Duquoc; London: Burns and Oates, 1968), 18–23.

Trummer, P., 'Warum gewaltlose selig sind. Exegetische Hinweise zum Verständnis von Mt 5,5' in *Gedanken des Friedens* (ed. P. Trummer; Grazer theologische Studien 7; Graz: Institut für Ökumenische Theologie und Patristik, 1982), pp. 203–36.

Tuckett, C. M., 'The Beatitudes: A Source-Critical Study. With a Reply by M. D. Goulder', *Novum Testamentum* 25 (1983), 193–216.

Waldron, T., 'For Yours is the Kingdom. The Beatitudes', *The Furrow* 33 (1982), 263–71.

Wansbrough, H., 'Blessed are the Peacemakers', *The Way* 22 (1982), 10–17.

Weren, W., 'Het bestaansrecht van de zwakste. De samenhang tussen Mt 5, 3–12 en Mt 25, 31–46', *Ons Geestelijk Leven* 59 (1982), 28–36.

Zimmerli, W., 'Die Seligpreisungen der Bergpredigt und das Alte Testament' in *Donum Gentilicium. New Testament Studies in Honour of David Daube* (ed. E. Bammel *et al.*; Oxford: Clarendon Press, 1978), pp. 8–26.

3. Salt and Light (Mt 5:13–16)

Berger, P.-R., 'Die Stadt auf dem Berge. Zum kulturhistorischen Hintergrund von Mt 5,14' in *Wort in der Zeit. Neutestamentliche Studien. Festgabe für K. H. Rengstorf* (Leiden: E. J. Brill, 1980), pp. 82–5.

Campbell, K. M., 'The New Jerusalem in Matthew 5.14', *Scottish Journal of Theology* 31 (1978), 335–63.

Deatrick, E. P., 'Salt, Soil, Savor', *The Biblical Archaeologist* 25 (1962), 41–8.

Fensham, F. C., 'Salt as Curse in the Old Testament and the Ancient Near East', *ibid.*, 48–50.

Grayston, K., 'Matthew 5:16: An Interpretation', *Epworth Review* 6 (1979), 61–3.

Hahn, F., 'Die Worte vom Licht. Lk 11,33–36' in *Orientierung an Jesus* (ed. P. Hoffmann; Freiburg/Basel/Vienna: Herder, 1973), pp. 107–38.

Isshiki, N., 'Looking for the Energy of the Salt of the Earth', *International Review of Mission* 66 (262, 1977), 135–9.

Krämer, M., 'Ihr seid das Salz der Erde . . . Ihr seid das Licht der Welt. Die vielgestaltige Wirkkraft des Gotteswortes für das Leben der Kirche aufgezeigt am Beispiel Mt 5, 13–16', *Münchener Theologische Zeitschrift* 28 (1977), 133–57.

Latham, J. E., *The Religious Symbolism of Salt* (Théologie Historique 64; Paris: Beauchesne, 1982).

Légasse, S., 'Les chrétiens, "sel de la terre", "lumière du monde". Mt 5, 13–16', *Assemblées du Seigneur* 36 (1974), 17–25.

Schwarz, G., 'Matthäus V 13a und 14a: Emendation und Rückübersetzung', *New Testament Studies* 17 (1970–71), 80–6.

Souček, J. B., 'Le sel de la terre et la lumière du monde', *Communio Viatorum* 6 (1963), 5–12.

Souček, J. B., 'Salz der Erde und Licht der Welt. Zur Exegese von Mt 5, 13–16', *Theologische Zeitschrift* 19 (1963), 169–79.

Sparks, H. F. D., 'The Doctrine of the Divine Fatherhood in the Gospels' in *Studies in the Gospels. Essays in Memory of R. H. Lightfoot* (ed. D. E. Nineham; Oxford: Basil Blackwell, 1957), pp. 241–62.

4. Jesus and the Law (Mt 5:17–20)

Banks, R., 'Matthew's Understanding of the Law: Interpretation in Matthew 5:17–20', *Journal of Biblical Literature* 93 (1974), 226–42.

Barth, G., 'Matthew's Understanding of the Law' in G. Bornkamm, G. Barth and H. J. Held, *Tradition and Interpretation in Matthew* (Philadelphia: The Westminster Press/London: SCM Press, 1963), pp. 58–164.

Condon, R. D., 'Did Jesus Sustain the Law in Matthew 5?', *Bibliotheca Sacra* 135 (1978), 117–25.

Davies, W. D., 'Matthew 5:17, 18' in *Christian Origins and Judaism. A Collection of New Testament Studies* (London: Darton, Longman and Todd, 1962/Philadelphia: Westminster Press), pp. 31–66.

Descamps, A., *Les justes et la justice dans les évangiles et le christianisme primitif hormis la doctrine proprement paulinienne* (Gembloux: Éditions J. Duculot, 1950).

Descamps, A., 'Essai d'interprétation de Mt 5, 17–48. Formgeschichte ou Redaktionsgeschichte?' in *Studia Evangelica* I (ed. F. Cross; Berlin: Akademie-Verlag, 1959), pp. 156–73.

Feuillet, A., 'Morale Ancienne et Morale Chrétienne d'après Mt V, 17–20; Comparaison avec la doctrine de l'Épître aux Romains', *New Testament Studies* 17 (1970–71), 123–37.

Fuchs, E., 'L'imaginaire et le symbolique. Réflexions hasardeuses sur Matthieu 5, 17–20', *Bulletin du Centre Protestant d'Études* 30 (1978), 21–8.

Hamerton-Kelly, R. G., 'Attitudes to the Law in Matthew's Gospel: a Discussion of Mt 5:18', *Biblical Research* 17 (1972), 19–32.

Heubült, C., 'Mt 5:17–20. Ein Beitrag zur Theologie des Evangelisten Matthäus', *Zeitschrift für die neutestamentliche Wissenschaft* 71 (1980), 143–9.

Hoffmann, P., 'Die bessere Gerechtigkeit. Auslegung der Bergpredigt III (Mt 5, 17–37)', *Bibel und Leben* 10 (1969), 175–89.

Honeyman, A. M., 'Matthew V. 18 and the Validity of the Law', *New Testament Studies* 1 (1954–55), 141–2.

Johnston, R. M., '"The Least of the Commandments": Deuteronomy 22:6–7 in Rabbinic Judaism and Early Christianity', *Andover University Seminary Studies* 20 (1982), 205–15.

Lange, H., 'The Greater Righteousness: Theological Reflections on Matthew 5:17–20', *Currents in Theology and Mission* 5 (1978), 116–21.

Légasse, S., 'Mt 5, 17 et la prétendue tradition paracanonique' in *Begegnung mit dem Wort. Festschrift für H. Zimmermann* (ed. J. Zmijewski and E. Nellessen; Bonner biblischer Beiträge 53; Bonn: Hanstein, 1980), pp. 11–21.

Luz, U., 'Die Erfüllung des Gesetzes bei Matthäus (Mt 5, 17–20)', *Zeitschrift für Theologie und Kirche* 75 (1978), 398–435.

McEleney, N. J., 'The Principle of the Sermon on the Mount', *The Catholic Biblical Quarterly* 41 (1979), 552–70.

Martin, B. L., 'Matthew on Christ and the Law', *Theological Studies* 44 (1983), 53–70.

Meier, J. P., *Law and History in Matthew's Gospel. A Redactional Study of Mt 5:17–48* (Analecta Biblica 71; Rome: Biblical Institute Press, 1976).

Pregeant, R., 'Torah and Salvation: Matt 5:17–20' in *Christology Beyond Dogma. Matthew's Christ in Process Hermeneutic* (Philadelphia: Fortress Press, 1978/Sheffield: JSOT Press, 1983), pp. 63–83.

Rothfuchs, W., 'Die sogenannten Antithesen des Matthäus-evangeliums und ihr Gesetzverständnis – untersucht im Zusammenhang Mt 5, 17–48', *Lutherischer Rundblick* 16 (1968), 95–109.

Sabourin, L., 'Matthieu 5, 17–20 et le rôle prophétique de la Loi (cf. Mt 11, 13)', *Science et Esprit* 30 (1978), 303–11.

Schürmann, H., ' "Wer daher eines dieser geringsten Gebote auflöst . . ." Wo fand Matthäus das Logion Mt 5, 19?' in *Traditionsgeschichtliche Untersuchungen zu den synoptischen Evangelien* (Düsseldorf: Patmos-Verlag, 1968), pp. 126–36.

Schweizer, E., 'Mt 5, 17–20 – Anmerkungen zum Gesetzverständnis des Matthäus', *Theologische Literaturzeitung* 77 (1952), 479–84.

Schweizer, E., 'Observance of the Law and Charismatic Activity in Matthew', *New Testament Studies* 16 (1969–70), 213–30.

Schweizer, E., 'Noch einmal Mt 5, 17–20' in *Das Wort und die Wörter. Festschrift für Gerhard Friedrich* (ed. H. Balz and S. Schulz; Stuttgart: W. Kohlhammer, 1973), pp. 69–73.

Seynaeve, J., 'La justice nouvelle (Mt 5, 17–20)' in *Message et Mission. Recueil commémoratif du Xe anniversaire de la Faculté de Théologie de l'Université Lovanium de Kinshasa* (Louvain: Nauwelaerts, 1968), pp. 52–75.

Strugnell, J., ' "Amen, I Say Unto You" in the Sayings of Jesus and in Early Christian Literature', *Harvard Theological Review* 67 (1974), 177–84.

Tilborg, S. van, 'Jezus in het krachtenspel van de wetsuitleg (over Matteüs 5, 17–20)', *Ons Geestelijk Leven* 58 (1981), 282–94.

Wenham, D., 'Jesus and the Law: an Exegesis on Matthew 5:17–20', *Themelios* 4 (1979), 92–96.

5. The Antitheses (Mt 5:21–48)

Bauer, J. B., 'De conjugali foedere quid adixerit Matthaeus (Mt 5:31s.; 19:3–9)', *Verbum Domini* 44 (1966), 74–8.

Blinzler, J., 'Die Strafe für Ehebruch in Bibel und Halacha', *New Testament Studies* 4 (1957–58), 32–47.

Broer, I., 'Die Antithesen und der Evangelist Matthäus: Versuch, eine alte These zu revidieren', *Biblische Zeitschrift* 19 (1975), 50–63.

Bruppacher, H., 'Was sagte Jesus in Mt 5, 48?', *Zeitschrift für die neutestamentliche Wissenschaft* 58 (1967), 145.

Bussby, F., 'A Note on *raka* (Mt 5, 22) and *battalogeō* (Mt 6, 7) in the Light of Qumran', *Expository Times* 76 (1964–65), 26.

Caron, G., 'Did Jesus Allow Divorce? (Mt 5:31–32). A Preaching Problem', *African Ecclesiastical Review* 24 (1982), 309–16.

Coiner, H. G., 'Those "Divorce and Remarriage" Passages (Mt 5, 32; 19:9; I Cor 7:10–16). With Brief Reference to the Mark and Luke Passages', *Concordia Theological Monthly* 39 (1968), 367–84.

Crossan, J. D., 'Jesus and Pacifism' in *No Famine in the Land. Studies in Honor of John L. McKenzie* (ed. J. W. Flanagan *et al.*; Missoula, Mont.: Scholars Press, 1975), pp. 195–208.

Crouzel, H., 'Le texte patristique de Matthieu 5:32 et 19:9', *New Testament Studies* 19 (1972–73), 98–119.

Dautzenberg, G., 'Ist das Schwurverbot Mt 5, 33–37; Jak 5, 12 ein Beispiel für die Torakritik Jesu?', *Biblische Zeitschrift* 25 (1981), 47–66.

Deiss, L., 'La loi nouvelle. Mt 5, 38–48; cf. Lc 6, 27–38', *Assemblées du Seigneur* 38 (1970), 60–78.

Descamps, A., 'Les textes évangéliques sur le mariage', *Revue Théologique de Louvain* 9 (1978), 259–86.

Descamps, A., 'Les textes évangéliques sur le mariage (suite)', *Revue Théologique de Louvain* 11 (1980), 5–50.

Dietzfelbinger, C., *Die Antithesen der Bergpredigt* (Theologische Existenz heute 186; Munich: Chr. Kaiser, 1975).

Dietzfelbinger, C., 'Die Antithesen der Bergpredigt im Verständnis des Matthäus', *Zeitschrift für die neutestamentliche Wissenschaft* 70 (1979), 1–15.

Dupont, J., ' "Soyez parfaits" (Mt V. 48) – "Soyez miséricordieux" (Lc VI. 36)' in *Sacra Pagina* II (ed. J. Coppens, A. Descamps and E. Massaux; Gembloux: Éditions J. Duculot, 1959), pp. 150–62.

Elliott, J. H., 'Law and Eschatology: The Antitheses of the "Sermon on the Mount" ', *Lutheran World* 15 (1968), 16–24.

Farla, P., 'Trouw in liefde en vrijheid. De beteekenis van de synoptische teksten over het huwelijk', *Schrift* no. 79 (1982), 16–32.

Fitzmyer, J. A., 'The Matthean Divorce Texts and Some New Palestinian Evidence', *Theological Studies* 37 (1976), 197–226.

Geldard, M., 'Jesus' Teaching on Divorce: Thoughts on the Meaning of *porneia* in Matthew 5:32 and 19:9', *Churchman* 92 (1978), 134–43.

George, A., 'Soyez parfaits comme votre Père céleste (Matth 5, 17–48)', *Bible et Vie Chrétienne* no. 19 (September-November 1957), 84–90.

George, A., 'Le disciple fraternel et efficace. Lc 6, 39–45', *Assemblées du Seigneur* 39 (1972), 68–77.

Guelich, R. A., 'Mt 5:22: Its Meaning and Integrity', *Zeitschrift für die neutestamentliche Wissenschaft* 64 (1973), 39–52.

Guelich, R. A., 'The Antitheses of Matthew V. 21–48. Traditional and/or Redactional', *New Testament Studies* 22 (1975–76), 444–57.

Guillet, J., 'Aimez vos ennemis (Lc 6, 27)', *Christus* 15 (1968), 360–70.

Haacker, K., 'Der Rechtssatz Jesu zum Thema Ehebruch (Mt 5, 28)', *Biblische Zeitschrift* 21 (1977), 113–16.

Hasler, V., 'Das Herzstück der Bergpredigt. Zum Verständnis der Antithesen in Matth. 5.21–48', *Theologische Zeitschrift* 15 (1959), 90–106.

Hoffmann, P., 'Die bessere Gerechtigkeit. Die Auslegung der Bergpredigt IV (Mt 5, 38–48)', *Bibel und Leben* 10 (1969), 264–75.

Hoffmann, P., 'Jesus' Saying About Divorce and Its Interpretation in the New Testament Tradition', *Concilium* 55 (V. 6: *The Future of Marriage as Institution*; 1970), 51–66.

Hruby, K., 'L'amour du prochain dans la pensée juive', *Nouvelle Revue Théologique* 91 (1969), 493–516.

Jensen, J., 'Does *porneia* mean Fornication? A Critique of Bruce Malina', *Novum Testamentum* 20 (1978), 161–78.

Jeremias, J., '*raka*' in *Theological Dictionary of the New Testament* VI (ed. G. Friedrich; Grand Rapids: Eerdmans/London: SCM Press, 1968), pp. 973–6.

Kilgallen, J. J., 'To what are the Matthean Exception-Tests (5, 32 and 19, 9) an Exception?', *Biblica* 61 (1980), 102–5.

Lapide, P. E., 'Es geht um die Entfeindungsliebe. Realpolitik, wie sie die Bergpredigt eigentlich meint', *Lutherische Monatshefte* 20 (1981), 505–8.

Leeming, B., and Dyson, R. A., 'Except it be for Fornication?', *Scripture* 8 (1956), 75–85.

Löbmann, B., 'Das Ehescheidungsverbot Jesu im Hinblick auf die Eheauffassung in der orientalischen und lateinischen Kirche' in *Dienst der Vermittlung* (ed. W. Ernst; Leipzig: St. Benno Verlag, 1977), pp. 673–89.

Lövestam, E., 'Die funktionale Bedeutung der synoptischen Jesusworte über Ehescheidung und Wiederheirat' in *Theologie aus dem Norden* (ed. A. Fuchs; Studien zum Neuen Testament und seiner Umwelt, Ser. A. 2; Linz: SNTU, 1976), pp. 19–28.

Lohfink, G., 'Jesus und die Ehescheidung. Zur Gattung und Sprachintention von Mt 5,32' in *Biblische Randbemerkungen* (ed. H. Merklein and J. Lange; Würzburg: Echter Verlag, 1974), pp. 207–17.

Lohfink, G., 'Der ekklesiale Sitz im Leben der Aufforderung Jesu zum Gewaltsverzicht (Mt 5,39b–42/Lk 6,29f.)', *Theologische Quartalschrift* 162 (1982), 236–53.

Lührmann, D., 'Liebet eure Feinde (Lk 6,27–36/Mt 5,39–48)', *Zeitschrift für Theologie und Kirche* 69 (1972), 412–38.

Mahoney, A., 'A New Look at the Divorce Clauses in Mt 5,32 and 19,9', *The Catholic Biblical Quarterly* 30 (1968), 29–38.

Malina, B., 'Does *Porneia* Mean Fornication?', *Novum Testamentum* 14 (1972), 10–17.

Marguerat, D., 'Matthieu 5,21–26', *Études Théologiques et Religieuses* 53 (1978), 508–13.

Miller, C. H., 'Old Testament Law: Abrogated by Jesus?', *The Bible Today* no. 80 (November 1975), 510–13.

Minear, P. S., 'Yes or No: The Demand for Honesty in the Early Church', *Novum Testamentum* 13 (1971), 1–13.

Moingt, J., 'Le divorce "pour motif d'impudicité" (Mt 5,32; 19,9)', *Recherches de Science Religieuse* 56 (1968), 337–84.

Moulder, J., 'Who are my enemies? An exploration of the semantic background of Christ's command', *Journal of Theology for Southern Africa* 25 (1978), 41–9.

Moule, C. F. D., 'Uncomfortable Words: I. The Angry Word: Matthew 5:21f.', *Expository Times* 81 (1969), 10–13.

Mueller, J. R., 'The Temple Scroll and the Gospel Divorce Texts', *Revue de Qumran* 10 (1980), 247–56.

Neirynck, F., 'Het evangelisch echtscheidingsverbod', *Collationes Brugienses et Gandavenses* 4 (1958), 25–46.

Neirynck, F., 'Huwelijk en Echtscheiding in het Evangelie', *Collationes Brugienses et Gandavenses* 6 (1960), 123–30.

Neirynck, F., 'De Jezuswoorden over de echtscheiding' in *Evangelica. Gospel Studies – Études d'évangile* (ed. F. Van Segbroeck; Bibliotheca Ephemeridum Theologicarum Lovaniensium 60; Louvain: Leuven University Press, 1982), pp. 821–33, 833–4 (note).

Neuhäusler, E., 'Mit welchem Masstab misst Gott die Menschen? Deutung zweier Jesussprüche', *Bibel und Leben* 11 (1970), 104–13.

O'Rourke, J., 'A Note on an Exception: Mt 5,32 (19,9) and I C 7,12 Compared', *Heythrop Journal* 5 (1964), 299–302.

Rausch, J., 'The Principle of Nonresistance and Love of Enemy in Mt 5:38–48', *The Catholic Biblical Quarterly* 28 (1966), 31–41.

Sabourin, L., 'Notes and Views: The Divorce Clauses (Mt 5,32; 19:9)', *Biblical Theology Bulletin* 2 (1972), 80–6.

Sabourin, L., 'Why is God called "perfect" in Mt 5,48?', *Biblische Zeitschrift* 24 (1980), 266–8.

Sahlin, H., 'Traditionskritische Bemerkungen zu zwei Evangelieperikopen', *Studia Theologica* 33 (1979), 69–84.

Schedl, C., 'Zur Ehebruchklausel der Bergpredigt im Lichte der neue gefundenen Tempelrolle', *Theologisch-praktische Quartalschrift* 130 (1982), 362–5.

Schmall, G., 'Die Antithesen der Bergpredigt. Inhalt und Eigenart ihrer Forderungen', *Trierer Theologische Zeitschrift* 83 (1974), 284–97.

Schottroff, L., 'Gewaltverzicht und Feindesliebe in der urchristlichen Jesustradition. Mt 5,38–48; Lk 6,27–36' in *Jesus Christus in Historie und Theologie* (ed. G. Strecker; Tübingen: J. C. B. Mohr, 1975), pp. 197–221.

Schreurs, P., 'La paternité divine dans Mt V,45 et VI,26–32', *Ephemerides Theologicae Lovanienses* 36 (1960), 593–624.

Seitz, O. J. F., 'Love your Enemies. The Historical Setting of Matthew V.43f.; Luke VI.27f.', *New Testament Studies* 16 (1969–70), 39–54.

Sidebottom, E., '"Reward" in Matthew 5:46, etc.', *Expository Times* 67 (1955–56), 219–20.

Stählin, G., 'Zum Gebrauch von Beteuerungsformeln im Neuen Testament', *Novum Testamentum* 5 (1962), 115–43.

Stein, R. H., 'Is It Lawful for a Man to Divorce His Wife?', *Journal of the Evangelical Theological Society* 22 (1979), 115–21.

Stock, A., 'Matthean Divorce Texts', *Biblical Theology Bulletin* 8 (1978), 24–33.

Strecker, G., 'Die Antithesen der Bergpredigt (Mt 5:21–48 par.)', *Zeitschrift für die neutestamentliche Wissenschaft* 69 (1978), 36–72.

Strecker, G., 'Compliance – Love of One's Enemy – The Golden Rule', *Australian Biblical Review* 29 (1981), 38–46.

Suggs, M. J., 'The Antitheses as Redactional Products' in *Jesus Christus in Historie und Theologie* (ed. G. Strecker; Tübingen: J. C. B. Mohr, 1975), pp. 432–44.

Taylor, R. J., 'Divorce in Matthew 5:32; 19:9', *The Clergy Review* 55 (1970), 792–800.

Theissen, G., 'Gewaltverzicht und Feindesliebe (Mt 5,38–48/Lk 6,27–38) und deren sozialgeschichtlichen Hintergrund' in *Studien zur Soziologie des Urchristentums* (Tübingen: J. C. B. Mohr, 1979), pp. 160–97.

Thurston, T., 'Did Jesus Allow Divorce?', *Religious Studies Journal* 3 (1979), 69–80.

Trilling, W., 'Die neue und wahre "Gerechtigkeit" (Mt 5,20–22)' in *Christus-*

verkündigung in den synoptischen Evangelien (Munich: Kösel-Verlag, 1969), pp. 86–107.

Trudinger, P., 'A Much Misunderstood Commandment', *The Bible Today* no. 56 (November 1971), 501–4.

Unnik, W. C. van, 'Die Motivierung der Feindesliebe in Lk VI, 32–35', *Novum Testamentum* 8 (1966), 284–300.

Vawter, B., 'The Divorce Clauses in Mt 5,32 and 19,9', *The Catholic Biblical Quarterly* 16 (1954), 155–67.

Vawter, B., 'Divorce and the New Testament', *The Catholic Biblical Quarterly* 39 (1977), 528–42.

Veerkamp, T., 'Nicht Widerstreben und nicht Zurückweichen', *Texte und Kontexte* no. 11 (1981), 10–22.

Walker, W. O., 'Jesus and the Tax Collectors', *Journal of Biblical Literature* 97 (1978), 221–38.

Wambacq, B. N., 'Matthieu 5, 31–32. Possibilité de divorce ou obligation de rompre une union illégitime', *Nouvelle Revue Théologique* 104 (1982), 34–49.

Weise, M., 'Mt 5,21f. – ein Zeugnis sakraler Rechtssprechung in der Urgemeinde', *Zeitschrift für die neutestamentliche Wissenschaft* 49 (1958), 116–23.

Wernberg-Moeller, P., 'A Semitic Idiom in Matt. V.22', *New Testament Studies* 3 (1956–57), 71–3.

Wolbert, W., 'Bergpredigt und Gewaltlosigkeit', *Theologie und Philosophie* 57 (1982), 498–525.

6. Almsgiving, Prayer, Fasting (Mt 6:1–18)

Althoff, K. F., *Das Vaterunser. Die Wortgestalt des Menschengebetes auf ihrem Weg durch die Kulturen der Völker* (Stuttgart: Urachhaus, 1978).

Angénieux, J., 'Les différents types de structure du "Pater" dans l'histoire de son exégèse. Section I – De Tertullien aux grands scolastiques', *Ephemerides Theologicae Lovanienses* 46 (1970), 40–77; 'Section II – De Saint Thomas d'Aquin aux exégètes récents – Essai de synthèse', *ibid.*, 325–9.

Arichea, D. C., Jr., 'Translating the Lord's Prayer (Matthew 6:9–13)', *The Bible Translator* 31 (1980), 219–23.

Ashley, B. M., 'What Do We Pray in the Lord's Prayer?', *Spirituality Today* 31 (1979), 121–36.

Ashton, J., 'Le Notre Père', *Christus* 24 (96: 1977), 459–70.

Ashton, J., 'Our Father', *The Way* 18 (1978), 83–91.

Bahr, G. J., 'The Use of the Lord's Prayer in the Primitive Church', *Journal of Biblical Literature* 84 (1965), 153–9.

Baker, A., 'Lead Us not into Temptation', *New Blackfriars* 52 (609; 1971), 64–9.

Baker, A., 'What Sort of Bread did Jesus want us to pray for?', *New Blackfriars* 54 (634; 1973), 125–9.

Bammel, E., 'A New Text of the Lord's Prayer', *Expository Times* 73 (1961–62), 54.

Bandstra, A. J., 'The Original Form of the Lord's Prayer', *Calvin Theological Journal* 16 (1981), 15–37.

Bandstra, A. J., 'The Lord's Prayer and Textual Criticism. A Response', *Calvin Theological Journal* 17 (1982), 88–97.

Bergerac, Groupe de, 'Lecture critique de Matthieu 6, 9–13', *Études Théologiques et Religieuses* 55 (1980), 536–59.

Bertrangs, A., 'Het Onze Vader', *Getuigenis* 6 (1961–62), 210–20.

Betz, H. D., 'Eine judenchristliche Kult-Didache in Matthäus 6, 1–18. Überlegungen und Fragen im Blick auf das Problem des historischen Jesus' in *Jesus Christus in Historie und Theologie* (ed. G. Strecker; Tübingen: J. C. B. Mohr, 1975), pp. 445–57.

Bouma, H., *Het Onze Vader. Matteüs 6* (Verklaring van een Bijbelgedeelte; (Kampen: J. H. Kok, n.d.).

Bourgoin, H., '*epiousios* expliqué par la notion de préfixe vide', *Biblica* 60 (1979), 91–6.

Braun, F.-M., 'Le pain dont nous avons besoin. Mt 6, 11; Lk 11, 3', *Nouvelle Revue Théologique* 100 (1978), 559–68.

Brooke, G. J., 'The Lord's Prayer Interpreted Through John and Paul', *Downside Review* 98 (333; 1980), 298–311.

Brown, R. E., 'The Pater Noster as an Eschatological Prayer', *Theological Studies* 22 (1961), 175–208.

Brown, R. E., 'Meaning of the Our Father', *Theology Digest* 10 (1962), 3–13.

Bruggen, J. van, 'The Lord's Prayer and Textual Criticism', *Calvin Theological Journal* 17 (1982), 78–87.

Bussche, H. van den, *Understanding the Lord's Prayer* (Stagbooks; New York: Sheed and Ward, 1963/London: Sheed and Ward, 1964).

Cambe, M., and Lucas, N., 'Le "Notre Père" (Matthieu 6, 9–13). Éléments d'analyse structurale', *Foi et Vie* 78 (1979), 113–17.

Carmignac, J., ' "Fais que nous n'entrions pas dans la tentation." La portée d'une négation devant un verbe au causatif', *Revue Biblique* 72 (1965), 218–26.

Carmignac, J., 'Hebrew Translations of the Lord's Prayer: An Historical Survey' in *Biblical and Near Eastern Studies* (ed. G. A. Tuttle; Grand Rapids: Eerdmans, 1978), pp. 18–79.

Collins, R. F., ' "Thy Will be done on earth as it is in heaven" – Mt 6:10', *The Bible Today* no. 14 (November 1964), 911–17.

Crosby, M. H., *Thy Will Be Done. Praying the Our Father as Subversive Activity* (Maryknoll, New York: Orbis Books, 1977/London: Sheed & Ward, 1979).

Dahms, J. V., 'Lead Us Not Into Temptation', *Journal of the Evangelical Theological Society* 17 (1974), 223–30.

Dewailly, L.-M., ' "Donne-nous notre pain": quel pain? Notes sur la quatrième demande du Pater', *Revue des Sciences Philosophiques et Théologiques* 64 (1980), 561–88.

Dupont, J., and Bonnard, P., 'Le Notre Père: notes exégétiques', *Maison-Dieu* 85 (1966), 7–35.

Duquoc, C., 'The Prayer of Jesus', *Concilium* 159 (1982), 11–17.

Ebeling, G., *On Prayer. The Lord's Prayer in Today's World* (Philadelphia: Fortress Press, 1978).

Elliott, J. K., 'Did the Lord's Prayer Originate with John the Baptist?', *Theologische Zeitschrift* 29 (1973), 215–16.

Evely, L., *We Dare to Say Our Father* (London: Burns and Oates, 1965/New York: Herder and Herder, 1967).

Fensham, F. C., 'The Legal Background of Mt VI, 12', *Novum Testamentum* 4 (1960), 1–2.

Ford, J. M., 'Yom Kippur and the Matthean Form of the Pater Noster', *Worship* 41 (1967), 609–19.

Ford, J. M., 'The Forgiveness Clause in the Matthean Form of the Our Father', *Zeitschrift für die neutestamentliche Wissenschaft* 59 (1968), 127–31.

George, A., 'La justice à faire dans le secret (Matthieu 6, 1–6 et 16–18)', *Biblica* 40 (1959), 590–98.

Gerhardsson, B., 'Geistiger Opferdienst nach Matth 6, 1–6, 16–18' in *Neues Testament und Geschichte* (ed. H. Baltensweiler and B. Reicke; Tübingen: J. C. B. Mohr, 1972), pp. 69–78.

Goulder, M. D., 'The Composition of the Lord's Prayer', *Journal of Theological Studies* N.S. 14 (1963), 32–45.

Grelot, P., 'La quatrième demande du "Pater" et son arrière-plan sémitique', *New Testament Studies* 25 (1978–79), 299–314.

Hadadian, D. Y., 'The Meaning of *epiousios* and the Codices Sergii', *New Testament Studies* 5 (1958–59), 75–81.

Hirschmann, H., *Vater unser – erlöse uns* (Würzburg: Echter Verlag, 1979).

Hoffmann, P., 'Der ungeteilte Dienst. Die Auslegung der Bergpredigt V (Mt 6,1 – 7,27)', *Bibel und Leben* 11 (1970), 89–104.

Hoffmann, P., ' "Er weiss was ihr braucht" (Mt 6, 7)' in *'Ich will euer Gott werden.' Beispiele biblischen Redens von Gott* (Stuttgarter Bibelstudien 100; Stuttgart: KBW Verlag, 1981), pp. 151–76.

Holleran, J. W., 'Christ's Prayer and Christian Prayer', *Worship* 48 (1974), 171–82.

Jacob, T., 'The Daily Bread in the Teaching of Jesus', *Jeevadhara* 32 (1976), 187–97.

Jacquemin, M. E., 'La portée de la troisième demande du Pater', *Ephemerides Theologicae Lovanienses* 25 (1949), 61–76.

Jeremias, J., 'The Lord's Prayer in Modern Research', *Expository Times* 71 (1959–60), 141–6.

Jeremias, J., *The Lord's Prayer* (Facet Books; Biblical Series 8; Philadelphia: Fortress Press, 1964).

Jeremias, J., *The Prayers of Jesus* (Studies in Biblical Theology, 2nd ser. 6; Naperville, Ill.: A. R. Allenson/London: SCM Press, 1967).

John, M. P., 'Give us this day our . . . bread', *The Bible Translator* 31 (1980), 245–7.

Kistemaker, S. J., 'The Lord's Prayer in the First Century', *Journal of the Evangelical Theological Society* 21 (1978), 323–8.

Klostermann, E., 'Zum Verständnis von Mt 6,2', *Zeitschrift für die neutestamentliche Wissenschaft* 47 (1956), 281–2.

Koch, K., 'Offenbaren wird sich das Reich Gottes. Die Malkuta Jahwäs im Profeten-Targum', *New Testament Studies* 25 (1978–79), 158–65.

Kuhn, K. G., 'New Light on Temptation, Sin, and Flesh in the New Testament' in *The Scrolls and the New Testament* (ed. K. Stendahl; New York: Harper and Row: 1957/London: SCM Press, 1958), pp. 94–113.

Lachs, S. T., 'On Matthew VI. 12', *Novum Testamentum* 17 (1975), 6–8.

Lambrecht, J., 'Jesus and Prayer', *Louvain Studies* 6 (1976), 128–42.

LaVerdière, E. A., 'The Prayer of Jesus', *The Bible Today* no. 66 (April 1973), 1165–72.

Limbeck, M., *Von Jesus beten lernen. Das Vaterunser auf dem Hintergrund des Alten Testamentes* (Stuttgart: Religiöse Bildungsarbeit, 1980).

Lohmeyer, E., *Our Father. An Introduction to the Lord's Prayer* (New York: Harper and Row, 1965)/*The Lord's Prayer* (London: Collins, 1965).

Maartens, P. J., 'The Cola Structure of Mt 6', *Neotestamentica* 11 (1977), 48–76.

Marchel, W., *Abba, Père! La Prière du Christ et des Chrétiens* (Rome: Biblical Institute Press, 1971).

Megivern, J., 'Forgive us our debts', *Scripture* 18 (1966), 33–47.

Metzger, B. M., 'How Many Times Does "Epiousios" Occur Outside the Lord's Prayer?', *Expository Times* 69 (1957–58), 52–4.

Morneau, R., *Our Father Revisited* (Collegeville, Minn.: The Liturgical Press, 1980).

Moule, C. F. D., 'An Unsolved Problem in the Temptation-Clause in the Lord's Prayer', *The Reformed Theological Review* 33 (1974), 65–75.

O'Hara, J., 'Christian Fasting (Mt 6:16–18)', *Scripture* 19 (1967), 3–18.

Orchard, B., 'The Meaning of *ton epiousion* (Mt 6:11 = Lk 11:3)', *Biblical Theology Bulletin* 3 (1973), 274–82.

Petuchowski, J., and Brocke, M., *The Lord's Prayer and Jewish Liturgy* (New York: The Seabury Press/London: Burns and Oates, 1978).

Rordorf, W., 'Le "pain quotidien" (Matth 6,11) dans l'histoire de l'exégèse', *Didaskalia* 6 (1976), 221–35.

Rordorf, W., 'Le "pain quotidien" (Matth 6,11) dans l'exégèse de Grégoire de Nysse', *Augustinianum* 17 (1977), 193–200.

Rordorf, W., '"Our daily bread": Shifts in Exegesis', *Theology Digest* 28 (1980), 43–4.

Schürmann, H., *Praying with Christ. The 'Our Father' for Today* (New York: Herder and Herder, 1964).

Schürmann, H., *Das Gebet des Herrn als Schlüssel zum Verstehen Jesu* (6th ed.; Leipzig: St. Benno-Verlag, 1981).

Schwarz, G., 'Mt 6,9–13/Lk 11,2–4. Emendation und Rückübersetzung', *New Testament Studies* 15 (1968–69), 233–47.

Schweizer, E., ' "Der Jude im Verborgenen . . . dessen Lob nicht von Menschen, sondern von Gott kommt." Zu Röm 2,28f. und Mt 6,1–18' in *Neues Testament und Kirche* (ed. J. Gnilka; Freiburg: Herder, 1974), pp. 115–24.

Shriver, D. W., 'The Prayer That Spans the World. An Exposition: Social Ethics and the Lord's Prayer', *Interpretation* 21 (1967), 274–88.

Smith, G., 'The Matthean "Additions" to the Lord's Prayer', *Expository Times* 82 (1970–71), 54–5.

Sobrino, J., 'The Prayer of Jesus and the God of Jesus in the Synoptic Gospels', *Listening* 13 (1978), 189–213.

Strecker, G., 'Vaterunser und Glaube' in *Glaube im Neuen Testament. Festschrift für H. Binder* (ed. F. Hahn and H. Klein; Biblisch-theologische Studien 7; Neukirchen-Vluyn: Neukirchener Verlag, 1982), pp. 11–28.

Swetnam, J., 'Hallowed Be Thy Name', *Biblica* 52 (1971), 556–63.

ten Kate, R., 'Geef ons heden ons "dagelijks" brood. *Epiousios*: een crux interpretum', *Nederlands Theologisch Tijdschrift* 32 (1978), 125–39.

Thompson, G. H. P., 'Thy Will be Done on Earth, as it is in Heaven (Matt VI. 11): A Suggested Re-interpretation', *Expository Times* 70 (1958–59), 379–81.

Tilborg, S. van, 'A Form-criticism of the Lord's Prayer', *Novum Testamentum* 14 (1972), 94–105.

Vögtle, A., 'Der "eschatologische" Bezug der Wir-Bitten des Vaterunser' in *Jesus und Paulus. Festschrift für W. G. Kummel* (ed. E. E. Ellis and E. Grasser; Göttingen: Vandenhoeck & Ruprecht, 1975), pp. 344–62.

Walker, W. O., Jr, 'The Lord's Prayer in Matthew and John', *New Testament Studies* 28 (1982), 237–56.

Willis, G. G., 'Lead us not into Temptation', *Downside Review* 93 (1975), 281–8.

7. Treasures and Anxieties (Mt 6:19–34)

Barclay, W., '*Merimna* and *Merimnan*' in *New Testament Words* (London: SCM Press, 1964), pp. 198–203.

Benoit, P., 'L'oeuil, la lampe du corps', *Revue Biblique* 60 (1953), 603–6.

Betz, H. D., 'Matthew VI.22f. and Ancient Greek Theories of Vision' in *Text and Interpretation. Studies in the New Testament presented to M. Black* (ed. E. Best; Cambridge: University Press, 1979), pp. 43–56.

Bultmann, R. '*merimnaō*, etc.' in *Theological Dictionary of the New Testament* VI (ed. G. Kittel and G. Friedrich; Grand Rapids: Eerdmans/London: SCM Press, 1967), pp. 589–93.

D'Sa, F. X., '"Dhvani" as a Method of Interpretation', *BibleBhashyam* 5 (1979), 276–94.

Fenham, F. C., 'The Good and Evil Eye in the Sermon on the Mount', *Neotestamentica* 1 (1967), 51–8.

France, R. T., 'God and Mammon', *Evangelical Quarterly* 51 (1979), 3–21.

Jacquemin, P.-E., 'Les options du chrétien. Mt 6,24–34', *Assemblées du Seigneur* 39 (1972), 18–27.

Mees, M., 'Das Sprichwort Mt. 6,21f./Lk. 12,24 und seine ausserkanonische Parallelen', *Augustinianum* 14 (1974), 67–90.

Olsthoorn, M. F., *The Jewish Background and the Synoptic Setting of Mt 6,25–33 and Lk 12,22–31* (Studium Biblicum Franciscanum Analecta 10; Jerusalem: Franciscan Printing Press, 1975).

Pax, E., 'Essen und Trinken', *Bibel und Leben* 10 (1969), 275–91.

Pesch, R., 'Zur Exegese von Mt 6,19–21 und Lk 12,33–34', *Biblica* 41 (1960), 356–78.

Powell, J. E., 'Those "Lilies of the Field" Again', *Journal of Theological Studies* 33 (1982), 490–2.

Rüger, H. P., 'Mamonas', *Zeitschrift für die neutestamentliche Wissenschaft* 64 (1973), 127–31.

Safrai, S., and Flusser, D., 'The Slave of Two Masters', *Immanuel* 6 (1976), 30–3.

Schwarz, G., '*Prostheinai epi tēn hēlikian auto pēchyn hena*', *Zeitschrift für die neutestamentliche Wissenschaft* 71 (1980), 244–7.

Schwarz, G., 'Zum Vokabular von Matthäus 6,19f.', *Biblische Notizen* no. 14 (1981), 46–9.

8. Judging and Praying (Mt 7:1–12)

Brox, N. 'Suchen und Finden: Zur Nachgeschichte von Mt 7,7b/Lk 11,9b' in *Orientierung an Jesus* (ed. P. Hoffmann; Freiburg: Herder, 1973), pp. 17–36.

Couroyer, B., 'De la mesure dont vous mesurez il vous sera mesuré', *Revue Biblique* 77 (1970), 366–70.

Marquardt, F. W., 'Matthäus 7,12' in . . . *aus der Sklaverei befreit. Zwölf Predigten zu den Zehn Geboten* (ed. H. Gollwitzer *et al.*; Stuttgart: Radius Verlag, 1979), pp. 105–14.

Maxwell-Stuart, P. G., ' "Do not give what is holy to dogs" (Mt 7:6)', *Expository Times* 90 (1978–79), 341.

Nicol, W., 'The Structure of Mt 7', *Neotestamentica* 11 (1977), 77–90.

Piper, R., 'Matthew 7,7–11 par. Lk 11,9–13: Evidence of Design and Argument in the Collection of Jesus' Sayings' in *Logia. Les Paroles de Jésus – The Sayings of Jesus. Mémorial Joseph Coppens* (ed. J. Delobel; Bibliotheca Ephemeridum Theologicarum Lovaniensium 59; Louvain: Leuven University Press, 1982), pp. 411–18.

Rüger, H. P., 'Mit welchem Mass ihr messt, wird euch gemessen werden', *Zeitschrift für die neutestamenliche Wissenschaft* 60 (1969), 174–84.

Schüssler-Fiorenza, E., 'Judging and Judgment in the New Testament Communities', *Concilium* 107 (1977), 1–8.

Schwarz, G., 'Matthäus VII. 6a. Emendation und Rückübersetzung', *Novum Testamentum* 14 (1972), 18–25.

Strecker, G., 'Compliance – Love of One's Enemy – The Golden Rule', *Australian Biblical Review* 29 (1981), 38–46.

9. The Disciple in the face of Judgment (Mt 7:13–27)

Abou-Chaar, K., 'The Two Builders: A Study of the Parable in Lk 6:47–49', *Near East School of Theology Theological Review* 5 (1982), 44–58.

Betz, H. D., 'Eine Episode im jüngsten Gericht (Mt 7,21–23)', *Zeitschrift für Theologie und Kirche* 78 (1981), 1–30.

Bligh, J., 'The "Two Ways" at Qumran and in the Early Church', *The Bible Today* no. 22 (February 1966), 1470–4.

Bornkamm, G., '*lukos*' in *Theological Dictionary of the New Testament* IV (ed. G. Kittel; Grand Rapids: Eerdmans/London: SCM Press, 1967), pp. 308–11.

Cothenet, É., 'Les prophètes chrétiens dans l'Évangile selon saint Matthieu' in *L'Évangile selon Matthieu. Rédaction et Théologie* (ed. M. Didier; Bibliotheca Ephemeridum Theologicarum Lovaniensium 29; Gembloux: Éditions J. Duculot, 1972), pp. 281–308.

Denaux, A., 'Der Spruch von den zwei Wegen im Rahmen des Epilogs der Bergpredigt (Mt 7, 13–14 par Lk 13, 23–24)' in *Logia. Les Paroles de Jésus – The Sayings of Jesus. Mémorial Joseph Coppens* (ed. J. Delobel; Bibliotheca Ephemeridum Theologicarum Lovaniensium 59; Louvain: Leuven University Press, 1982), pp. 305–35.

Derrett, J. D. M., 'The Merits of the Narrow Gate (Mt 7:13–14; Lk 13:24)', *Journal for the Study of the New Testament* 15 (1982), 20–9.

Geist, H., 'Die Warnung vor den falschen Propheten – eine ernste Mahnung an die heutige Kirche. Zu Mt 7,15–20; 24:11f. 24' in *Biblische Randbemerkungen* (ed. H. Merklein and J. Lange; Würzburg: Echter Verlag, 1974), pp. 139–49.

Gerhardsson, B., '"An ihren Früchten sollt ihr sie erkennen." Die Legitimitätsfrage in der matthäischen Christologie', *Evangelische Theologie* 42 (1982), 113–26.

Hill, D., 'On the Evidence for the Creative Role of Christian Prophets', *New Testament Studies* 20 (1973–74), 262–74.

Hill, D., 'False Prophets and Charismatics: Structure and Interpretation in Mt 7:15–23', *Biblica* 57 (1976), 327–48.

Jeremias, J., '*pulē, pulōn*' in *Theological Dictionary of the New Testament* VI (ed. G. Kittel and G. Friedrich; Grand Rapids: Eerdmans/London: SCM Press, 1968), pp. 921–8.

Krämer, M., 'Hütet euch für dem falschen Propheten. Eine überlieferungsgeschichtliche Untersuchung zu Mt 7, 15–23/Lk 6, 43–46/Mt 12, 33–37', *Biblica* 57 (1976), 349–77.

Kretzer, A., 'Die Übereinstimmung von Hören, Reden und Tun als Fundament unseres Christsein' in *Am Tisch des Wortes* N.S. 150 (ed. K. Jockwig and W. Massa; Stuttgart: KBW Verlag, 1975), pp. 31–40.

Mattill, A. J., 'The Way of Tribulation', *Journal of Biblical Literature* 98 (1979), 531–46.

Michaelis, W., '*hodos*, etc.' in *Theological Dictionary of the New Testament* V (ed. G. Kittel and G. Friedrich; Grand Rapids: Eerdmans/London: SCM Press, 1967), pp. 42–96.

Minear, P. S., 'False Prophecy and Hypocrisy in the Gospel of Matthew' in *Neues Testament und Kirche* (ed. J. Gnilka; Freiburg: Herder, 1974), pp. 76–93.

Ornella, A., 'Les chrétiens seront jugés. Mt 7, 21–27', *Assemblées de Seigneur* 40 (1972), 16–27.

Schwarz, G., 'Matthäus VII. 13a. Ein Alarmruf angesichts höchster Gefahr', *Novum Testamentum* 12 (1970), 229–32.

Schweizer, E., 'Observance of the Law and Charismatic Activity in Matthew', *New Testament Studies* 16 (1969–70), 213–30.

Schweizer, E., 'Matthäus 7, 15–23' in *Matthäus und seine Gemeinde* (Stuttgarter Bibelstudien 71; Stuttgart: KBW Verlag, 1974), pp. 126–31.

Tooley, W., 'The Shepherd and the Sheep Image in the Teaching of Jesus', *Novum Testamentum* 7 (1964), 15–25.